AF254773

WHAT GREAT LEADERS SAY

A manager oversees processes. A leader grows people. Leadership Is Tough reminds us that the most enduring leaders are not those who accumulate authority, but those who develop others, hold firm to their values under pressure, and leave every organization stronger than they found it.

– Nido Qubein, President
High Point University

Kelly and Stark are spot on: Leadership is Tough. Leaders are always watched and scrutinized. Thank goodness "popularity" is not a leadership requirement. Leaders deal with difficult decisions and difficult people. Yet beneath chaos and constant change lies opportunity. Leaders can create high-performing teams, tackle important missions, and have a positive impact on their communities and society. Leadership is Tough covers every aspect of executive work. Reading this book caused me to reflect on past errors and rethink how I could have handled a few situations. Importantly, Kelly and Stark's advice will help me better navigate future challenges.

– Andy Lennon, Rear Admiral
US Navy (Ret.)

Leadership at the highest levels demands strategy and discipline, and Leadership is Tough helps with both.

– Mark McWilliams, President
The Gold Medal Team

Leadership is vision. If you don't know your objective, you and everyone involved will be lost!

– William Jacobs, CEO
White Sands Credit Union

Leadership is simple, but it is not easy. It requires discipline, courage, and the humility to keep learning. In Leadership Is Tough, Mary Kelly and Peter Stark remind us that great leadership is not about authority or titles. It is about responsibility. The responsibility to make tough decisions, build trust, develop people, and create an environment where others can succeed. This book offers practical wisdom for leaders who understand that real leadership is practiced every day, especially when it is hard.

– Garry Ridge, Chairman Emeritus
WD-40 Company

Leadership is not only tough, it can feel lonely. Moments of key decision-making feel unique and isolating. Here is a critical truth: it does not follow that you must be alone as you lead. Seek mentors, advisors, peers, and resources - many others have walked the path you walk. This book is a fantastic resource to guide you - don't try to lead in isolation.

– Dave Welch, Rear Admiral
US Navy (Ret.)

In today's rapidly evolving business environment, the leaders who thrive are those who communicate with clarity, embrace change, and build cultures of trust and open dialogue. Leadership Is Tough delivers a practical, no-nonsense framework for developing exactly those skills.

– Lorry Bottrill, Division President
Aetna/CVS

After 31 years as a naval officer—six of those years in communist prison camps—I know leadership is best tested in adversity. This book delivers the hard-hitting lessons every leader needs when the going is tough and the stakes are high.

– Charlie Plumb, Captain
US Navy (Ret), POW 1967–1973

I have been a fan of Peter's work for many years, and it has guided my thoughts and decisions throughout my career. Leadership is Tough gets right to the core of why leadership is so difficult by highlighting that the decisions we make as leaders affect the lives of people. From associates to clients, to partners and investors, and the marketplace in general. If more leaders understood the weight of this responsibility, the marketplace would have a very different impact in our communities, culture, and our daily lives.

– Kevin Carroll, General Manager
Southern California Lexus Dealer

One of my favorite leadership quotes is "A leader is best when people barely know he exists, when his work is done, his aim fulfilled, they will say: we did it ourselves"- Lao Tzu. It speaks to the nuanced nature of leadership and the aim to elevate others. While it is not easy and very trying at times, as Stark & Kelly lay out in Leadership is Tough, those who do it well make it look easy. I have always appreciated Peter Stark's support in making it look easier.

– Don Cates, CEO
3Rivers Credit Union

Stark and Kelly have written the most pragmatic leadership guide that I have ever read. Courage, Clarity and consistency are not only what they explain, but also how they prepared this book. Drawing from their own tough leadership experiences, they lay out a clear path for sustainable leadership with practical tips on developing personal courage and delivering consistent performance results.

– Barry Banther, Chairman
Florida State Board of Independent Colleges and Universities

If you need something TOUGH done NOW, task Mary Kelly, the EPITOME of leadership, organization, and motivation!

– Bill Rigby, Captain
US Navy (Ret.)

Leadership Is Tough captures what every leader eventually discovers: that connecting with clarity, humanity, and consistency across an entire organization is one of the hardest things we are asked to do. The insights and real-world examples in this book speak directly to

v

the complexity of leadership culture and why getting it right is never optional, especially when the stakes are highest.

– Todd Lane, CEO
California Coast Credit Union

Leadership is Tough...What Great Leaders Do Differently goes beyond typical leadership theory to serve as a practitioner's field guide for everyday situations. Peter's results-through-relationships philosophy has consistently helped me make sense of complex situations and take the next best step to address them. Practical and encouraging, this book is a must for anyone who wants to lead with integrity and a heart for serving others.

– Brian Mills, CEO
Powder River Energy Cooperation

Leadership is about getting your people to embrace the difficult.

– Harold T. Fields, Jr., Lieutenant General
U.S. Army (Ret.)

This is the best leadership book I've ever seen because it presents perspectives that leaders need to know, but probably have never focused on. Character, courage, and commitment are the core of great leaders, and courage is at the center of all leadership behavior and performance. Our leaders in the Vietnam POW camps suffered the most torture and isolation, but they always bounced back to resist, survive, and return with honor. They were a great example and inspired all of us.

– Leon "Lee" Ellis, Colonel
US Air Force (Ret.), Vietnam POW

The Leadership is Tough book is an outstanding, practical, and effective guide. It captures the essence of what every great leader contends with: the need to make tough, thoughtful, and enduring decisions when the stakes are high and the circumstances are imperfect. The most effective and strategic leaders lead with connection, inclusion, respect, and care. These habits command respect, not demand it.

vi

Having had the opportunity to work directly with Peter for more than a decade, I have always seen him underscore and model the critical importance of remaining humble and building strong teams across every facet of leadership, and this book offers direct insights into how to achieve that and so much more.

– Michelle D. Gonzalez, President & CEO
TrueCare

True leadership means guiding people toward growth and accountability, even when the path is difficult or unpopular. Leadership Is Tough speaks directly to that responsibility, reminding us that the best outcomes are achieved when leaders lead with integrity, humility, and a shared sense of purpose, creating the conditions where patients, teams, and organizations all strive for a win-win.

– Kenneth Morris, MD, FAAP, President & CEO
Children's Primary Care Medical Group

Leadership is tough because you are accountable for outcomes you don't fully control, in environments that rarely stand still. What resonated most in this book is the idea that great leaders don't have all the answers – they create clarity when others see noise, and they make decisions when certainty doesn't exist. In my experience, leadership isn't about having the right answers; it's about building the structure, discipline, and trust that allow organizations to move forward anyway.

– Mike Boden, President & CEO
OneAZ Credit Union

In a world defined by rapid change and constant complexity, practical leadership guidelines help turn good intentions into meaningful action.

– Rob Grabill, President
Chief Executive Network

Mary and Peter nail it in their book, Leadership is Tough, when they said leadership is Accountability without complete control. Most leaders ascended because they got things done, solved problems, and innovated out of necessity, often because they'd been left on their own or suffered under poor leadership. That's what makes striving for great leadership so difficult. Empowerment, sensitivity, emotional intelligence, and trust are keys to great leadership, but I'd bet 90% of leaders were not developed in those environments, and that's what makes leadership so tough.

– Talbot H. Gee, CEO
Heating, Air-conditioning & Refrigeration
Distributors International (HARDI)

Leadership today is indeed tough! In many respects, it is more difficult today than at any other point in my forty-year career. From the start of the first chapter, Kelly and Stark clearly describe the current difficult leadership environment. The balance of "Leadership is Tough" takes a deep dive into the issues we face as leaders and offers focused ideas for addressing these challenges. I look forward to sharing this great resource with my leadership team!

– Doran J. Barnes, CEO
Foothill Transit

In a world where leadership feels heavier, faster, and more complex than ever, Leadership Is Tough delivers exactly what leaders need: honesty, perspective, and practical guidance. This book doesn't romanticize leadership. It tells the truth about its weight while showing readers how to lead with resilience, clarity, and heart.

– Tom Koning, President
Intelliguard

Leadership means making hard decisions with incomplete information while others look to you for clarity—and this book captures that responsibility with rare honesty.

– Samantha A. Roe, IOM, CEO
International Erosion Control Association

I've been fortunate to work with many types of leaders. I've learned from each of them, either what to do or what not to do. As this book highlights so well, the best leaders focus on developing their people. Hire people smarter than you and help them to shine. Combine that with creating a culture of collaboration towards a shared vision, and your organization achieves great things!

– Terry Shirey, President & CEO
Nevada State Bank

After thirty years of leading others, I know that the most defining moments in leadership rarely come with a roadmap. Leadership Is Tough provides exactly that, an honest, practical guide for developing the skills and navigating the decisions, relationships, and disciplines that distinguish good leaders from truly great ones.

– Karen Timmins, SVP of HR
Western Growers

Leadership is being resourceful and giving credit to the team when and where credit is due. I was taught early in my career that a good leader needs to utilize their network (internal and external) who have the right experience. There is no possible way to know everything there is to know for every scenario.

– Jean Thomas, CMPE, Executive Director
Iowa Healthcare Leaders Association

Leadership is tough because people are watching, the stakes are high, and the margin for avoidance is small. This book doesn't offer shortcuts. It offers discipline, perspective, and the kind of guidance leaders actually need when the job gets heavy.

– Sparkle Barnes, President and CEO
Health Center Partners Family of Companies

Trust provides the foundation of leadership. Leaders must earn, through their words and deeds, the trust of their employees. Leaders earn this trust by providing training and the information needed to safely and efficiently accomplish the organization's established mission. They earn this trust by demonstrating that they care about their people and empower them to demonstrate initiative, make good decisions, and take accountable actions.

– Don Nelson, Colonel, US Air Force (ret)
Former Assistant Director of Admission, US Naval Academy

Leadership is Tough…What Great Leaders Do Differently provides the blueprint for the skills necessary to build a solid organization. As described in the book, the success achieved at IRE Development required vision. Still more importantly, our team members enthusiastically and skillfully handled every detail and nuance required for successful growth and exceptional customer service. Similar to the skills covered in the mentorship and succession planning chapters. Recognizing and empowering your team members is essential for scalable achievement.

– Mike Vogt, President
IRE Development

Great leaders who truly care have to have the managerial courage to be honest and willingly have those difficult conversations. Truly caring is gifting your employees with the opportunity to get better.

– Kim Schaefer, Director of People Strategy
Watkins Manufacturing

Leadership can be tough, but when you surround yourself with talented people who share your passion for the mission, even the hardest challenges become opportunities to move forward together.

– Kimberlie E. Prior, CPPT, CEO
Florida Public Pension Trustees Association

In Leadership is Tough, I really enjoyed the chapter on empathetic leadership. Your point that 'courtesy, respect, and intentionality are not soft skills, but strategic disciplines' is absolutely spot on. Thank you for such an insightful read!

– Carol Camarda, Chief Human Resources Officer
Vista Community Clinics

Great leaders surround themselves with people they can trust to be candid and courageous, who are great teammates.

– Peg Klein, Rear Admiral
US Navy (Ret.)

The most important thing about leadership at any level is finding leaders with integrity who care about the company almost to a fault. This type of leader, who believes deeply in the company's philosophy, ends up as invested as an owner.

– Amy S. Woody, CEO
Mountain Credit Union

It's so refreshing to see how Mary and Peter captured and then reinforced how hard it is to make the tough look easy. This professional insight will be an invaluable compass for both current and future leaders. Bravo Zulu!

– John Fuller, Vice Admiral,
US Navy (Ret.)

Showing empathy, building trust, working well with others, Mary Kelly and Peter Stark hit the nail on the head with every word of this exquisitely-written, conversational masterpiece! Yes, the pace of change is dizzying, and yes, adopting technology is a must. But effective leadership will always come down to human-to-human relationships, and these two masterful storytellers not only explain why but also provide us a roadmap to get better.

– Bill Byrne, Rear Admiral
U.S. Navy (Ret.)

LEADERSHIP IS TOUGH

MARY KELLY & PETER STARK

Paperback ISBN: 978-1-935733-43-0
Hardcover ISBN: 978-1-935733-42-3
Kindle ISBN: 978-1-935733-44-7
Audio ISBN: 978-1-935733-45-4

First Edition: 2026

ISBN: 978-1-935733-43-0

Published by Productive Leaders

Printed in the United States of America

LEGAL DISCLAIMER
FOR LEADERSHIP IS TOUGH

This book is intended for informational and educational purposes only. The authors make no representations or warranties with respect to the accuracy, applicability, or completeness of the contents of this book. The information provided is based on the authors' experience, research, and opinions and is not intended to be, nor should it be construed as, professional, legal, financial, or other specific advice.

Readers are advised to consult with appropriate professionals before making any decisions or taking any actions based on the information contained in this book. The strategies, frameworks, and examples presented are illustrative and may not be suitable for every individual, organization, or situation.

The authors disclaim any liability for any loss, damage, or adverse consequences that may result, directly or indirectly, from the use or application of any information contained in this book. This includes, but is not limited to, business decisions, employment actions, organizational changes, or personal conduct based on the material presented.

Any references to organizations, individuals, or situations are for illustrative purposes only. While some examples may be based on real experiences, identifying details have been changed to protect confidentiality, and any resemblance to actual persons or entities is coincidental.

All content is provided "as is," without warranty of any kind, either express or implied, including but not limited to implied warranties of merchantability or fitness for a particular purpose.

By reading this book, you acknowledge and agree that you are solely responsible for your decisions, actions, and results.

DEDICATION

This book is dedicated to the leaders we have had the privilege to work with throughout our careers.

You challenged us.

You trusted us.

You allowed us into the rooms where decisions were hard, consequences were real, and leadership truly mattered.

Through your successes, your stories, and your struggles, you gave us the experiences and insights that made this book possible. You reminded us that leadership is learned in moments of responsibility and refined through humility, discipline, and accountability.

We are deeply grateful for the opportunity to walk alongside you, to learn with you, and to help you think through the decisions that shape organizations and transform lives.

We are better because of you. You know who you are.

We are also profoundly grateful to our spouses, Greg and Kathleen, whose patience, support, and steady belief made the long hours, deep thinking, and demanding work behind this book happen. We appreciate and love you!

With respect and gratitude,

Mary Kelly & Peter Stark

ACKNOWLEDGEMENT

Dusty Tockstein

Twenty-five years is more than a career milestone. It's a testament to loyalty, dedication, and the kind of partnership that makes difficult work possible.

Dusty has been with us through every evolution of our work, and this book would not exist without her. She's done far more than keep things running. She's made the work better.

Dusty has the courage to tell us when our writing misses the mark. That kind of honesty is rare and invaluable. She doesn't soften the truth to protect egos. She tells us what needs fixing, and we're better writers because of it.

She's spent countless hours proofreading every page and helping the book flow. That's meticulous, exhausting work, and she's done it with skill and patience.

Great leaders surround themselves with people who make them better. Dusty does exactly that. We're grateful for her partnership, her candor, and her commitment to excellence.

Thank you, Dusty.

Peter and Mary

TABLE OF CONTENTS

Dedication xviii

Acknowledgement xix

Chapter 1 Why Leadership Is Tough Today 1

Chapter 2 Leading Change
In an Uncertain and Change-Fatigued World 17

Chapter 3 Strategic Decision-Making
Make the Call Before the Call Is Made for You 39

Chapter 4 Working Well with Others
How You Treat People Defines You 57

Chapter 5 Building Trust
Communicate and Connect with Others 79

Chapter 6 Empathy Is a Discipline
Understand Without Lowering the Bar 97

Chapter 7 Priorities and Values
Align Purpose with What Actually Gets Done 121

Chapter 8 Accountability
Hold the Line Without Breaking Trust 143

Chapter 9 Leadership Gets Lonely
Lead Yourself When You're the One In Charge 167

Chapter 10 Resilience Is Earned
Develop Capacity, Withstand Pressure, Avoid Burnout 189

Chapter 11 Managing Time and Energy
Achieve the Most Important Results 207

Chapter 12 Succession Planning
Build Your Bench and Future-Proof the Organization 225

Chapter 13 Mentorship Is a Decision
Advice For Purposeful Development 247

Chapter 14 Leading Your Board
Without Losing Control 269

Chapter 15 Becoming a Transformative Leader 281

About the authors 298

CHAPTER 1

WHY LEADERSHIP IS TOUGH TODAY

The phone rang at 6:27 a.m.

That's the moment you realize leadership isn't what you thought it would be. Not when you accepted the promotion. Not when you practiced your first all-hands speech in the mirror. Not even after the congratulatory emails stopped arriving. Leadership isn't the title. It's the weight.

It's the early-morning call telling you the product launch failed, the key client is walking away, or someone on your team just quit. It's the email you open on Sunday morning that changes everything you planned for Monday. It's the decision you have to make right now, based on information that won't be complete until next week.

From the outside, leadership looks like power, prestige, and corner offices. From the inside? It's accountability without complete control. It's being responsible for outcomes you can't entirely dictate, with people you didn't entirely choose, in circumstances that shift faster than you can respond.

Anyone who tells you leadership is easy either isn't actually leading or is lying to make themselves feel good.

Here's the truth: leadership has always been hard. But right now? It's harder than ever. Not just psychologically demanding, though it is that. Not just emotionally exhausting, though it is that too. Leadership today is structurally more complex, more volatile, and more relentless than at any point in modern history. This chapter explains why, and more importantly, what it actually takes to lead effectively in this environment.

FROM THE OUTSIDE, LEADERSHIP LOOKS LIKE POWER, PRESTIGE, AND CORNER OFFICES. FROM THE INSIDE? IT'S ACCOUNTABILITY WITHOUT COMPLETE CONTROL.

THE MYTHS THAT SET YOU UP TO FAIL

Before we examine what makes leadership uniquely difficult today, we need to dismantle the myths that make the job even harder than it needs to be. These aren't just unhelpful ideas. They're traps that undermine effectiveness, erode confidence, and set leaders up for failure.

Myth #1: Leaders Must Have All the Answers

This is the lie that traps more leaders than any other. Somewhere along the way, we decided that leaders are supposed to be omniscient. Admitting "I don't know" feels like a sign of weakness. Asking for help seems like proof you're not qualified for the role. Nonsense. We once worked with a CEO

THE BEST LEADERS AREN'T THE ONES WITH ALL THE ANSWERS. THEY'RE THE ONES WHO KNOW WHICH QUESTIONS TO ASK AND WHO TO ASK.

who prided himself on never saying "I don't know." In every meeting, he had an answer. Sometimes it was the right answer. Often, it wasn't. But he couldn't help himself. His ego demanded that he appear infallible. The result? His executive team stopped bringing him problems because they knew he'd make something up rather than admit uncertainty. Innovation died. Trust eroded. And when the company hit a real crisis, nobody believed him anymore.

Contrast that with another CEO we coached who made it a habit to say, "I don't know, but let's figure it out together." Her team respected her more, not less. Why? Because she was honest. She created space for collaboration instead of pretending to be the smartest person in the room.

Here's the reality: the best leaders aren't the ones with all the answers. They're the ones who know which questions to ask and who to ask them to.

Myth #2: Good Leaders Are Always Liked

If your primary goal as a leader is to be liked, you've already lost.

Leadership requires making decisions that sometimes disappoint people. Saying no to good ideas because resources are limited. Holding someone accountable even though it's uncomfortable. Choosing one strategic direction, which means saying no to three others.

In one organization we worked with, a mid-level manager admitted she avoided giving critical feedback because she "didn't want people to think she was mean." The result? Performance declined. Deadlines slipped. And her team lost respect for her. Not because she was mean, but because she wasn't leading.

During a restructuring at a large manufacturing company, the plant manager had to eliminate an entire shift. It was brutal. People lost jobs. Families were affected. But he handled it honestly, transparently, and with as much compassion as the situation

RESPECT BEATS POPULARITY EVERY SINGLE TIME. PEOPLE DO NOT FOLLOW PEOPLE THEY DO NOT TRUST OR RESPECT.

allowed. Months later, several of those same employees reached out to thank him for treating them with dignity. They didn't like the decision, but they respected how it was made, and they trusted the plant manager. That's the difference.

Myth #3: The Hardest Part Is the Workload

If believing you need all the answers is the first trap, and chasing popularity is the second, here's the third: believing that the difficulty of leadership is primarily about how much work there is. Wrong.

Yes, leaders work long hours. Yes, the to-do list is endless. But the real challenge isn't the volume of work; it's the weight of responsibility.

Your decisions affect people's livelihoods. Their families. Their futures. One wrong call can cost someone their job, tank a project that dozens of people worked on for months, or damage relationships with clients who trusted you. That's what keeps you up at night. Not the emails. The stakes.

We've seen executives with decades of experience admit they still feel the pressure of that weight. One senior leader told us, "I've made a thousand decisions in my career, but every time I have to let someone go, it still guts me. Because I know I'm not just affecting them. I'm affecting their spouse, their kids, their mortgage payment." That's the part nobody tells you about leadership. The workload is manageable. The weight is not.

These three myths have plagued leaders for generations. But they're more damaging now because today's leaders face challenges that previous generations didn't. The myths promised that if you were smart enough, likable enough, and worked hard enough, leadership would be manageable. But those assumptions were built for a world that no longer exists. The reality leaders face today is fundamentally different.

WHY LEADERSHIP IS UNIQUELY DIFFICULT NOW

If you feel like leadership is harder than it used to be, you're not imagining it. The data backs you up. According to recent global surveys, 40 to 55 percent of senior leaders report experiencing burnout or near-burnout, with over 70 percent describing their roles as increasingly demanding due to crises, economic uncertainty, and rapid technological change. Nearly one-third are actively considering career changes due to relentless stress.

That's not a morale problem. That's a structural problem. Leadership today requires navigating a convergence of forces that compound and accelerate each other. Let's break down what's actually happening.

EXTERNAL DISRUPTION: THE GROUND KEEPS SHIFTING

In the past, leaders could plan with some degree of predictability. Markets moved in understandable patterns. Business cycles were recognizable. Strategic plans had a shelf life measured in years. Not anymore.

Today, approximately 70-80% of global CEOs list macroeconomic volatility and inflation as their top concerns. Supply chains collapse overnight. Interest rates swing wildly. Competitors emerge from unexpected corners. Regulatory environments shift without warning. Leaders are forced to plan for multiple scenarios simultaneously because no one knows which will actually happen.

One CEO we worked with described it this way: "I used to build a five-year strategic plan and then execute it. Now, I build five different plans and keep all of them ready, because I don't know which version of reality we'll be living in six months from now."

This volatility is exhausting, but it's compounded by a second force: technological disruption that's rewriting the rules faster than organizations can adapt. Artificial intelligence is transforming how work is done, how decisions are made, and how value is created, often faster than organizations can absorb the change.

Consider this: over 40 percent of workers will need new skills in the next five years due to AI, and the majority of large enterprises are actively adopting or planning to integrate AI. But here's the kicker: 70 to 80 percent of executives see AI as a strategic priority, yet face significant barriers, including skills gaps and ethical concerns. Meanwhile, 40 to 60 percent of employees express anxiety about AI-related job security.

So, leaders are expected to integrate game-changing technology, reskill their workforce, address fears of job displacement, and do it all while the technology itself evolves monthly. One manufacturing executive told us, "I'm supposed to lead my team through an AI transformation, but I barely understand AI myself. How do I build confidence in something I'm still learning?" That's the challenge. You're leading through change you haven't fully figured out yet, in an economic environment where the old playbooks no longer work.

INTERNAL CHALLENGES: YOUR PEOPLE ARE EXHAUSTED

While external forces create instability, internal challenges drain the organizational energy needed to respond. Start with the talent crisis. Here's the uncomfortable truth: 60 to 70 percent of HR leaders cite talent shortages and engagement issues as critical internal constraints.

You need skilled people, but they are hard to find and even harder to keep. When you do have them, keeping them engaged is a full-time job. Why? Because the workforce has fundamentally changed. Employees today expect more than a paycheck. They want purpose, flexibility, growth opportunities, and leaders who actually care about their well-being. If they don't get it, they leave. And in many industries, they have plenty of options.

During a consulting project with a technology firm, the VP of Engineering admitted he spent more time trying to retain top performers than he did on product development. "I'm not running an engineering team anymore," he said. "I'm running a retention strategy with some engineering on the side." That's the new reality. Leadership isn't just about the work; it's about keeping the people who do the work engaged enough to stay.

PEOPLE DON'T QUIT JOBS. THEY QUIT THEIR LEADERS.

But engagement is collapsing across organizations. Let's talk about one of the most troubling trends in leadership today: only 20 to 25 percent of employees globally are highly engaged, 60 percent are not engaged, and 15 to 20 percent are actively disengaged. Read that again. In most organizations, most people are just going through the motions, and some are actively working against you.

Why? Engagement is influenced by career development, leadership quality, workload, and the perceived disconnect between what leaders say and what employees actually experience. In other words, people don't leave jobs. They leave leaders.

During a leadership assessment for a mid-sized professional services firm, we surveyed 250 employees, and the results were sobering. When asked, "Do you trust your immediate supervisor?" only 34 percent said yes. When asked, "Do you believe leadership cares about your development?" the number dropped to 28 percent. The managing partner was shocked. "We talk about development all the time!" he protested.

Exactly. They talked about it. But talking about it isn't the same as doing something about it. Employees didn't see real investment in their growth; they just saw lip service. That's the engagement crisis in a nutshell. Leaders think they're communicating care and commitment. Employees experience something else.

Then there's change fatigue. Here's a statistic that should alarm every leader: over 70% of organizations report that change fatigue is affecting their workforce. Think about it. In the past few years alone, organizations saw a shift to remote or hybrid work, adopted new technologies, restructured teams, and dealt with economic uncertainty. People are exhausted. And yet, the pace of change isn't slowing down. It is accelerating.

Leaders are caught in an impossible bind: they need to drive change to stay competitive, but their people are already burned out from too much change. Push too hard, and you lose your best people. Move too slowly, and you lose market share. This is the daily tightrope walk of modern leadership.

STRUCTURAL TENSIONS: THE IMPOSSIBLE BALANCING ACT

External disruption creates instability. Internal challenges drain energy. But there's a third force that makes leadership uniquely difficult today: the competing demands from stakeholders who want fundamentally different, often contradictory outcomes.

Leaders are expected to deliver results, build culture, develop talent, manage risk, and prepare the next generation of leaders, all while answering to boards, stakeholders, customers, and employees who may want very different things. Let's be blunt: these demands often conflict.

Shareholders want short-term profits. Employees want long-term investment in their development. Customers want lower prices. Your team wants higher wages. The board wants aggressive growth. Your people are already maxed out. You can't make everyone happy. Someone will always be disappointed. And guess who gets blamed when expectations aren't met? You.

A senior executive at a healthcare organization described it perfectly: "I wake up every morning knowing I'm going to disappoint someone today. My only choice is deciding who." That's leadership. Navigating trade-offs that don't have clear answers, where every decision creates winners and losers, and you're accountable for all of it.

This is the convergence. Economic volatility makes planning nearly impossible. AI disruption that requires leading through uncertainty. Talent challenges consume enormous energy. Burned-out teams. Disengaged employees. Stakeholders who want contradictory outcomes. These forces don't exist in isolation. They compound each other, creating a level of complexity that previous generations of leaders simply didn't face.

The question becomes: what does leadership actually look like in this environment? Not the sanitized version in leadership books, but the real thing.

WHAT TOUGH LEADERSHIP ACTUALLY LOOKS LIKE

Let's be clear about something: tough leadership is not about being cold, harsh, or unapproachable. It's not about yelling in meetings, ruling by fear, or crushing dissent. Real toughness is entirely different. It's the discipline to do what's necessary even when it's uncomfortable, the consistency to show up when others are falling apart, and the capacity to sustain effort over the long haul.

Given the realities we've just outlined, effective leadership today requires five core qualities.

YOU'RE ALWAYS BEING WATCHED

One of the most underestimated realities of leadership is this: you are always being watched. Always. Every word. Every email. Every facial expression in a meeting. Even your silence communicates something. Your people watch you constantly, scanning for clues about whether things are okay, whether they should worry, and whether you actually know what you're doing.

When the CEO walks into the room looking stressed, the entire executive team tenses up. When a manager snaps at someone in the hallway, it ripples through the department for days. When a leader goes quiet during a crisis, people assume the worst.

During one consulting engagement with a Fortune 500 company, we watched a senior VP deliver what he thought was a straightforward update on a restructuring plan. His tone was measured. His slides were clear. But halfway through, someone raised a hand and asked, "Are we all getting laid off?"

The VP was stunned. "What? No. Where did that come from?"

Turns out, he'd used the phrase "rightsizing our operations" three times without explaining what it meant. In the absence of clarity, people filled in the blanks with their worst fears. That's what happens when leaders forget they're on stage. Your team isn't just listening to your words; they're reading between the lines, watching your body language, and trying to decode what you're not saying.

In the military, this is even more pronounced. When you're commanding a unit, and things go wrong, and they will, your people are watching to see if you panic. If you lose your composure, they lose theirs. If you stay calm and focused, they follow your lead. One night aboard a Navy vessel, an engine malfunction triggered alarms throughout the ship. The crew looked to the bridge. The commanding officer didn't yell or get overly excited. Just calmly issued orders, asked the right questions, and kept everyone focused on the solution. The crisis was averted. Not because the problem was easy, but because the leader stayed steady.

That's the hidden weight of leadership. You don't get to have a bad day in public. You don't get to vent in the group chat. You don't get to visibly fall apart when things go sideways, because the moment you do, everyone else does too. You carry the team's confidence on your shoulders, whether you feel confident or not. Which leads directly to the first requirement of tough leadership.

CLARITY IN THE FOG

Tough leaders provide direction even when the path isn't clear. They don't wait for perfect information. They make the best decision they can with what they have, communicate it clearly, and adjust as new information emerges.

In the military, this is called "commander's intent." You tell your people what needs to be accomplished and why, even if you don't know exactly how it will unfold. That clarity gives them the confidence to act, even in chaos. The same principle applies in business. When everything is uncertain, your job isn't to pretend you have all the answers. Your job is to provide enough clarity that people know what to do next.

This requires comfort with ambiguity. You will never have all the data you want. Waiting for certainty is the same as choosing indecision. The leaders who succeed in volatile environments are the ones who can make the best call with incomplete information, communicate it decisively, and course-correct as conditions change.

COURAGE TO DISAPPOINT

Clarity alone isn't enough. Leaders also need courage. Tough leaders make decisions that might be unpopular, but necessary. They say no to good ideas because resources are finite. They hold people accountable, even when it's uncomfortable. They deliver bad news directly instead of sugarcoating it.

During one consulting engagement, a division president had to shut down a beloved product line that hadn't been profitable in years. The team was devastated. But he didn't hide from the decision or blame someone else. He stood before the group, explained the reasoning, and took full ownership. People respected him for it.

This is where the myth about being liked becomes dangerous. If your primary concern is popularity, you'll avoid the hard calls. You'll soften feedback. You'll delay necessary confrontations. And in doing so, you'll lose the respect that actually matters. Tough leaders understand that disappointing people occasionally is part of the job. What's unforgivable is failing to lead because you're afraid of their reaction.

CONSISTENCY THAT BUILDS TRUST

Courage gets you through individual decisions. Consistency keeps you in the game long-term. Tough leaders show up prepared to lead, day after day. They don't let their mood dictate their leadership. They don't play favorites. They don't blow up one day and act like nothing happened the next.

Why? Because trust is built through predictability. Your team needs to know they can count on you, not just on the good days, but especially during the difficult days. When you're consistent in your values, your standards, and your demeanor, people feel safer. They know what to expect. That stability becomes the foundation for everything else.

One CEO we worked with had a simple rule: "I never make a decision when I'm angry, and I never celebrate a win until the work is done." That discipline kept him steady when everyone else was roller-coasting between panic and euphoria. His team learned they could trust his judgment because he didn't operate on emotion. He operated on principle.

This doesn't mean you suppress your humanity or pretend to be a robot. It means you manage yourself first so you can lead others effectively. Your emotions matter, but they can't drive your decisions. Your energy matters, but it can't be erratic. Consistency in leadership creates the psychological safety teams need to perform under pressure.

CAPACITY TO GO THE DISTANCE

Yet even the most consistent leader will burn out without one final ingredient: the capacity to sustain the effort over time. Tough leaders take care of themselves so they can take care of their team. They protect their energy, set boundaries, and build routines that sustain them for the long haul.

This is where many leaders fail. They burn hot and fast, working 80-hour weeks, skipping sleep, ignoring their health, and then they crash. And when the leader crashes, the team suffers. Leadership is a marathon, not a sprint. If you don't build capacity, you won't finish the race.

Protecting your capacity isn't selfish. It's strategic. You cannot give what you don't have. If you're running on empty, you can't support your team through their exhaustion. If you're mentally fried, you can't make good decisions. If you're emotionally depleted, you can't regulate yourself when others need you to be steady.

The leaders who last are the ones who treat their resilience as a renewable resource that requires intentional maintenance. They sleep. They exercise. They set boundaries. They protect time for recovery. Not because they're soft, but because they understand the math: sustainable leadership requires sustainable practices.

THE REALITY CHECK

If you want to know whether you're prepared for the toughness leadership requires, ask yourself these questions.

Can I make decisions with incomplete information? You will never have all the data you want. Waiting for certainty is the same as choosing indecision.

Am I willing to have the hard conversations? Avoiding conflict doesn't make it go away; it makes it worse.

Do I set boundaries to protect my time and focus? If you say yes to everything, you're saying no to the things that actually matter.

Can I maintain composure when others are losing theirs? Your team's confidence is directly tied to your ability to stay calm under pressure.

Am I committed to developing my own resilience? You can't give what you don't have. If you're not investing in your own growth, you can't expect your team to invest in theirs.

These aren't theoretical questions. They're diagnostic. Your honest answers reveal where you're strong and where you need to build capacity. Because here's what we know after decades of working with leaders across industries, from boardrooms to battlefields: leadership is hard. It's supposed to be hard. If it were easy, everyone would do it. If it didn't require sacrifice, it wouldn't be worth doing.

But here's the other thing we know: you're capable of more than you think. The leaders who thrive aren't the ones who avoid the tough parts. They are the ones who accept the weight, face the challenges head-on, and keep showing up anyway.

They don't pretend to have all the answers. They ask better questions. They don't chase popularity. They earn respect. They don't avoid discomfort. They lean into it.

YOU'RE TOUGHER THAN YOU THINK

The phone rang at 6:27 a.m. Maybe it was today. Maybe it was last week. Maybe it will be tomorrow. It doesn't matter. What matters is what you did when it rang. Did you answer it? Did you take ownership of the problem on the other end? Did you lead, even when it was hard?

Leadership is tough. But so are you. The question isn't whether leadership is hard. The question is: are you willing to do it anyway? Because the world doesn't need more people sitting on the sidelines, wishing things were easier. It needs leaders, real leaders who are tough enough to stand in the fire and lead others through it.

That's you. That's why you're here. And that's why this book exists. To help you become the leader your people need, even when it's tough. Especially when it's tough.

The chapters that follow will give you the frameworks, tools, and practices to lead effectively in this environment. We'll explore how to lead through change without burning out your team. How to build cultures of accountability and trust. How to develop others while protecting your own capacity. How to make decisions under pressure. How to have the hard conversations that move organizations forward.

But it all starts here, with this truth: leadership is harder now than it's ever been. And you're capable of rising to meet it.

KEY TAKEAWAYS:

- **Accept That You Don't Need All the Answers.** Stop pretending you know everything. When you don't have the answer, say, "I don't know, but let's find out." This opens the door to collaboration, learning, and building trust. Your team respects honesty far more than false confidence.

- **Choose Respect Over Popularity.** Recognize that making tough calls will sometimes disappoint people. That's the job. If your primary goal is to be liked, you'll avoid necessary decisions. Focus on earning respect by doing what's right for the mission, not what's comfortable.

- **Understand That You're Always Being Watched.** Every word, email, silence, and decision sends a signal. Your team is constantly reading you for cues about whether things are okay. Be intentional about what you communicate, even nonverbally. Show up intentionally and consistently so your people know what to expect from you.

- **Get Comfortable Making Decisions with Incomplete Information.** Perfect clarity rarely exists in leadership. Waiting for all the facts often means waiting too long. Train yourself to make the best call you can with what you have, then adapt as new information emerges. Decisiveness, even imperfect decisiveness, builds momentum.

- **Have the Hard Conversations Early.** Avoiding difficult conversations doesn't make them go away. Ignoring problems makes them worse. Address performance issues, misalignment, and conflicts quickly and directly. Your willingness to lean into discomfort sets the tone for accountability across the team.

- **Build Consistency That Creates Trust.** Your team needs to know they can count on you regardless of circumstances. Don't let your mood dictate your leadership. Manage yourself first so you can lead others effectively. Trust is built through predictable values, standards, and presence.

- **Protect Your Capacity for the Long Haul.** Leadership is a marathon, not a sprint. Protect your time, set boundaries, and prioritize what actually matters. If you burn out, your team suffers. Sustainable leadership requires that you maintain your energy, focus, and stamina so you can keep showing up when it counts.

REFLECTION QUESTIONS:

1. When was the last time you felt the weight of leadership rather than the status of leadership? What specifically made it heavy?

2. What signals are you sending, intentionally or unintentionally, when you walk into a room, respond to an email, or go silent during uncertainty?

3. Which leadership myth do you struggle with most: "I must have all the answers," "I need to be liked," or "the hardest

part is the workload"?

4. Think about a recent decision you delayed or softened to avoid disappointing someone. What did that avoidance cost you, or your team?

5. Where are you choosing short-term harmony over long-term respect?

6. How would you describe the level of change fatigue on your team right now? What evidence supports your assessment?

7. Where might there be a gap between what you say you value, such as development, well-being, or growth, and what people actually experience?

8. What routines or disciplines help you stay steady when others are not? Which ones need strengthening?

9. Are you making decisions based on incomplete information, or are you waiting for certainty that may never come?

10. What would it look like to lead in a way that allows you to be still effective five years from now?

CHAPTER 2

LEADING CHANGE
IN AN UNCERTAIN AND
CHANGE-FATIGUED WORLD

The CEO stopped mid-sentence during our consulting session. "I don't understand," she said, frustration edging into her voice. "We've explained the changes. We've shown them the data. We've answered their questions. Why are they still resisting?"

We've heard some version of this from clients in nearly every organization. Leaders are baffled. They've done everything the playbook says to do. They communicated the vision, outlined the strategy, provided resources, held town halls, and sent follow-up emails. Yet people remain stuck. Productivity drops. Morale tanks. High performers start updating their résumés. The confusion is genuine: if we did everything right, why isn't it working?

Here's what most leaders miss: the problem isn't communication. It's biology.

Change has always been part of leadership, but what's different now is the speed, the stacking, and the stakes. Leaders are no longer managing one change at a time. They're navigating continuous

17

disruption involving new technologies, shifting labor markets, economic volatility, regulatory pressure, social expectations, and AI, often all at once. Many leaders look around and ask: Why are people struggling so much to keep up? The answer is not a lack of intelligence, work ethic, or commitment. The answer is neurobiology.

To understand why traditional change management fails, we need to start where change actually happens: in the neurobiology of the human brain. When leaders understand how the brain reacts to uncertainty and disruption, they can stop mislabeling normal human responses as resistance, laziness, or incompetence and instead lead with clarity, structure, and purpose. This is how leaders move people forward during times of accelerating change without burning them out or losing them along the way.

THE BRAIN IS WIRED FOR SURVIVAL, NOT SPEED

The human brain evolved to keep us alive, not to keep us comfortable during quarterly reorganizations or technological upheaval. At its core, the brain's primary job is threat detection. Long before spreadsheets, dashboards, or AI tools existed, the brain was scanning for danger: predators, scarcity, and social exclusion.

Modern change activates those same ancient systems. When people experience changes, especially rapid or poorly explained changes, the brain asks three immediate questions, often subconsciously: Am I safe? Do I still belong? Do I still matter?

If the brain cannot quickly answer "yes" to those questions, it shifts into a defensive state. This is not a character flaw. It's neurology.

From a scientific perspective, uncertainty increases cognitive load. The brain must work harder to predict outcomes, assess risks, and decide how to respond. That additional effort consumes energy. Over time, sustained uncertainty leads to mental fatigue, slower decision-making, emotional volatility, and reduced creativity. People are not resisting change. They are protecting themselves.

Neuroscience research shows that the amygdala, the brain's alarm system, becomes hyperactive during periods of uncertainty. According to a study published in Nature Neuroscience, ambiguous situations trigger stronger stress responses than clearly negative ones. In other words, not knowing what's coming feels worse than knowing something bad is coming. This explains why vague announcements like "there will be changes soon" create more anxiety than clear, direct communication about difficult realities.

WHY UNCERTAINTY FEELS SO UNCOMFORTABLE

The brain is a prediction machine. It constantly compares what it expects to happen with what actually happens. When predictions are accurate, the brain is efficient. When predictions are disrupted by new systems, new leaders, new rules, or unclear priorities, the brain goes into overdrive.

Research in neuroscience shows that uncertainty activates the same brain regions as physical pain. That helps explain why people often react emotionally to change that seems, on the surface, relatively minor. A new reporting structure, a new software platform, or a new performance metric may not be physically dangerous, but neurologically, it feels painfully destabilizing.

This is why people crave routines during times of chaos. Habits reduce the number of decisions the brain must make. Familiar processes create a sense of control. When change disrupts routines without providing a new structure, people feel like they are drifting. Productivity drops, not because people are unwilling, but because their brains are overloaded.

During one military deployment, we implemented a new communication protocol mid-mission. Simple change on paper. The crew had operated under the previous system for years. The old system was automatic and effortless. The new protocol required conscious thought for every transmission. Within 48 hours, we saw errors spike. Not because sailors didn't care. Because their cognitive bandwidth was maxed out managing everything else while simultaneously learning new procedures. Once we recognized the overload and built in structured training time, performance recovered. The lesson? Never underestimate the mental cost of what leaders perceive as simple changes.

CHANGE THREATENS IDENTITY, NOT JUST TASKS

One of the most overlooked aspects of change is its impact on identity. Work is not just what people do; it is often how they define themselves. Titles, expertise, seniority, and routines provide a sense of competence and value. Change alters those elements. New technology replaces familiar skills, new leadership shifts expectations, or new strategies deprioritize past successes. As a result, people experience a subtle but powerful threat to their identity.

The brain interprets threats to identity as social threats. Social threats trigger the same stress responses as physical danger. This is why people may cling to "the way we've always done it," even when they intellectually understand the need for change. The resistance is not about logic. It's about loss. Effective leaders recognize this and address it directly.

In one consulting engagement with a healthcare organization, we worked with a team of experienced nurses as they implemented a new electronic health records system. These were seasoned professionals with an average of 20-plus years of experience, deeply respected by colleagues and patients alike. Yet when the new system rolled out, several refused to engage. Management labeled them "resistant to change," "old-fashioned," and "set in their ways."

When we dug deeper, the real issue surfaced. These nurses had built their professional identity on their ability to remember patient details, anticipate needs, and move quickly through documentation so they could spend more time providing direct care. The new system, which was clunky and time-consuming in the early stages, made them feel incompetent. Their resistance wasn't about technology. It was about preserving their sense of professional worth by providing excellent patient care. Once leadership acknowledged this and provided mentorship pairings that allowed administrative assistants to help refine the system's workflow, engagement shifted. People need to see how they still matter in the new reality.

COGNITIVE OVERLOAD IS THE SILENT PRODUCTIVITY KILLER

Accelerating change creates another problem: stacked demands. People are asked to learn new systems, adapt to new expectations, deliver the same or better results, support teammates who are also struggling, maintain customer satisfaction, and absorb constant communication, all while continuing their regular work. The human brain can only process so much information at once. When demand exceeds capacity, performance declines. Not because people don't care, but because the brain is triaging.

In this state, people default to familiar behaviors, short-term thinking, risk avoidance, reduced collaboration, and a tendency to protect their silos. Leaders who interpret this as disengagement often respond with pressure. Pressure, however, increases the release of stress hormones such as cortisol, which further impair learning, memory, and decision-making. The cycle accelerates in the wrong direction.

According to research from the Harvard Business Review, employees experiencing chronic stress make 50% more errors and take 19% longer to complete tasks. The math is straightforward: overloaded brains produce worse outcomes, slower.

This overloaded state explains why the behaviors leaders observe during change are so predictable. What gets labeled as resistance falls into four scientifically documented stress responses.

WHY PEOPLE APPEAR "RESISTANT" TO CHANGE

What leaders often label as resistance usually falls into one of four scientifically predictable responses: fight, where people argue, challenge decisions, or criticize leadership; flight, where people disengage, check out, or leave; freeze, where people become quiet, withdrawn, or indecisive; and fawn, where people agree publicly, but resist privately.

All four are stress responses. None of these is a sign of incompetence. Leaders who understand this stop taking resistance personally and start leading strategically.

We witnessed this firsthand during a consulting engagement with a regional hospital system implementing a new patient management platform. The project had stalled for months. Leadership blamed resistance from the physician staff. When we interviewed the physicians, we discovered something entirely different.

The most vocal resister was one of their best physicians. He had 20 years of experience, was beloved by patients, and respected by staff. In meetings, he asked pointed questions, challenged timelines, and questioned decisions. Leadership interpreted this as obstruction.

What was really happening? He was in fight mode, his brain's stress response to uncertainty. He'd seen three previous technology rollouts fail. Each failure meant more work, more frustration, and worse patient care during the transition. His questions weren't resistant. They were his brain trying to assess threats and predict outcomes.

Once physician leadership recognized this, they changed their approach. Instead of sidelining him, they invited him onto the implementation team. His difficult questions became valuable insights that helped design a better rollout. Within weeks, he became one of the system's strongest advocates for the change. The lesson? What appears to be resistance often masks legitimate concern. Your job is to decode the stress response and address the underlying need.

THE PREDICTABLE PATH OF CHANGE: UNDERSTANDING THE J-CURVE

Understanding these stress responses explains why change follows such a predictable emotional pattern. Once you recognize it, you can stop being surprised by it and start preparing for it. Every significant change, whether it's a new technology platform, a leadership transition, or a strategic pivot, follows an emotional pattern called the J-curve.

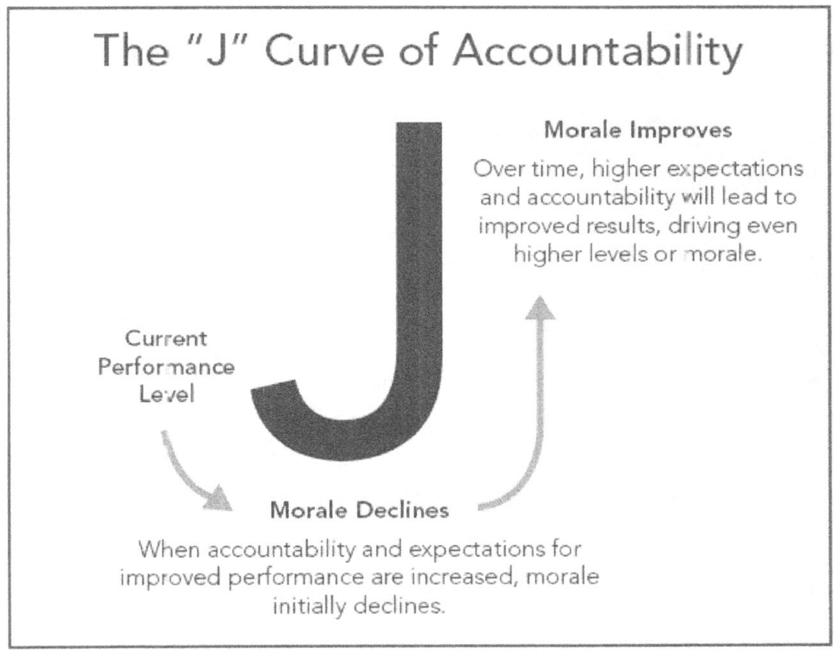

Every change moves through four distinct stages, each with its own characteristics and leadership requirements.

Stage 1: Denial. People hear about the change but don't believe it will happen. "This too shall pass," they conclude. They keep doing what they've always done, waiting for things to blow over.

Stage 2: Resistance. Reality sets in. The change is happening. Now comes pushback. Sometimes the resistance is overt, oftentimes it is subtle. Productivity drops. Complaints increase. People dig in their heels. They don't want to change, so they don't.

Stage 3: Exploration. This is the turning point. People start experimenting in a new way. They ask questions. They test possibilities. Energy begins to shift from defensive to mildly curious.

Stage 4: Commitment. People fully adopt the change. New

behaviors become routine. Confidence returns. Performance often exceeds pre-change levels.

Here's the problem: most leaders focus all their energy on Stage 1. They announce the change, explain the rationale, and expect immediate buy-in. When people hit Stage 2, the resistance phase, leaders panic. They assume something is wrong. They weren't clear enough. They didn't sell it hard enough. They need another all-hands meeting. Wrong.

Stage 2 isn't a failure. It's expected. The J-curve dips before it rises. Performance will temporarily decline. That's not abnormal. It's a feature of how human beings process change. Leaders who understand this can prepare their teams instead of being blindsided. Great leaders actually promise problems when implementing a change, so their people know what to expect.

> **PREDICTABILITY REDUCES COGNITIVE LOAD. IT FREES MENTAL ENERGY FOR ADAPTATION.**

During a deployment, we had to shift a reporting protocol mid-mission. The announcement went out at 8:00 am. By 2:00 pm, I was getting reports of frustration, confusion, and errors. A young officer approached me, clearly concerned. "Commander, I think people aren't getting it. Should we delay implementation?"

I pulled out a piece of paper and drew the J-curve. "What you're seeing is Stage 2. This is exactly what's supposed to happen. If people weren't pushing back, I'd be worried. It would mean they aren't taking it seriously. Give them 48 hours. Keep supporting them. Keep reassuring them. Be kind. This will pass."

It did. Within three days, the team moved into exploration. Within a week, the new system was running smoother than the old one. The difference? We expected the dip and didn't let it derail us.

In contrast, we've seen organizations abandon necessary changes simply because leadership couldn't tolerate the discomfort of Stage 2. One manufacturing client we worked with had attempted to restructure their production process three times in 18 months. Each time, when resistance surfaced, the CEO backed down. "It's not working," he'd say. "People hate it." So, he stopped the process. This is a mistake. The worst thing a leader can do is go backward in the J-curve.

What he really meant was, "I can't handle resistance and watching my people struggle." That's understandable, but it's not leadership. When we finally convinced him to push through the resistance phase, to stay steady, provide support, and trust the process, the transformation succeeded. Six months later, productivity was up 23%, employee satisfaction had improved, and the CEO admitted, "I almost quit again at week two. I'm glad you stopped me."

WHAT EXCEPTIONAL LEADERS DO DIFFERENTLY DURING CHANGE

Understanding the neuroscience and recognizing the J-curve gives leaders a significant advantage. Knowledge alone doesn't move organizations forward; action does. The question becomes: what specifically do exceptional leaders do differently when they understand how change affects people?

Exceptional leaders do not eliminate uncertainty; they cannot. But they address the brain's needs directly through nine consistent practices.

1. Leaders Create Predictability Where They Can

Even when the future is unclear, leaders can create stability in the present. They clarify what is actually changing, what is not changing, what decisions have already been made, what timelines look like, even if tentative, and what success looks like right now.

Predictability reduces cognitive load. It frees mental energy for adaptation. One of the most powerful phrases a leader can use during change is: "Here's what I know for certain right now." Then list it. Even if the list is short, it gives people something solid to hold onto.

During the 2008 financial crisis, we worked with a credit union CEO facing massive uncertainty. Markets were crashing. Members were panicking. Her board was divided on strategy. Every day brought more bad news. In her weekly all-staff meetings, she started with the same opening: "Here's what I know for certain today." Then she'd list those things.

"We are solvent. Our reserve ratios are strong. No one is losing their job this month. We will make payroll. Your benefits are secure. We are open for business."

Then she'd follow with: "Here's what I don't know yet." And she'd be honest about the uncertainties, things like loan default rates, regulatory changes, and market recovery timelines.

This simple practice created an anchor. Employees stopped spiraling into worst-case scenarios because they had facts to hold onto. The predictable structure of the meetings became a stabilizing rhythm during chaos. Productivity stayed remarkably high. Employee turnover was minimal. The credit union not only survived but also emerged stronger than many competitors. When we asked the CEO what made the difference, she said, "I gave them the truth they could hang on to."

2. Leaders Over-Communicate With Purpose

In times of change, silence is interpreted as danger. Strong leaders communicate early, often, clearly, and consistently. They repeat messages, knowing that stressed brains do not absorb information the first time. They explain why, not just what. They acknowledge uncertainty instead of pretending it does not exist.

According to research from Towers Watson, companies with highly effective communication practices are 3.5 times more likely to outperform their peers. Communication isn't soft. It's strategic. Importantly, they listen. Listening restores a sense of agency, which calms the brain.

We've seen the catastrophic results of under-communication too many times. A mid-sized tech company we consulted with was planning a major reorganization. Leadership decided to keep it quiet until all decisions were finalized. "We don't want to cause unnecessary worry," the CEO explained.

What happened instead? Rumors filled the void. Speculation ran wild. People assumed the worst. By the time leadership finally announced the changes, employee trust had evaporated. The talented people they wanted to retain had started interviewing elsewhere. The reorganization they'd carefully planned became a crisis they had to manage.

Compare that to a retail chain CEO who took the opposite approach. Facing store closures due to market shifts, he sent a video message to all employees the day the board approved the decision. "We're going to close underperforming locations. I don't have all the answers yet. I don't know which stores or when. But I will update you every Friday at 3 PM until we do. You deserve to hear from me, not the rumor mill."

He kept that promise. Every Friday. Sometimes the update was 90 seconds: "No new decisions this week. Still analyzing data. I'll keep you posted." Other times it was longer. But the consistency mattered. When closures were finally announced, employees felt respected. Many chose to relocate to other stores. Some left, but they left without bitterness. Leadership isn't about having all the answers. It's about consistently showing up with the truth.

3. Leaders Involve People Early, Especially the Resisters
Communication creates the foundation, but exceptional leaders go further. They recognize that the most vocal critics often hold the keys to successful implementation. Here's a counterintuitive truth: the people most resistant to change are often the organization's informal leaders. They have influence. They set the tone. They are often the most committed. They care, which is why they are not afraid to speak up. Leaving them out of the process until you have to include them is a fatal mistake. Involve them upfront.

Get your most resistant people into the room early. Not to convince them. To learn from them. They will tell you what the roadblocks are.

They will surface concerns others are too afraid to voice. They will help you design better implementation strategies. And here's what happens next: when people are involved in shaping change, they shift from being resistors to co-creators. They are involved. They're more likely to support it.

WHEN PEOPLE HAVE OWNERSHIP, RESISTANCE TRANSFORMS INTO COMMITMENT.

During a merger between two professional services firms, we noticed the integration was stalling. One partner, David, was openly skeptical. In meetings, he questioned everything. Other partners complained about his negativity. The managing partner had two choices: sideline David or engage him.

He chose engagement. He asked David to lead the culture integration workgroup. David was stunned. "You want me to lead this? I've been fighting you at every turn." The managing partner smiled. "Exactly. You see problems others miss. I need that. Help me make this work."

David accepted. Within weeks, his entire demeanor shifted. The insights he'd been using to criticize became tools to strengthen the integration. He identified potential conflicts before they erupted. He built bridges between teams. By the end of the process, David had become one of the merger's strongest advocates. When people have ownership, resistance transforms into commitment.

4. Leaders Promise Problems, Not Perfection

Most leaders try to sell change by making it sound easy. "This transition will be seamless." "You'll love the new system once you get used to it." "It's going to make everything better." Stop. Change is hard. It's disruptive. It will create temporary pain. Tell people that.

One of the most effective change leaders we've ever worked with opened his kickoff meeting with this: "This is going to be messy. You're going to be frustrated. Some days you're going to want to quit. I'm not going to pretend otherwise. But here's what I can promise. We're going to work through it together, and on the other side, we'll be stronger."

People exhaled. He didn't insult their intelligence. He acknowledged reality. And when the inevitable frustrations surfaced, no one said, "You didn't tell us it would be this hard." He had. Promising problems does something counterintuitive. It builds trust. When leaders are honest about difficulty, people believe them about everything else. When leaders pretend that change will be painless, credibility evaporates the moment reality hits.

5. Leaders Reduce Competing Priorities

Honesty about difficulty matters, but so does protecting people's capacity to handle that difficulty. One of the most powerful leadership moves during change is subtraction. Great leaders ask: What can we pause? What can we simplify? What no longer matters right now?

By narrowing focus, leaders protect cognitive capacity. People perform better when expectations are clear and achievable.

During one particularly intense period of transformation in a financial services firm, the COO made a bold call. He suspended all non-critical projects for 90 days. "We're going all-in on this," he said. "Everything else waits." The pushback was immediate. "But what about this project or that initiative?" His answer: "It waits."

That singular focus allowed the team to channel energy into learning the new processes without the mental drain of juggling a dozen other initiatives. The transformation succeeded because people had the bandwidth to absorb it.

6. Leaders Reinforce the Mission and Vision

Creating focus through subtraction matters. But focus alone isn't enough. People also need to know why their focused effort matters. During change, people need to know they matter. During turmoil, people are not just trying to figure out what to do differently; they are trying to determine whether their effort still matters. Change disrupts routines, expectations, and often confidence. When familiar markers of success disappear, people naturally begin to question their value, their role, and their future. In these moments, leaders play a critical role in anchoring individuals and teams to something larger than the disruption itself.

Leaders who lead change well consistently reconnect people with the organization's mission and vision. They help employees understand that while methods may change, the purpose remains the same. This matters deeply from a neurological standpoint. When people can link their work to a meaningful outcome, the brain shifts from threat mode to engagement mode. Meaning provides context, and context reduces anxiety.

Effective leaders do several things intentionally during change. They connect the change to purpose, explaining not only what is happening but also why it matters and why it supports the organization's long-term mission, values, and goals. They take the time to show how individual roles contribute, even when job duties are evolving or temporary inefficiencies exist. People do not need to be told they are important in vague terms; they need to see how their work directly supports the bigger picture.

Strong leaders also recognize progress, not just final outcomes. During change, wins may be smaller, slower, or less visible. When leaders acknowledge effort, learning, adaptation, and incremental improvement, they reinforce momentum and confidence. This recognition signals that growth is valued, not just perfection. It also reinforces psychological safety, an essential condition for learning and innovation in uncertain times.

Equally important, great leaders frame challenges as collective rather than personal. Instead of asking, "Why can't you handle this?" they ask, "What are we learning?" and "How do we solve this together?" This subtle shift reduces defensiveness and preserves trust. People are far more willing to stretch, experiment, and persevere when they believe they are not facing change alone.

The research supports this approach. According to McKinsey, employees who find meaning in their work are three times more likely to stay with their organization and report 1.7 times higher job satisfaction. During times of change, that sense of purpose becomes even more critical. When uncertainty is high, meaning becomes a stabilizer. It reminds people that their effort has value beyond the immediate disruption and that their contribution still counts.

In the end, reinforcing mission and vision is not a soft leadership practice; it is a strategic one. Leaders who consistently connect change to purpose help people move forward with clarity, motivation, and resilience. They turn disruption into direction. And in doing so, they preserve not just performance, but commitment, the resource organizations can least afford to lose during times of accelerating change.

7. *Leaders Invest in Capability, Not Just Compliance*

Change often fails because leaders announce new expectations without building new skills. One of the most common and costly mistakes leaders make during periods of change is assuming that announcing new expectations automatically creates new capability. It does not. Change initiatives frequently fail not because people are unwilling to comply, but because they are unprepared to perform. When leaders demand results without first equipping their teams with the skills, knowledge, and confidence required to deliver them, they create frustration, fear, and ultimately disengagement.

Exceptional leaders understand that capability must precede compliance. They recognize that asking people to work in new ways, adopting new technologies, processes, or performance standards, requires intentional investment in learning. Training is not a perk or an afterthought; it is a prerequisite for success. Leaders who lead change well ensure that education and skill development come before accountability measures are enforced, not after performance falters.

This approach matters because learning is cognitively demanding. When individuals are required to master new skills under pressure, the brain experiences stress that can impair memory, focus, and problem-solving. Effective leaders account for this reality by allowing time for learning curves. They understand that temporary dips in productivity are a normal part of growth, not evidence of failure. By setting realistic expectations and acknowledging the effort required to learn something new, leaders reduce anxiety and increase persistence.

Great leaders also normalize mistakes as part of the development process. During change, errors are not only inevitable but also helpful. Mistakes provide feedback about what is working, what is unclear, and where additional support is needed. Leaders who respond to mistakes with curiosity rather than punishment create an environment where people are willing to experiment, ask questions, and refine their approach. This accelerates learning and strengthens long-term performance.

Crucially, investing in capability requires psychological safety. People must believe they can admit what they do not know without risking embarrassment, blame, or career consequences. Without psychological safety, individuals often resort to performing competence rather than building it. They nod in meetings, avoid asking questions, and quietly hope problems will resolve themselves. This illusion of understanding is far more dangerous than open learning gaps, especially during change.

Exceptional leaders pair accountability with support. They are clear about expectations and outcomes, but they also provide the tools, coaching, feedback, and resources necessary to meet those expectations. Accountability without support feels punitive. Support without accountability breeds complacency. The balance between the two creates ownership and confidence.

SLOW CHANGE IS NOT KINDER. IT'S CRUELER. DRAGGING OUT A TRANSITION PROLONGS THE PAIN.

Ultimately, leaders who invest in capability build organizations that can adapt repeatedly, not just once. They develop people who can learn, unlearn, and relearn as conditions evolve. In times of accelerating change, that capacity may be the most sustainable competitive advantage an organization can possess.

8. Leaders Move Fast

Building capability is essential, but timing matters too. Leaders face a paradox: people need time to learn, but prolonged transitions create their own problems. Here's a truth that surprises many leaders: slow change is not kinder. It's crueler. Dragging out a transition prolongs the pain. It extends the period of uncertainty. It gives resistance time to calcify. Our advice? Rip off the Band-Aid.

Research supports this. According to the Harvard Business Review, fast implementations have significantly higher success rates than phased ones. Speed creates momentum. Momentum creates confidence. This doesn't mean reckless. It means decisive.

9. Leaders Manage Their Own Emotions First

Perhaps the most overlooked truth of leadership during change is this: leaders set the emotional tone. People unconsciously mirror the behavior of those in authority. Leaders who are frantic, reactive, or inconsistent amplify stress. Leaders who are calm, transparent, and steady create stability, even in chaos. This doesn't mean pretending everything is fine. It means responding with intention rather than emotion.

Before every high-level briefing during major military deployments, we had a quick focus exercise: Take deep breaths. Check in mentally. Intentional grounding. Because the moment you step into that room, every eye is on you. Your energy becomes their energy. If you bring panic, they absorb panic. If you bring calm resolve, they absorb that instead.

LEADING CHANGE IS A DISCIPLINE, NOT A PERSONALITY TRAIT

The myth of the "naturally good change leader" does real damage. Leading through change is not about charisma. It's about understanding human behavior and consistently applying that understanding.

The best leaders are not those who push hardest. They are those who understand how people think under pressure, design systems that reduce friction, communicate with clarity and empathy, and balance urgency with humanity.

Change will not slow down. Change will continue to accelerate. Leaders who fail to adapt their leadership will burn out their people and themselves. Leaders who understand the science of change will build resilient, adaptable organizations that thrive in uncertainty.

Before you can lead anyone else through change, you must lead yourself. Change exhausts leaders, too. The difference is, you don't get the luxury of checking out. You're the steady hand. The calm voice. The source of direction when everyone else feels lost. That requires discipline.

Protect your own resilience. Sleep matters. Exercise matters. Boundaries matter. You cannot pour from an empty cup, and leadership during change is an endurance event, not a sprint. Stay connected to your purpose. Why does this change matter? Who benefits? What becomes possible on the other side? When the resistance is loud and the progress feels slow, reconnect to the reason you're doing this in the first place.

Stay informed and never stop learning. One of the most distinguishing traits of effective leaders during times of change is that they do not retreat into isolation or rely solely on past experience. They read broadly and intentionally. They network with other leaders across industries. They seek out perspectives that challenge their assumptions rather than reinforce them.

From a cognitive standpoint, learning restores a sense of control. When leaders actively gather information, the brain shifts from a reactive threat response to a problem-solving mode. Knowledge reduces uncertainty, not by eliminating risk, but by improving judgment. Leaders who continue to learn are better able to contextualize change, anticipate second and third-order effects, and make decisions grounded in reality rather than fear or speculation.

Great leaders also understand that learning is contagious. When employees see leaders investing time in reading, asking thoughtful questions, attending industry events, and engaging in professional networks, it signals that adaptation is expected and supported.

Learning becomes a shared value rather than a remedial activity. In contrast, leaders who stop learning often default to outdated mental models, overconfidence, or rigid thinking, precisely when flexibility is most needed.

In times of accelerating change, leadership is not about having all the answers. It's about staying curious enough to keep asking better questions. Leaders who remain informed, connected, and intellectually engaged are far better equipped to guide their organizations through uncertainty with credibility, confidence, and clarity.

And remember, you don't have to have all the answers. But you do have to stay present, stay engaged, and keep moving forward.

WHY THIS CHAPTER MATTERS

Leadership is tough because change never stops, and the leaders who misread resistance as attitude or lack of commitment make the work harder than it needs to be. They push when they should support, communicate once when they should communicate repeatedly, and abandon necessary change at precisely the moment when staying the course would have turned the corner. The cost is not just a failed initiative. It is eroded trust, depleted teams, and a culture that learns to wait out leadership rather than follow it. When leaders recognize that resistance is biology before it is behavior, they stop taking it personally and start leading strategically. Change will not slow down. The leaders who thrive are not the ones who find ways to avoid its difficulty. They are the ones who understand it well enough to lead others through it without losing them along the way.

MOVING FORWARD

Leadership is tough. But when leaders learn how the brain responds to change, tough does not have to mean chaotic, exhausting, or destructive. It can mean intentional, disciplined, and effective, even amid relentless transformation.

That's leadership. And that's what gets people through.

KEY TAKEAWAYS:

- **Change is not a communication problem; it's a biological one.** Resistance to change is rarely about attitude or intelligence. It is the brain's natural response to uncertainty, threat, and overload. Leaders who understand this stop blaming people and start leading more effectively.

- **Uncertainty activates the brain's threat system.** When people cannot quickly answer "Am I safe, do I belong, and do I still matter?" their brains shift into defense mode. Productivity, creativity, and collaboration decline. Not because people don't care, but because their cognitive resources are strained.

- **What appears to be resistance is often a stress response.** Fight, flight, freeze, and fawn are predictable human reactions to change. Exceptional leaders decode these responses instead of taking them personally or attempting to suppress them.

- **The J-Curve is predictable and temporary.** Performance dips during change are normal and expected. Leaders who understand the J-curve prepare their teams for the dip, support them through it, and avoid the costly mistake of retreating mid-change.

- **Clarity reduces cognitive load.** Leaders cannot eliminate uncertainty, but they can reduce it by clarifying what is changing, what is not, what is known, and what is still being decided. Even partial certainty stabilizes people.

- **Silence is interpreted as danger.** In times of change, people fill information gaps with fear. Leaders must communicate early, often, and consistently, even when there is no new information to share.

- **Involving resisters early strengthens change.** Those who push back are often the most committed and influential people in the organization. When involved early, they shift from critics to co-creators, improving implementation outcomes.

- **Promising problems builds trust.** Leaders who acknowledge that change will be difficult preserve credibility. Pretending change will be painless erodes trust the moment reality sets in.

- **Capability must precede compliance.** Expecting new performance without building new skills creates frustration and failure. Training, time, and psychological safety are prerequisites for sustainable change.

- **Leaders set the emotional tone.** People mirror leadership behavior. Calm, steady leaders create stability. Reactive leaders amplify stress. Leading change requires emotional discipline, not emotional suppression.

- **Purpose anchors people during disruption.** When leaders connect change to mission and meaning, people move from threat to engagement. Purpose restores motivation when routines and confidence are disrupted.

- **Leading change is a discipline, not a personality trait.** Effective change leadership is learned, practiced, and repeatable. It requires understanding human behavior and consistently applying that understanding, especially when it's uncomfortable.

REFLECTION QUESTIONS:

1. Where have you recently labeled behavior as resistance instead of asking what stress response might be driving it?

2. What signals, intentional or not, might be increasing anxiety during current or upcoming changes?

3. What uncertainty are you unintentionally amplifying by delaying communication or waiting for perfect clarity?

4. How often do you explicitly separate what you know for certain from what is still undecided?

5. Where could additional structure, routine, or predictability reduce cognitive overload for your team?

6. Which stage of the J-curve is your team currently in, and how do you know?

7. How do you personally react when performance dips during change: with patience or panic?

8. Have you ever abandoned a necessary change because you couldn't tolerate Stage 2 discomfort? What did that cost?

9. Whose identity might be most threatened by the changes you are leading, and how are you addressing that directly?

10. Who are the informal leaders or resisters you should be involving earlier rather than managing around?

11. Where might acknowledging loss or honoring the past help people let go and move forward?

12. What competing priorities could you pause, simplify, or eliminate to protect learning capacity?

13. How well are you regulating your own stress before leading others through uncertainty?

14. What habits, boundaries, or routines do you need to strengthen to lead change sustainably?

15. How are you staying informed and continuing to learn rather than relying solely on experience?

16. What is one behavior you will stop doing that increases stress during change?

17. What is one behavior you will start doing to create clarity, stability, or trust?

18. If change continues at this pace (and it will), how must you evolve as a leader to keep your people engaged and resilient?

CHAPTER 3

STRATEGIC DECISION-MAKING
MAKE THE CALL BEFORE THE CALL IS MADE FOR YOU

Leadership is not tested when decisions are easy. It is tested when the decision is obvious, but the consequences are painful. When you know what must be done, and you also know someone will be disappointed, inconvenienced, reassigned, demoted, let go, or told no.

That is where leadership gets real. And that is why leadership is tough.

Most people want to believe that good leadership means finding a way for everyone to win. Sometimes that is possible, but often it is not. The uncomfortable truth is that every meaningful decision creates winners and losers, even if the losses are temporary or indirect. Strategic decision-making requires the courage to accept that reality and the discipline to move forward anyway.

This chapter is not about being cold, callous, or indifferent. It is about being clear-eyed, principled, and accountable when emotions, relationships, and pressure tempt you to delay, dilute, or dodge the decision altogether. Because indecision is a decision, and avoidance has consequences too.

THE LEADERSHIP MYTH THAT CONFUSES RISING LEADERS

One of the most damaging myths in leadership is that strong leaders always have confidence and clarity. The truth is far messier. The best leaders often feel doubt, discomfort, and moral tension, but they move forward anyway.

In the military, we say that perfect information does not exist. Waiting until you have all the information before you make a decision means you will never make a decision, and that hurts people. In corporate leadership, the same rule applies. Waiting for the market to stabilize, the employee to self-correct, the culture to magically improve, or the numbers to rebound without intervention usually makes the eventual outcome worse. Good leaders don't eliminate risk. They manage it using the best available information.

We've surveyed more than 250,000 managers and employees over our combined careers. One pattern consistently emerges: the leaders people respect most are not the ones who never make mistakes. They're the ones who make tough calls, communicate clearly, own the outcomes, and learn publicly from what went wrong.

Unpopular decisions are often avoided because leaders fear damaging relationships, being perceived as uncaring, losing trust or morale, or being wrong. Here's what the data shows: avoiding the decision often causes all four.

WHY LEADERS HESITATE: THE NEED TO BE LIKED

Let's be direct about what stops leaders from making tough calls. It's rarely a lack of information. It's the deeply human need to be liked.

We once worked with a city manager. Fantastic person. Came to work every day with genuine enthusiasm. His team loved him. When we conducted a 360-degree assessment, the feedback was overwhelmingly positive. Everyone said he was a great guy. Then we dug deeper.

While he was well-liked, he wasn't always respected. The reason?

He wanted to make everyone on the team happy, which got in the way of making decisions, either in a timely manner or at all. He had one problematic team member. Everyone knew it. Everyone talked about it privately. But this manager didn't want to address it because he needed to be liked.

> **PEOPLE CAN ENDURE DIFFICULTY - WHAT THEY CANNOT ENDURE IS UNCERTAINTY WITHOUT PURPOSE.**

Six months later, three of his best employees left, not because of the problem employee directly, but because their leader wouldn't deal with it. They lost respect for him. They questioned his judgment. They decided to work somewhere else where leadership meant something. That manager eventually made the decision he should have made months earlier. By then, the damage was done. His reputation took years to rebuild.

The truth is, we all want to be liked on some level. That's human. But when a leader's desire to be liked overrides their responsibility to be respected, everyone loses. The leader. The team. The organization. Even the person who should have been held accountable months ago.

WHAT THE MILITARY TEACHES ABOUT DECISIVENESS

In uniform, decisions were rarely about comfort. They were about mission, people, and risk, in that order. Leaders who reversed those priorities endangered everyone. We've watched officers struggle with orders that would separate families, extend deployments, put people in harm's way, or cancel long-planned leave and personal plans. The hardest decisions were not tactical. They were human.

But here's the lesson many corporate leaders miss: clarity is kindness. Waffling, hedging, or attempting to soften reality erodes trust far faster than a hard but honest decision. People can endure difficulty. What they cannot endure is uncertainty without purpose.

A military memory that stands out was during a command briefing, a senior officer had to tell his team that their current deployment schedule was being extended. Families needed to be notified that their plans, weddings, births, holidays, and vacations would be affected. People were angry, frustrated, and exhausted.

The officer didn't sugarcoat it. He didn't promise it wouldn't happen again. He didn't blame higher command or deflect responsibility. He said, "This is the mission. This is why it matters. This is what we're doing. I know it's hard. I'm asking you to trust that we wouldn't do this unless it was necessary."

The room was silent. But the trust held. Why? Because he respected them enough to tell the truth. This principle, clarity over comfort, applies equally in corporate environments where leaders face decisions about layoffs, restructuring, budget cuts, or strategic pivots. The medium changes, but the human need for honest communication remains constant.

THE COST OF DELAY: LEARNING FROM NOKIA'S DECLINE

Understanding why we hesitate is the first step. The next step is recognizing what the delay actually costs. Few corporate stories illustrate this better than Nokia's decline. At its peak in the early 2000s, Nokia was not just successful; it was dominant. The company controlled more than 40 percent of the global mobile phone market. Internally, however, trouble was brewing.

Smartphones were emerging. Software ecosystems mattered more than hardware. Apple and Android were redefining consumer expectations. Nokia saw the change coming. That was not the problem. The problem was that leadership hesitated to act decisively because the necessary decisions were organizationally painful and politically explosive.

Nokia's internal culture was risk-averse, hierarchical, and deeply protective of legacy systems. Engineers knew the software platform was lagging. Middle managers feared delivering bad news to their superiors. Senior leaders feared disrupting a still-profitable machine. This created a dangerous illusion: we still have time.

TRUTH OFTEN FEELS LIKE BETRAYAL TO THOSE WHO BENEFITED FROM THE STATUS QUO.

By the time Stephen Elop became CEO in 2010, that illusion was gone. Elop inherited a company that needed radical change, and fast. The decisions required were deeply unpopular: abandon Nokia's proprietary operating systems, partner externally rather than build internally, lay off thousands of employees, and publicly acknowledge that the company was falling behind. None of these choices was culturally acceptable at the time. But avoiding them had already put the company in existential danger.

Elop's now-famous "burning platform" memo was blunt, uncomfortable, and brutally honest. He told employees that Nokia was standing on a burning platform, and that jumping into icy waters was the only option for survival. The message acknowledged failure, created urgency, and eliminated denial. Internally, the reaction was swift and emotional. Morale dropped. Trust fractured. Critics accused Elop of demoralizing the workforce and accelerating the decline.

Here is the leadership lesson many miss: truth often feels like betrayal to those who benefited from the status quo. Elop then made the ultimate unpopular decision to partner with Microsoft and abandon Nokia's legacy platforms. It was a strategic gamble made under intense time pressure, with no guarantee of success.

The strategy ultimately failed to save Nokia's handset business, which was sold to Microsoft in 2014. From a simplistic view, this looks like leadership failure. It wasn't. Nokia's downfall was not caused by decisive action. It was caused by years of indecision before decisive action became unavoidable. By the time Elop made the hard calls, the window for a smooth transition had closed. Market momentum, developer ecosystems, and consumer loyalty had already shifted.

Here is an uncomfortable truth for leaders: some decisions cannot undo the cost of previous avoidance. Courage delayed becomes damage control. Leaders everywhere have seen the warning signs in their own organizations. "We know this isn't working, but it's still profitable." "The organization

COURAGE DELAYED BECOMES DAMAGE CONTROL.

isn't ready for that conversation." "We'll fix it next year." "We don't want to scare people." Those statements feel reasonable. They are not. They are the language of delay.

The hardest decisions often involve dismantling systems that once worked. They require leaders to disappoint people who not only built them but also benefited from them, and to identify with them emotionally. That is not a failure of empathy. That is the burden of leadership. From Nokia, leaders should remember this: seeing reality early is not enough. You must act on information while the decisions still matter. Cultural resistance is not a reason to delay strategic change. When decisions are postponed to preserve comfort, the eventual decision will be harsher, faster, and more damaging. Leaders are rarely judged for making tough decisions too early. They are almost always judged for being too late.

THE DISCIPLINE OF ACTING EARLY: SIEMENS AND STRATEGIC FOCUS

If Nokia represents the cost of waiting too long, Siemens represents what leaders must be willing to pay early, before decline becomes unavoidable. Siemens is one of the world's oldest and most complex industrial organizations, with deep roots in engineering, manufacturing, energy, healthcare, and infrastructure. For decades, its size and diversity were considered strengths. Internally, however, that complexity created a familiar leadership problem: too many businesses, competing priorities, and diluted accountability.

By the early 2010s, Siemens faced mounting pressure, though none was yet catastrophic. And that is precisely when leadership decisions become hardest. They faced slowing growth in legacy businesses, rising global competition, and capital tied up in underperforming units, which increased scrutiny from investors and regulators. Under Joe Kaeser's leadership, Siemens made a series of decisions that were strategically necessary but politically painful.

These included divesting long-standing business units, restructuring large portions of the workforce, separating iconic divisions such as

Siemens Healthineers and Siemens Energy, forcing capital discipline across the organization, and publicly acknowledging that tradition was no longer a sufficient strategy. Internally, these decisions were deeply unpopular. Many employees viewed them as a betrayal of Siemens' heritage. Communities feared job losses. Leaders who had built careers inside certain divisions saw their influence, and sometimes their roles, disappear.

> **LEADERS ARE RARELY JUDGED FOR MAKING TOUGH DECISIONS TOO EARLY. THEY ARE ALMOST ALWAYS JUDGED FOR BEING TOO LATE.**

This is the moment where many executives hesitate. Siemens did not. What Siemens leadership understood is something many leaders avoid admitting: legacy can become a liability. The organization was not broken, but it was unfocused. Capital was spread too thin. Accountability was diffused. The strategy had become descriptive rather than decisive.

By acting early, Siemens accomplished what delayed leaders rarely can. It controlled the pace of change. It preserved options. It avoided panic-driven restructuring. It protected long-term competitiveness. Yes, people were impacted. Jobs were lost. Long-standing assumptions were challenged. But those consequences were managed deliberately, not reactively. This is a critical distinction in leadership: proactive pain is almost always less damaging than reactive pain.

One of the most instructive elements of the Siemens case is how leaders handled cultural resistance. Rather than softening the message to preserve comfort, leadership consistently reinforced a simple truth: focus is not abandonment. It is a responsibility. Employees did not have to like the decisions. They had to understand them. That clarity, repeated, reinforced, and aligned with capital allocation, allowed Siemens to repositior itself around industrial software, automation, smart infrastructure, and healthcare technology. The company emerged leaner, more agile, and better aligned with global economic realities.

Siemens demonstrates how effective strategic decision-making looks when leaders accept three hard truths: not every business you love deserves to survive, waiting until the decline is visible removes your ability to choose, and short-term pain is the price of long-term relevance. This is not ruthless leadership. It is responsible leadership. Unlike Nokia, Siemens did not wait for the market to force its hand. Leaders made decisions when they still had leverage: financially, culturally, and strategically. That is the difference between managing decline and shaping the future.

Put Nokia and Siemens side by side, and the lesson becomes unavoidable. Nokia delayed to protect comfort and paid later at a far higher cost. Siemens acted early, absorbed criticism, and preserved control. Both faced disruptions. Both faced internal resistance. Only one acted while choice still existed.

THE FOUR TRAPS THAT PREVENT EARLY ACTION

Over decades of working with leaders across industries, sectors, and countries, we've identified the common traps that prevent good leaders from making great decisions. These traps explain why so many organizations end up like Nokia rather than Siemens.

Trap One: Hoping the Problem Will Solve Itself

Hope is not a strategy. Yet we've watched intelligent, experienced leaders convince themselves that if they wait a little longer, the difficult employee will change, the underperforming division will turn around, or the market will shift in their favor. It almost never happens. Problems left unaddressed don't disappear. They metastasize. They become more expensive, more complicated, and more damaging over time.

ANALYSIS BECOMES PROCRASTINATION WHEN IT IS SUBSTITUTED FOR ACTION.

Trap Two: Waiting for Perfect Information

Leaders who demand certainty before acting guarantee that they will act too late. In our work across military and corporate environments, we've consistently found that leaders who wait for

100 percent clarity end up with significantly fewer options. The best leaders we've studied operate differently. They gather information quickly. They consult trusted advisors. They analyze scenarios. Then they make the call once they reach 70-80% confidence. That remaining 20-30%? That's where leadership lives.

Trap Three: Mistaking Analysis for Progress

We've seen executive teams hold endless meetings, commission multiple studies, form task forces, and create steering committees, all while avoiding the actual decision. It feels productive. It looks responsible. But it is neither. Analysis becomes procrastination when it is substituted for action. Great leaders know the difference. They gather input efficiently. They move deliberately. Then they decide.

Trap Four: Letting Relationships Trump Results

This is perhaps the most emotionally challenging trap. Leaders hesitate to make tough calls because the person affected is loyal, likable, long-tenured, or a friend or relative. We've coached executives who kept underperforming senior leaders in place for years because "they've been with us since the beginning" or "they're going through a tough time personally." The cost? Other talented people left. Team performance suffered. Strategy stalled.

Loyalty matters. But loyalty cannot be the only thing that matters. When leaders prioritize relationships over results, everyone loses, including the person who should have been transitioned months or years earlier.

CORPORATE REALITY: THE STRATEGIC POWER OF SAYING NO

In business, the most common unpopular decision is not termination. It is saying no. No to another product line. Another initiative. Another exception. Another meeting. Another "just this once." Leaders who lack the discipline to say no slowly bankrupt their organizations, not just financially, but culturally. They exhaust their people. They dilute focus. They signal that priorities are negotiable.

We've worked with executive teams who were drowning in initiatives. Every quarter, something new got added. Nothing ever got removed.

Leaders kept saying yes because they didn't want to disappoint stakeholders, turn down opportunities, or admit that capacity was finite. The result? Burnout. Mediocrity. Projects that launched but never gained traction. Teams that worked incredibly hard but achieved very little.

One of the toughest calls a leader can make is to stop something that people enjoy but no longer serves the strategy. That decision often feels personal, even when it is not. And yet, strategy without trade-offs is not strategy at all. It is wishful thinking.

Steve Jobs understood this. When he returned to Apple in 1997, the company had dozens of products. Jobs cut the lineup to four. Four. People were furious. But that ruthless focus saved the company and created space for innovation that changed industries. Saying no is not about being difficult. It is about being clear.

WHEN GREAT LEADERS OWN THE CONSEQUENCES

Too many leaders try to make decisions without consequences. They want accountability without discomfort. That does not exist. Every decision carries intended outcomes, unintended consequences, and second and third-order effects. Strong leaders acknowledge this upfront. They do not promise that everything will be painless. They promise that the decision was thoughtful, aligned, and intentional. Owning consequences builds credibility. Deflecting blame destroys it.

We coached a leader who made a restructuring decision that eliminated a popular program. Employees were upset. Some left. Others openly questioned his judgment. He could have blamed the board, the budget, or market conditions. Instead, he said, "I made this decision. I believe it's right for where we're going. I know some of you disagree. I respect that. If you want to talk through why I made this call, my door is open."

Not everyone agreed with him. But everyone respected that he owned it. Six months later, the organization was healthier. Twelve months later, even the skeptics acknowledged the decision had been necessary.

Mary Barra demonstrated the same principle when she became CEO of General Motors and inherited a crisis no leader wants: a fatal ignition switch defect that had been known internally for years and had been quietly ignored. The easy choice would have been to minimize exposure, blame legacy leadership, or quietly settle claims while moving on. Many organizations do exactly that. Barra did the opposite.

She made a series of deeply unpopular decisions. She publicly acknowledged GM's failures. She ordered an independent investigation. She fired employees, even senior leaders, who had failed to act. She testified before Congress, knowing the reputational risk. The internal back ash was real. Careers ended. Longtime employees felt betrayed. The company took a financial hit.

But here is the leadership lesson: Barra chose institutional trust over institutional comfort. She signaled that safety, accountability, and transparency were not slogans. They were standards. GM survived not because the decision was painless, but because it was decisive. Avoiding that decision would have cost far more in credibility, litigation, and long-term viability.

A PRACTICAL FRAMEWORK FOR TOUGH DECISIONS

When facing a difficult, unpopular decision, disciplined leaders work through five essential questions. These questions don't eliminate the difficulty, but they provide clarity about what matters most.

1. What problem am I really solving?

Not the symptom, but the root cause. Too many leaders solve the surface issue without addressing what created it in the first place, which guarantees the problem will return.

2. What happens if I do nothing?

This is the most ignored question and often the most revealing. Leaders overestimate the risk of action and underestimate the cost of inaction. Research by business professors Peter Dickson and Joseph Giglierano shows that not making a decision is far riskier than taking a bold risk that ultimately fails. They

> PEOPLE
> DON'T NEED
> YOU TO BE
> PERFECT.
> THEY NEED
> YOU TO BE
> HONEST.

refer to the major difference in these two scenarios as "missing the boat" versus "sinking the boat." What boat are you missing because you're too comfortable with your current situation?

3. Who is affected, and how?

Compassion does not require denial. Map out the stakeholders. Understand the impact. Anticipate the reactions. This doesn't mean you avoid the decision; it means you prepare for the aftermath.

4. Does this align with our stated values and strategy?

If not, fix the strategy or reconsider the decision. One of the fastest ways to erode trust is to make decisions that contradict what you claim to care about.

5. Am I willing to be accountable for the outcome?

If the answer is no, you're not ready to make the decision. Leadership means your name goes on the decision. Own it or don't make it.

HOW TO COMMUNICATE THE UNPOPULAR DECISION

How you communicate a hard decision matters as much as the decision itself. Effective leaders speak plainly. They avoid jargon and corporate spin. They explain the why without over-explaining. They listen without renegotiating. They stay present after the announcement.

Here's what doesn't work: calling a meeting, announcing a decision, and disappearing. That signals you're afraid of the reaction. It signals you don't believe in what you just said. It signals you're not willing to face the people affected by your choice. Great leaders lean into the discomfort. They take questions. They acknowledge emotions. They clarify misunderstandings. They don't get defensive when people push back.

The goal is not universal agreement. The goal is to earn respect. People don't need you to be perfect. They need you to be honest.

Making unpopular decisions does not mean ignoring emotions. It means managing them effectively. Emotionally intelligent leaders understand that people need time to process change, space to express concerns, and clarity about what happens next. They don't rush the human side of hard decisions. But they also don't let emotions prevent necessary action.

Here's what that looks like in practice. Before the decision, they anticipate reactions. They think through who will be most affected and why. They prepare for difficult conversations. They line up support resources if needed. During the announcement, they communicate with empathy but not ambiguity. They acknowledge that the decision is difficult. They explain the reasoning clearly. They take questions without getting defensive.

After the decision, they stay present. They don't delegate the hard conversations or disappear while people process the change. They reinforce the decision without apologizing for it. They support people through the transition. This is not a weakness. This is a strength. Leaders who combine decisiveness with emotional intelligence build trust even when people disagree with their choices.

THE ROLE OF ADVISORS AND TRUSTED COUNSEL

No leader should make major decisions in isolation. The best leaders we've worked with actively seek input from people who will challenge their thinking, not just validate their instincts. Some leaders have found the benefits of having a trusted executive advisor who helps with questions like: "What am I not seeing?" What are the unintended consequences I should consider? Where is my bias showing up? What would you do in my position?

They listen without justifying. They probe without defensiveness. They provide honest feedback, even when it's uncomfortable to hear. This does not mean decisions get made by committee. Final accountability still rests with the leader. But well-thought-out decisions are almost always better than ones made in isolation.

BUILDING DECISION-MAKING CAPACITY OVER TIME

Decision-making is a skill. Like any skill, it improves with deliberate practice and experience. The leaders who make the best decisions consistently do several things differently. They regularly reflect on past decisions, asking what went well, what didn't, and what they would do differently next time.

They study how other leaders handled similar situations. They read case studies. They ask mentors about their toughest calls. They learn from both successes and failures. They practice making decisions under time pressure. They simulate scenarios. They role-play difficult conversations. They prepare systematically so they can respond effectively when the stakes are high and time is short.

Most importantly, they build confidence through repetition—every decision they make and own builds capacity for the next one. Sam Walton, founder of Walmart, captured this perfectly. When a reporter asked how he became so successful, Walton answered, "I've made a lot of good decisions." When asked how he learned to make good decisions, Walton replied, "By making a lot of bad decisions."

That's the truth most leadership books won't tell you. You will make mistakes. You will get some decisions wrong. What separates great leaders from struggling ones is not perfection. It is learning.

WHAT TO DO WHEN YOU GET IT WRONG

Bad decisions will happen. The question is not if, but when, and what you do next. Great leaders conduct post-mortems without blame. They ask: What did we expect to happen? What actually happened? Where did our assumptions break down? What signals did we miss? What would we do differently?

They document lessons learned. They share insights with their teams. They adjust their decision-making process based on what they discover. This is not a weakness. This is wisdom. Leaders who pretend they never make mistakes quickly lose credibility. Leaders who acknowledge mistakes, learn from them, and adjust accordingly earn lasting respect.

THE PATTERN LEADERS MUST FACE

If you're facing a difficult decision right now, work through these questions honestly. What decision am I avoiding? Why am I avoiding it? What will it cost me, my team, and my organization if I delay another month? Another quarter? Another year? Who am I protecting by not deciding, and is that protection serving them or just making me feel better? What would I tell someone else to do if they came to me with this exact situation?

If I got fired today and my replacement arrived tomorrow, what decision would they make in their first week? That last question is particularly clarifying. New leaders make tough calls quickly because they're not protecting legacy relationships, past decisions, or comfortable patterns. Sometimes you need to permit yourself to lead like you just arrived.

LEADING WHEN THE ROOM GOES QUIET

Anyone can lead when the path is clear, and applause is guaranteed. Leadership is revealed when the room goes quiet, the stakes are high, the decision is unpopular, and the responsibility is yours alone. That is when character matters. That is when preparation pays off. That is when leaders prove they deserve the role.

You don't have to make all of your own mistakes. Learn from those who delayed too long, avoided accountability, or chose comfort over clarity. Then do better. Leadership is not about protecting yourself from criticism. It is about protecting the mission, the organization, and the people, even when they don't immediately agree with you. Especially then.

Because leadership is not about ease, it is about earning the right to decide, especially when it is tough.

WHY THIS CHAPTER MATTERS

Leadership is tough because the decisions that define it are rarely comfortable, and the leaders who avoid that discomfort do not protect their organizations. They expose them. As Nokia demonstrated, the cost of delay is not neutrality. It is compounding damage that arrives later, faster, and with far fewer options attached. As Siemens demonstrated, acting early while the decisions are painful, but the leverage still exists, is what separates leaders who shape the future from those who are eventually forced to react to it. Every leader reading this chapter has a decision they are currently avoiding, a conversation they are postponing, or a reality they are softening to preserve short-term comfort. The framework in this chapter exists for that decision. Strategic decision-making is not about being hard. It is about being honest, timely, and accountable enough to act while acting still matters.

KEY TAKEAWAYS:

- **Indecision is a decision.** Choosing not to act is still a choice, and it often carries the most damaging consequences. Delay rarely reduces pain; it usually compounds it.

- **Unpopular decisions are often the most necessary ones.** Leadership is revealed when the right decision creates discomfort, resistance, or disappointment. Popularity is not a leadership metric.

- **Perfect information does not exist.** Waiting for certainty is a luxury that leaders do not have. Strong leaders make informed decisions with incomplete data and accept responsibility for the outcome.

- **Clarity is kindness.** People can endure hard news, change, and even loss, but they cannot endure prolonged uncertainty without purpose. Honest, direct communication builds trust faster than hedging or delay.

- **All decisions have consequences; own them.** Effective leaders acknowledge second and third-order effects up front. Accountability strengthens credibility; deflection destroys it.

- **Strategy requires trade-offs.** If everything is a priority, nothing is. Saying no is one of the most underused and most powerful leadership tools.

- **Timing matters as much as correctness.** A good decision made too late will fail. Leaders who act while they still have options preserve control; those who wait surrender it.

- **Cultural resistance does not mean the decision is wrong.** Resistance is often proof that the decision matters. Leaders must not confuse emotional pushback with strategic error.

- **Learn from others so you don't repeat their mistakes.** History, case studies, and lived leadership experience exist for a reason. You do not earn credibility by suffering unnecessarily.

- **Respect matters more than popularity.** The true obligation of leadership is to act in the long-term best interest of the organization and its people, even when that choice is lonely.

- **Tough decisions do not get easier with time.** You either make them deliberately, or they get made for you by markets, competitors, regulators, or crises.

- **The hardest decisions define your legacy.** Leaders are remembered not for the easy calls, but for the moments when they chose clarity over comfort and responsibility over relief.

REFLECTION QUESTIONS:

1. What decision am I currently delaying because it will be unpopular or uncomfortable? Be specific. What, exactly, am I avoiding, and why?

2. If I make no decision, what is the most likely outcome six months from now? One year from now? Am I underestimating the cost of delay?

3. Who benefits from my indecision, and who pays the price for it? Is my hesitation protecting people, or protecting me?

4. What signals am I ignoring because they threaten the status quo? Data, behavior, culture, performance, morale. What evidence am I rationalizing away?

5. If this issue belonged to another organization, what advice

would I give its leader? Why am I holding myself to a lower standard than I would expect from others?

6. What values or strategic priorities should guide this decision? Am I aligning my actions with our stated values, or contradicting them to preserve comfort?

7. Am I confusing compassion with avoidance? How might clarity serve people better than delay?

8. What second and third-order consequences should I anticipate? If this decision succeeds or fails, what ripple effects will follow?

9. How will I communicate this decision clearly, honestly, and without over-explaining? What must people understand, even if they don't agree?

10. Am I prepared to stay present after the decision is made? Or am I tempted to announce it and disappear?

11. What would "acting too late" look like in this situation? How will I know if I have crossed from thoughtful deliberation into negligence?

12. What is the most principled version of this decision, even if it costs me personally? Reputation, comfort, relationships, approval. What am I willing to risk to do the right thing?

13. If this decision defines my leadership legacy, am I comfortable with that? When people look back, will they say I chose clarity or comfort?

14. What lesson from the case studies in this chapter applies most directly to me right now? Am I more at risk of acting too late like Nokia, or do I have the opportunity to act early like Siemens?

15. What is one decisive action I will take within the next 30 days? Not a plan. Not a discussion. A decision.

WORKING WELL WITH OTHERS
HOW YOU TREAT PEOPLE DEFINES YOU

How you treat people defines you. Leadership is never done in isolation. No matter how advanced the strategy, how elegant the plan, or how well-funded the initiative, nothing gets done without people. Leaders work through people. They depend on people. They succeed, or fail, because of people. That truth never changes. What changes is how easy it becomes to forget it.

As leaders advance, the work becomes more complex, the stakes become higher, and the pace of change accelerates. As demands multiply, time compresses, and pressure intensifies, something quietly shifts. Patience erodes. Courtesy slips. Listening shortens. The very behaviors that help leaders rise can be replaced by efficiency, urgency, and impatience. This is not a character flaw. It is a leadership hazard.

This chapter exists to guard against that drift. It is about remembering that leadership is not just about the decisions we make, but also about how we make them, how we communicate them, and how we treat the people affected by them. People are always watching and listening. And how you treat them will define you far more than any strategy you execute or any result you achieve.

> **CULTURE IS NOT WHAT LEADERS SAY. CULTURE IS WHAT LEADERS MODEL.**

THE UNAVOIDABLE REALITY: LEADERS ARE ALWAYS ON DISPLAY

Leaders are always being watched, and your ability to stay calm and steady under pressure directly impacts your team's confidence. That visibility requires emotional discipline and composure, especially during a crisis or uncertainty. But there's another dimension to this reality that matters just as much: people are not only watching how you handle stress. They are watching how you treat them.

Whether you like it or not, leadership is a public role, and people are always watching. They notice how you enter a room, who you acknowledge and who you do not, and how you speak to assistants, frontline employees, vendors, peers, board members, janitors, and wait staff. They pay attention to your tone under stress and your demeanor when things go wrong.

Leadership is not only performed in formal meetings or polished presentations. It shows up in hallways, emails, parking lots, restaurants, at the coffee machine, in text messages, and during moments when you believe no one is paying attention. It shows up in how quickly you respond or don't, whether you listen fully or read emails while someone is talking to you. You are an ambassador. Always.

You represent the organization when you are patient and when you are frustrated, when you are generous and when you are dismissive, when you are calm under pressure, and when you let stress leak into your interactions. People do not merely observe your behavior. They take cues from it. Your actions signal what is acceptable, what is valued, what is rewarded, and what is tolerated. Culture is not what leaders say. Culture is what leaders model.

We once worked with a senior executive who was strategically brilliant. Her presentations to the board were flawless. Her understanding of market dynamics was exceptional. Yet her administrative assistant quit.

Then her replacement quit. Then the third one quit.

The pattern was clear. She was an awful boss. She never said good morning. She never said thank you. She barked orders. She interrupted. She treated support staff as invisible unless she needed something. Her defense was simple: "I'm busy. I don't have time for small talk."

What she failed to understand was that those are not small moments. They are defining moments. Every interaction was observed by others. The message was unmistakable: "If you are not senior enough, you do not matter here." Within six months, two of her strongest managers left. Not because of strategy. Not because of compensation. Because they watched how people were treated and decided they did not want to work in that environment.

Leadership visibility is not something you can opt out of. The only question is whether you are intentional or careless with it. And what people observe in those visible moments shapes everything that follows.

WORKING WELL WITH OTHERS IS A LEADERSHIP SKILL, NOT A PERSONALITY TRAIT

Some leaders believe interpersonal effectiveness is a soft skill, something you either have or you don't, something that matters more when you are climbing the ladder but becomes less important as you gain authority. That belief is not only wrong; it is dangerous.

Working well with others is not about being agreeable, avoiding conflict, or trying to make everyone happy. It is about respect, clarity, emotional discipline, and intentionality. It is a skill set, one that needs to be practiced deliberately at every level of leadership.

Too often, leaders treat relational competence as optional. Strategy is studied. Finance is analyzed. Operations are optimized. Relationships are assumed. And yet, when organizations struggle, the root cause is rarely a lack of intelligence or effort. More often, it is a breakdown in trust, communication, or respect.

Working well with others is not a personality trait you are born with. It is a leadership discipline you choose to practice. This discipline applies everywhere leadership shows up: managing up with your boss, partnering with a board, leading peers, developing direct reports, interacting with frontline employees, and representing the organization externally.

At every level, leaders must balance decisiveness with humility, authority with approachability, and urgency with patience. That balance becomes harder, not easier, the more senior you become. Why? Because authority changes the dynamic. When you have positional power, people listen differently. They filter more. They hesitate longer. They are less likely to challenge, clarify, or push back. What feels like efficiency to you can feel like dismissal to them. What feels like confidence can land as arrogance. What feels like speed can be perceived as disrespect.

Leaders who work well with others understand this asymmetry. They do not rely solely on good intentions. They compensate deliberately.

THE SENIOR LEADER'S TRAP: WHEN EXPERIENCE TURNS INTO IMPATIENCE

One of the great paradoxes of leadership is that the more you know, the easier it is to forget what others do not. Senior leaders see patterns faster and connect dots more quickly because they have lived through cycles, crises, and consequences that give them context others lack. What feels obvious to them may be entirely new to someone else.

This gap creates temptation. The temptation to interrupt, rush explanations, and dismiss questions. The temptation to say, "We've already tried that," instead of asking, "Tell me more." Unchecked, experience turns into arrogance. Efficiency turns into impatience. Confidence turns into condescension.

When that happens, leaders may still get compliance, but they lose commitment. They may still get results, but at a higher human cost. They may still win in the short term, but they weaken long-term trust. This is how organizations slowly erode from the inside, not through dramatic failures, but through everyday interactions that, intentionally or not, signal that curiosity is inconvenient and that questions are unwelcome.

During a naval command briefing, a junior officer asked a seemingly basic question. I watched the room. Several senior officers rolled their eyes. One sighed audibly. Another checked his watch. The commanding officer noticed. He stopped the briefing.

"That's an excellent question," he said. "Here's why it matters." Then he answered it thoroughly. After the briefing, he pulled the senior officers aside. "Every question deserves respect," he said. "You knew that answer because you've been doing this for twenty years. He's been doing this for two years. The day you forget what it's like not to know something is the day you stop being an effective leader."

That moment mattered, not because it was dramatic, but because it was corrective. It reset the standard. It reminded everyone in the room that leadership is not about displaying superiority. It is about creating understanding.

Guarding against this trap requires self-awareness, discipline, and a willingness to slow down, even when you feel you do not have time. It requires remembering that your experience is an asset only if it makes others better, not smaller. Understanding this intellectually is one thing. Practicing it daily is another. It starts with something deceptively simple.

COURTESY AS A STRATEGIC ADVANTAGE

Courtesy is not weakness; it is strength under control. In leadership, courtesy is often mistaken for softness, a nice-to-have that seems expendable under pressure, but this perception misses the point entirely. Secure leaders do not need to belittle, rush, or dismiss others to prove their authority. Courtesy signals confidence without arrogance and authority without intimidation.

One of the true gentlemen in leadership today is Nido Qubein,

President of High Point University. Regardless of title, status, or circumstance, he models something increasingly rare: consistent courtesy. He is gracious with everyone. Attentive. Respectful. Present. Whether he is speaking with a student, a donor, a faculty member, or a visitor, his behavior communicates dignity and value. That is not accidental. It is intentional leadership.

PEOPLE RARELY REMEMBER EVERY DECISION YOU MAKE, BUT THEY ALWAYS REMEMBER HOW YOU MADE THEM FEEL.

Courtesy sends a powerful message: You matter here. That message shapes culture more effectively than policies, mission statements, or value posters ever will. Courtesy does not require agreement. It does not eliminate accountability. It does not weaken standards. What it does is create an environment where people are willing to engage, contribute, and take responsibility. Leaders who dismiss courtesy as unnecessary confuse urgency with importance. They believe results excuse behavior. Over time, that belief corrodes trust.

WHY COURTESY SCALES AND ARROGANCE DOES NOT

Courtesy scales beautifully. Arrogance does not. As organizations grow, leaders rely less on control and more on influence. Information moves faster. Reputations travel farther. Stories, both good and bad, spread instantly. A single dismissive comment can undo months of trust-building. A careless interaction can become someone else's defining story of your leadership.

People rarely remember every decision you make, but they always remember how you made them feel. That emotional memory shapes engagement, retention, willingness to speak up, willingness to challenge, and willingness to follow. Leaders who work well with others do not lower standards; they elevate them. They create environments where people think clearly, communicate honestly, and perform at their best.

Courtesy gives leaders leverage. It allows difficult messages to be heard. It enables accountability conversations to remain productive. It creates space for disagreement without degradation. Arrogance is the opposite. It may create short-term compliance, but it destroys long-term commitment as people withdraw, stop offering ideas, stop sharing bad news, and protect themselves instead of the organization. The math is simple. Courtesy compounds. Arrogance taxes.

Courtesy isn't abstract. It shows up in the specific language leaders use every day, especially in moments that seem too small to matter.

THE POWER OF SIMPLE WORDS

Over decades of corporate and military leadership, one pattern emerges consistently. The leaders people respect most are not necessarily the most eloquent. They are the ones who consistently use simple, powerful words. Leadership is not revealed in grand speeches as much as in everyday language. The words leaders choose, especially under pressure, shape trust, clarity, and commitment.

There is an old framework that captures this reality with remarkable precision:

- The most important six words: "I admit I made a mistake."
- The most important five words: "You did a good job."
- The most important four words: "What is your opinion?"
- The most important three words: "Would you please."
- The most important two words: "Thank you."
- The most important one word: "We."
- The least important word: "I."

These are not niceties. They are relationship builders. Each phrase reflects a deeper leadership discipline worth examining.

"I ADMIT I MADE A MISTAKE"

When leaders admit they made a mistake, they demonstrate two critical qualities: confidence and a commitment to growth. Leaders who lack confidence defend wrong decisions at all costs. Secure leaders take responsibility and move forward. Admitting mistakes creates an environment where problems surface early instead of being hidden. It signals that learning matters more than blame.

We coached a CEO who made a strategic decision that backfired badly. The company lost a major client. Revenue dropped. The board was worried and concerned. The CEO could have blamed market conditions, the client, or his team. Instead, he called a company-wide meeting.

"I made a decision," he said. "I believed it was right. I was wrong. Here's what I learned. Here's what we're doing differently. Here's how we recover."

The room was silent. Then something unexpected happened. Three senior leaders stood and said, "We supported that decision. We own this, too." That is what happens when leaders model accountability. Ownership spreads.

"YOU DID A GOOD JOB"

From our client surveys, we know that leaders most often provide feedback when something goes wrong, but positive feedback is rare. People need to know when they are doing well, not just at annual reviews or after extraordinary performance, but regularly. This is the basis of the One Minute Manager: catch people doing something right and let them know right away.

Recognition does not require grand gestures. It requires attention. A simple statement such as "You handled that difficult client situation beautifully" takes seconds, but the impact lasts far longer.

One manager we worked with adopted a daily habit. Before leaving work each day, she identified one person who had done something well. She sent a brief email or stopped by their desk to acknowledge it. Six months later, her team engagement scores had increased by fifteen points. When asked what changed, team members said, "She actually sees what we do."

"WHAT IS YOUR OPINION?"

This question signals respect, invites contributions, and acknowledges that leadership does not require having all the answers. Leaders who ask for opinions build stronger teams because people support what they help create.

We watched a director struggle with a policy decision. She had three options, each with drawbacks. She gathered her team. "Here's the situation," she said. "Here are the options I'm considering. What am I missing? What would you do?"

The discussion that followed challenged assumptions, surfaced risks, and produced a fourth option, stronger than any of the original three. She implemented that option. It worked. More importantly, the team owned it. When implementation became difficult, they solved problems rather than complaining.

"WOULD YOU PLEASE" AND "THANK YOU"

These phrases sound elementary. They are, and they are powerful.

During a consulting engagement with a manufacturing company, we observed a plant manager for a week. He barked orders. "Get me that report." "Fix that machine." "Handle that customer." Never "please." Never "thank you." When asked how it felt to work for him, one employee said, "He treats us like robots."

We challenged him to add "please" and "thank you" to every request for one month. He resisted. "I don't have time for pleasantries. We have production targets." We insisted he try. Just for a month. He did. Slowly, behavior shifted. People responded differently. They moved faster. They smiled more. They stopped avoiding him.

Three months later, production was up eight percent. Turnover declined. "I didn't realize how much those two words mattered," he said. Courtesy is not weakness. It is leadership.

"WE" VERSUS "I"

Leaders who default to "we" instead of "I" build stronger teams. "We accomplished this goal." "We overcame that challenge." "We learned from that mistake." "I" takes credit. "We" shares it.

We worked with a CEO who relished the spotlight. Every success story began with "I decided" or "I implemented." His team resented it. They worked long hours, delivered results, and watched him take the credit. Within two years, his top performers left, not for more money, but for leaders who valued their contributions.

> **THE LEADERS WHO EXCEL AT BUILDING RELATIONSHIPS ARE NOT PERFECT. THEY ARE DISCIPLINED.**

Contrast that with a leader who led a successful turnaround. At the board meeting, she said, "Our team made this happen. Let me tell you what they did." She named names and generously shared credit. One of her managers later said, "I would walk through fire for her." That is the power of one word.

These words matter because they reflect broader disciplines that effective leaders practice daily.

PRACTICAL DISCIPLINES FOR WORKING WELL WITH OTHERS

Working well with people does not require charisma. It requires intentional disciplines practiced consistently, especially when pressure is high and patience is low. The leaders who excel at building relationships are not perfect. They are disciplined. They recognize that behavior under stress is not accidental; it is practiced.

SLOW YOUR RESPONSE, ESPECIALLY WHEN YOU'RE CERTAIN

Certainty is not permission to be abrupt. When leaders know the answer quickly, the temptation is to respond quickly. But speed can signal disinterest, dismissal, or impatience, even when none is intended.

A senior leader once told us, "The faster I know the answer, the slower I respond." Why? Rushing signals that the other person's perspective does not matter. Pausing signals respect. Try this discipline: when someone asks a question, you can answer right away, or pause for three seconds before responding. Use that time to consider not only what you will say but also how you will say it. That three-second pause changes tone, posture, and outcome.

SEPARATE THE PERSON FROM THE PROBLEM

Slowing your response changes the dynamic of a conversation. But even when you've mastered pace, you still need to navigate disagreement without damage. Effective leaders challenge ideas vigorously without diminishing the individual. People can handle disagreement. They struggle with disrespect.

In one executive team meeting, two leaders clashed over budget allocation. The disagreement was legitimate. Both had valid points. But one leader said, "That's the dumbest idea I've heard all week." The other leader shut down. The conversation ended. The problem remained unresolved. Later, the first leader defended himself. "I was challenging the idea, not the person." It did not matter. The damage was done.

A better approach sounds like this: "I see your reasoning. Here's where I'm struggling with that approach." Same disagreement. Different delivery. Relationship intact.

LISTEN PAST THE FIRST LAYER

Often, what people say is not the real issue. Leaders who listen only to words miss concerns, fears, incentives, and context. Leaders who listen beyond the first layer uncover what needs to be addressed.

During a consulting engagement with a regional logistics company, a warehouse supervisor approached his director and said, "I don't think the new routing system is going to work for us." The director's first instinct was to defend the decision. The system had taken months to select and cost significantly more than the previous one. Instead, she paused and asked, "Walk me through what you're seeing. What specifically isn't working?"

What emerged had nothing to do with the system itself. The routing software was performing exactly as designed, but the team had received only a single two-hour training session before going live. Supervisors were expected to train their own people on the floor, in real time, while simultaneously managing daily operations. Nobody had raised this issue because they assumed pushing through was simply part of adopting something new. What appeared to be resistance to the system was actually a lack of proper instruction. Had the director stopped at the first layer, she would have sought a technology fix when what her people actually needed was time, structure, and more training.

EXPLAIN THE WHY, NOT JUST THE WHAT

Senior leaders see consequences others cannot. When leaders announce decisions without context, people fill the gaps with speculation, frustration, and fear.

A director once announced, "We're cutting travel by forty percent, effective immediately." No explanation. The team erupted. Had he explained, "Revenue is down eighteen percent year over year. We have three options: cut travel, cut staff, or cut development. I'm prioritizing keeping the team intact and protecting our product pipeline. That means travel takes the hit. Here's how we'll manage client relationships differently," the response would have been very different. Same decision. Different outcome.

MODEL THE BEHAVIOR YOU EXPECT

Leaders cannot demand behavior they do not model. If you want respect, show it. If you want accountability, demonstrate it. If you want professionalism, embody it.

A manager complained that her team did not respond to emails promptly. When we reviewed her inbox, we found seventeen unread messages from team members, some more than a week old. We asked, "Why should they respond quickly to you when you do not respond to them?" She did not have an answer. Modeling works both ways. If you want it, show it first.

These disciplines apply daily, often in moments that leaders overlook. Great relationships are not built during annual retreats or quarterly reviews. They are built through small, consistent actions that signal attention, respect, and care.

GREET PEOPLE BY NAME

This sounds simple. It is, and it is surprisingly rare. Leaders who greet people by name, make eye contact, and acknowledge their presence create an immediate connection. Leaders who rush past without acknowledgment communicate something entirely different.

We observed two executives at the same organization. One walked the floor every morning. He greeted people by name, asked about families, projects, and weekends, and knew what mattered to his team. The other stayed in his office. Door closed. Headphones on. Interaction only when necessary. The engagement difference between their teams was dramatic. The first leader was not more talented. He was more intentional.

CHECK IN BEFORE YOU CHECK OUT

At the end of the day, effective leaders check in with their teams, not to micromanage, but to connect. "How did today go?" "Do you have what you need for tomorrow?" "Anything I can help with?" These questions take minutes. They signal care, surface issues early, and build trust. Leaders who skip these moments often learn about problems only after they have grown large and costly.

CELEBRATE SMALL WINS

Do not wait for major milestones to recognize progress. When a team hits a weekly target, acknowledge it. When someone solves a nagging problem, recognize it. When a client sends positive feedback, share it. Small wins build momentum when they are consistently celebrated. They remind people that effort matters, progress counts, and leadership noticed.

APOLOGIZE WHEN YOU ARE WRONG

Leaders make mistakes. Great leaders own up to them right away.

"I was wrong about that."
"I should have handled that differently."
"I'm sorry. Let me fix this."

These statements do not weaken authority. They strengthen it.

> YOUR JOB AS A LEADER IS NOT TO BE THE SMARTEST PERSON IN THE ROOM. IT IS TO BUILD A ROOM FULL OF CAPABLE PEOPLE WHO CAN EVENTUALLY REPLACE YOU.

We worked with a leader who snapped at an employee during a meeting. The employee had made an error, but the leader's tone was harsh and unnecessary. After the meeting, the leader called the employee into his office. "I owe you an apology," he said. "The issue needed to be addressed. The way I handled it was wrong. I'm sorry."

The employee later told us, "That's when I decided I wanted to work for him long-term. He's tough, but he's fair. And he owns his mistakes."

These disciplines apply in every direction leadership flows: upward to those with authority over you, across to peers at your level, and downward to those you develop and lead.

MANAGING UP, DOWN, AND ACROSS WITH INTENTION

Leadership requires navigating multiple relationships simultaneously. Few leaders fail because they lack intelligence or effort. Many struggle because they underestimate the complexity of managing relationships in multiple directions at once. Managing up means respecting authority without surrendering judgment. Managing across means collaborating without competing for credit. Managing down means developing others without diminishing yourself.

Each direction requires emotional intelligence, situational awareness, and discipline. The most effective leaders adapt their communication without compromising their values. Different audiences may require different approaches, but they all deserve the same respect.

Managing Up: Your Boss Needs You, Too

Many leaders forget that their boss is human, too. Your boss has pressures you may not see. They have competing priorities, incomplete information, and accountability that flows both upward and downward. Great leaders do not merely comply; they contribute.

Leaders who effectively manage up bring solutions, not just problems. They deliver bad news early and offer options. They protect their boss's time by filtering out non-critical issues. They ask, "What's keeping you up at night?" and then help solve it.

One of the most useful pieces of advice we ever received was this: Your job is to make your boss successful. When your boss succeeds, you succeed. This does not mean blind loyalty. It means strategic support. It means having the courage to disagree respectfully and the discipline to align once a decision is made.

Managing Across: Your Peers Are Not Your Competition

In healthy organizations, peers collaborate. In unhealthy ones, they compete. Leaders who hoard information, undermine colleagues, or compete for credit create dysfunction that damages everyone, including themselves.

We coached a leadership team where infighting had become the norm. Every meeting turned into a turf battle. Every project became a power struggle. Energy was spent on protecting territory rather than serving customers. The CEO finally addressed it directly. "We are spending more energy fighting each other than serving our customers," he said. "That stops now."

He instituted a simple rule. At every leadership meeting, each leader had to publicly recognize another leader's contribution. At first, it felt forced. Over time, it changed the team's behavior. Collaboration improved. Information flowed more freely. Trust increased. The culture shifted, not because of a policy, but because leaders changed what they publicly valued.

Managing Down: Develop People, Don't Diminish Them

Your job as a leader is not to be the smartest person in the room. It is to build a room full of capable people who can eventually replace you. Leaders who feel threatened by talented team members create weak teams. Leaders who develop talent create legacies.

The worst thing a leader can do is position themselves as intellectually superior to their team. When leaders communicate, whether explicitly or implicitly, that they are smarter than everyone else, they create an environment in which people stop contributing ideas, taking risks, and challenging assumptions. This is not humility. This is ego masquerading as confidence.

One CEO we worked with announced to her direct reports, "I am tired of being the smartest person in the room." In reality, she is not. What she meant was that she wanted her people to develop creative solutions and present them at the weekly meetings. What manifested instead was that she was perceived as so arrogant that no one dared speak up. Words matter. Her statement, intended to encourage contribution, instead communicated superiority and dismissiveness. We worked with her to change her approach entirely, replacing the declaration with a simple question: 'What ideas are you working on that I haven't heard yet?' That small shift opened the door she had accidentally closed.

The leaders who build the strongest teams are those who genuinely believe they have something to learn from everyone around them. They value diverse expertise. They recognize that being the leader does not mean being the expert in everything. They understand that their role is to bring together people who collectively know more than any individual, including themselves, could know alone.

A different director once told us, "My best employee wants my job." Our response was immediate: "Good. That means you are doing something right. Now develop her so well that when she gets your job, you are ready for the next one."

That shift in mindset changed everything. Instead of seeing talent as a threat, the director saw it as proof of leadership effectiveness. Two years later, the employee was promoted. So was the director. The organization won because the leader understood that developing people is not about diminishing yourself. It is about multiplying impact.

When these relationships work well across all directions, organizations thrive. When they break down, the costs are measurable and expensive.

THE COST OF POOR RELATIONSHIPS

The consequences of poor relational leadership are measurable and expensive. When leaders fail relationally, turnover increases. Strong performers leave. Mediocre performers stay because they have fewer options. Over time, the talent pool weakens.

Engagement drops. People do only what is required. Discretionary effort disappears. Innovation slows. Initiative fades. Communication breaks down. People stop sharing bad news. Problems are hidden. Small issues become crises. Reputation suffers. Stories spread. "Don't work for that leader" becomes common advice. Recruiting becomes harder. Trust erodes. Performance declines. People are capable, but because so much unnecessary energy is spent managing relationships rather than accomplishing goals, productivity declines.

Poor relationships are expensive. Great relationships are profitable.

HOW TO RECOVER WHEN YOU'VE DAMAGED A RELATIONSHIP

Every leader will make mistakes. You will say the wrong thing, react poorly, or mishandle a situation. The question is not if, but when, and what you do next. Recovery begins with speed.

Acknowledge It Quickly

Do not wait. Do not hope the issue fades. Address it directly. "I handled that poorly." "I should have approached that differently." "I owe you an apology." Speed matters. The longer you wait, the deeper the damage becomes.

Take Full Responsibility

No excuses, no justifications, no deflection. Instead, simple ownership: "I was wrong. That was my mistake. I take full responsibility for how that went." People can forgive mistakes. They struggle to forgive leaders who refuse to own them.

Ask How to Make It Right

"What can I do to fix this?" "How can I make this right?" "What would help?" These questions demonstrate humility and restore agency. They signal that the relationship matters more than saving face.

Change Your Behavior

Words without action are empty. If you apologize for interrupting people but keep interrupting them, the apology means nothing. If you promise to listen but do not change your behavior, trust does not return. Recovery requires visible change.

LEADERSHIP IS TOUGH BECAUSE PEOPLE MATTER

Leadership is tough because people are complex, emotional, imperfect, and human. But leadership is also meaningful for the same reason. Every interaction is a decision. Every tone sends a signal. Every moment models leadership.

The question is not whether people are watching. They are. The question is: what are they learning from you? Are they learning that leadership means treating people as tools to accomplish goals, or are they learning that leadership means accomplishing goals by honoring the people who make them possible? Are they learning that success justifies poor behavior, or are they learning that how you win matters as much as whether you win? Are they learning that relationships are transactional, or that they are the foundation of everything that matters in organizations?

You get to choose. Every single day, in every single interaction. Choose wisely. Choose intentionally. Choose to remember that leadership is never done in isolation. It is done through people. With people. For people.

At the end of your career, people will not remember your quarterly reports. They will remember how you made them feel, whether you saw them, valued them, and treated them with dignity. Make it count.

WHY THIS CHAPTER MATTERS

Your workforce is watching your leadership more closely than ever before. Employees evaluate not only outcomes but also behaviors, not just results but also relationships, not just success but also sustainability. They pay attention to how decisions are made, how feedback is delivered, and how people are treated, especially under pressure.

Leaders who fail to work well with others may still succeed individually, but they leave behind damaged organizations. Leaders who master this discipline build enduring cultures.

The number one predictor of whether someone stays or leaves an organization is not compensation, benefits, or even career advancement opportunities. It is their relationship with their immediate supervisor. People do not leave organizations. They leave leaders. And they stay for leaders who treat them well, value their contributions, and make them feel like they matter.

KEY TAKEAWAYS:

- **Leadership is never done in isolation.** Every decision, interaction, and behavior sends a signal about what is valued and what is tolerated.

- **Working well with others is not a personality trait.** It is a leadership skill that must be practiced deliberately at every level.

- **Senior leaders struggle when experience quietly turns into impatience.** Guarding against that drift requires self-awareness and discipline.

- **Courtesy is not optional.** It is a strategic advantage that builds trust, credibility, and long-term commitment.

- **Simple words make a big impact.** Phrases like: "I made a mistake," "You did a good job," "What is your opinion?" "Would you please?" "Thank you," and "We" all build relationships when used consistently and sincerely.

- **Daily habits determine whether people feel respected and valued.** Yes, peak moments are important, but what happens day to day matters more.

- **Managing up, across, and down with intention matters.** It is essential for organizational health and personal credibility.

- **Poor relationships are costly.** Strong relationships are profitable. When relationships are damaged, recovery depends on speed, ownership, humility, and visible behavior change.

- **Your legacy is how you are remembered.** Your legacy will be defined less by what you accomplished and more by how you treated the people who helped accomplish it.

REFLECTION QUESTIONS:

1. When pressure is high, which of my leadership behaviors tend to slip first: patience, listening, courtesy, or curiosity?

2. How would the people who work most closely with me describe my tone, availability, and respect for their perspective?

3. Where might my experience be creating impatience instead of clarity for others?

4. When was the last time I publicly admitted a mistake? What effect did that have on my team?

5. How often do I provide specific, timely recognition for good work, and how intentional am I about using simple, powerful words like "thank you" and "you did a good job"?

6. How intentional am I about managing up, across, and down? Where do I need to improve?

7. Is there a relationship I have damaged or neglected that needs

to be repaired? What is one concrete step I can take this week?

8. If someone were describing my leadership legacy five years from now, what would I hope they would say about how I treated people?

CHAPTER 5

BUILDING TRUST
COMMUNICATE AND CONNECT
WITH OTHERS

Trust is the most valuable and fragile currency in leadership. It determines how fast decisions move, how honestly people speak, how resilient teams become under pressure, and how much discretionary effort people are willing to give when things get hard. Leaders often talk about trust as a cultural aspiration. Still, in practice, trust is built or broken through communication, consistency, and connection. Trust is not slogans, team-building exercises, or charisma; it is how we communicate and connect with others.

Trust is built through the daily interactions leaders have with others, especially when the message is difficult, the stakes are high, or the answer is no. This chapter is about how leaders deliberately build trust, how they unintentionally erode it, and how communication becomes the primary mechanism through which trust either compounds or collapses. Because leadership without trust is simply authority, and authority without trust does not scale.

WHY TRUST IS THE REAL LEADERSHIP CURRENCY

Every organization runs on trust, whether leaders acknowledge it or not. When trust is high, communication is efficient, conflict is productive, decisions are implemented quickly, people take ownership, and leaders

> **TRUST IS BUILT THROUGH PATTERNS, NOT MOMENTS.**

hear the truth sooner. When trust is low, information is filtered, people hedge their language, meetings become painful to attend, or a burden, or risk-taking disappears, and silence replaces candor.

Leaders often assume trust is present until results suffer. In reality, trust tends to erode quietly long before performance declines. Trust is not visible on dashboards. It shows up in behavior. Trust determines who speaks up and who does not, who challenges assumptions and who waits to be told. Leaders who understand this treat trust not as a soft issue, but as a strategic leadership responsibility.

Over our combined decades of consulting and military leadership, we have learned that when we ask employees what undermines their performance at work, lack of trust in leadership ranks at the top. The data is sobering. Research from the Harvard Business Review shows that 58 percent of workers say they trust perfect strangers more than they trust their own boss. Read that again. More than half of employees trust random people they have never met more than the person they report to every day. That statistic is not just discouraging. It is a leadership crisis.

WHAT TRUST IS AND WHAT IT IS NOT

Trust is frequently misunderstood. Trust is not being liked, avoiding conflict, oversharing personal details, always agreeing, or making people comfortable. Trust is reliability over time, consistency between words and actions, clear intent, predictable standards, and respectful communication, especially under stress. Trust is built through patterns, not moments.

A single inspiring speech cannot overcome months of inconsistency. Likewise, one difficult decision does not destroy trust if the leader's behavior has been steady and transparent over time. Leaders who confuse trust with likability often avoid necessary tension. Respect beats popularity every single time. Leaders who understand trust are willing to be direct because people trust clarity more than reassurance.

We worked with a CEO who believed his team trusted him because they never challenged his decisions. He interpreted silence as agreement. During a 360-degree assessment, the truth emerged. His team was silent because they had learned that disagreement was not welcome. One senior leader said, "I stopped offering input because every time I did, he explained why I was wrong. Eventually, I realized it was easier to stay quiet."

The CEO was stunned. He had no idea his behavior was shutting people down. He thought he was educating them. They experienced it as dismissal. Trust was not broken because he was harsh. It was broken because he was predictably unreceptive. This connects directly to what we will explore in Chapter 6: empathy requires genuine listening, not just waiting to respond.

SELF-TRUST: THE FOUNDATION LEADERS OVERLOOK

Before leaders can build trust with others, they must trust themselves. This is one of the most overlooked elements of trust-building. Leaders who do not trust themselves struggle to earn others' trust because uncertainty travels. When leaders constantly second-guess their decisions, avoid taking stands, or waffle between positions, their teams absorb that instability.

Self-trust comes from values alignment, decision clarity, willingness to stand by principled choices, and comfort with accountability. In Chapter 7, we will explore how, when priorities align with values, leaders can defend their decisions with conviction. That internal coherence translates into external credibility. People sense when leaders believe in what they are saying versus when they are performing leadership.

Self-trust does not mean arrogance or refusing to admit mistakes. It means having enough confidence in your judgment to make decisions with incomplete information, as we discussed in Chapter 3 on decision-making, and enough humility to adjust when new information emerges. Leaders who trust themselves can say "I don't know" without feeling diminished and "I was wrong" without losing credibility. That security creates the psychological safety others need to trust in return.

THE TRUST GAP LEADERS DON'T SEE COMING

As leaders rise, trust becomes harder to read. Power changes how people communicate. Employees begin to edit feedback, soften disagreement, avoid difficult conversations, and wait for direction instead of offering perspective. Leaders interpret this as alignment. It is often caution.

Many senior leaders believe they are approachable because they intend to be. But intention does not override perception, and perception is shaped by how leaders respond when people speak up. If the first person who challenges an idea gets shut down, even politely, others notice. Trust does not usually disappear because leaders are harsh. It disappears because leaders are unpredictable. People don't know when it is safe to speak, what will trigger frustration, or whether honesty will be rewarded or penalized. That uncertainty creates distance.

This dynamic is amplified in remote and hybrid work environments. Without the context that physical proximity provides, silence feels more personal, and delays feel more intentional. A message that goes unanswered for two hours in the office might go unnoticed. The same two-hour delay on Slack can feel like avoidance. Distance magnifies interpretation, and interpretation fills gaps with assumptions.

During a command assignment, I watched a senior officer respond to a junior officer's question during a briefing. The question was reasonable. The response was sharp. The officer said, "We already covered that. Pay attention." The room went silent. No one asked any more questions for the rest of the briefing. Later, the senior officer complained that his team was not engaged. He did not connect his response to their silence. He had shut down one person. Everyone else learned the lesson.

THE BEHAVIORS THAT QUIETLY DESTROY TRUST

In our research for Why Leaders Fail and the 7 Prescriptions for Success, we identified specific behaviors that consistently undermine trust. Many leaders engage in these behaviors without realizing the damage they cause. These failures often appear small in the moment but compound over time.

Lying or Lying by Omission

Nothing destroys trust faster than discovering a leader lied. It does not have to be a big lie. A small, seemingly inconsequential lie can completely shatter trust. If a leader is willing to lie about little things, what prevents them from lying about matters of real significance?

Lying by omission is equally damaging. Leaders often withhold information, believing they are protecting employees or waiting for better timing. Employees experience this as betrayal. We coached a leader who delayed sharing financial concerns, hoping conditions would improve. They did not. When the board finally learned the full scope of the problem, the reaction was less about the numbers and more about the delay. "What else don't we know?" became the silent question in every room. Boards and employees forgive bad outcomes more readily than they forgive withheld information.

Disrespecting Others' Time

As we discussed in Chapter 4, small behaviors send large signals. We worked with a well-liked technology executive who was admired by his boss, peers, and employees. A 360-degree assessment showed that everyone respected him, except for one pervasive problem. He was always late. To meetings, appointments, and even company-wide addresses. He regularly kept people waiting 10, 20, or 45 minutes while he finished with others. The result? People felt disrespected. They questioned his priorities. Trust eroded because his actions communicated that their time did not matter.

Being late is not a minor issue. It is a trust issue. In another organization, the CEO of a commercial banking group did his best thinking late in the day. As the afternoon wound down, his energy ramped up. His ideas came faster. His creativity clicked on. His routine was predictable. He refreshed his coffee, then called in a key team member to brainstorm. On the surface, it seemed fine, maybe even productive. The problem was timing.

These impromptu strategy sessions almost always began around 4:45 p.m., exactly when everyone else was trying to leave. People were thinking about daycare pickup deadlines, grocery runs, dinner plans, and the dog that had been home all day. Instead, they found themselves sitting in the CEO's office for 45 minutes to over two hours, nodding thoughtfully while silently recalculating their entire evening. They wanted to contribute. They wanted to be present. But their attention was divided, split between engaging in the conversation and managing the growing stress of commitments waiting outside the office door. The CEO was operating at his peak. His team was operating under pressure.

While no one overtly complained, the cost showed up in quiet resentment, diminished engagement, and a growing sense that leadership priorities mattered more than personal realities. Small patterns of disrespect accumulate into significant trust deficits.

Withholding Information

Some leaders defend their lack of communication by saying they are too busy or that the timing is not right. They believe waiting will allow them to provide more accurate information when employees are better prepared to receive it. What these leaders fail to understand is that efforts to deliver information at the "right time" usually result in information arriving too late. Employees learn through coworkers, the media, or social media. When information does not come directly from their leader, trust collapses. It appears the leader either did not know what was happening or did not care enough to communicate in a timely manner.

This problem intensifies in remote work settings where informal information channels disappear. In physical offices, leaders overhear conversations and can course-correct rumors before they spread. In distributed teams, information voids persist longer, and speculation fills them faster. Remote leaders must communicate more proactively, not less, to maintain trust.

As General Tom Fields said, "I would rather have 90 percent of the information now than 100 percent in six months." Employees feel the same way.

Gossiping

When leaders gossip, trust erodes for two reasons. First, people wonder, "If this leader talks like this about others when they are not present, what are they saying about me?" Second, it communicates that the leader does not truly care about the people they are speaking negatively about. Employees do not trust leaders who they believe do not care about their people.

Being Disloyal

A leader's job is to serve and support the people on their team. This means the needs of employees and customers must come before the leader's own needs. We worked with one manager who publicly took sole credit for his team's work. He loved the praise. His team resented him. Within two years, his top performers left, not for more money, but for leaders who valued their contributions.

Not Trusting Employees

When leaders do not trust their people, they send unmistakable signals. They withhold information. They micromanage. They require approval for minor decisions. They check in excessively. Every one of these actions communicates distrust. In Chapter 8, we further clarify that accountability and micromanagement are not the same. Micromanagement is about control. Accountability is about clarity. When leaders confuse the two, they undermine trust while believing they are ensuring quality.

Employees respond to perceived distrust by pulling back. They stop trying. They stop making decisions. They assume the leader will find fault regardless. The result is that both the leader and the employee begin taking actions that confirm each other's beliefs, creating a downward spiral in which no one trusts anyone.

COMMUNICATION AS THE TRUST VEHICLE

Every leadership communication does one of two things. It builds trust or spends it. Leaders often focus on content and ignore context. They ask: Is the information accurate? Is the message efficient? Is the decision justified? Those questions matter, but they are incomplete.

People also ask: Was I considered? Was I respected? Was I informed early or after the fact? Was this explained or simply announced? Trust grows when people feel both informed and respected. A leader can make the right decision and still lose trust if they communicate it poorly. When discussing leading through change, people can endure difficulty, but they cannot endure uncertainty without purpose. Communication provides that purpose.

This is why explaining the why matters as much as communicating the what. Leaders who take time to explain the rationale, acknowledge the impact, and connect decisions to the larger strategy build trust, even when delivering unwelcome news. Leaders who simply announce decisions without context create confusion and resentment.

SAYING HARD THINGS WITHOUT BREAKING TRUST

Some of the most trust-defining moments in leadership involve bad news: budget cuts, role changes, strategy shifts, performance issues, and unpopular decisions. Leaders who try to soften these moments with vague language often do more damage than those who communicate directly. Clarity builds trust faster than comfort.

People may not like the decision, but they respect leaders who explain the rationale, acknowledge impact, avoid defensiveness, and do not hide behind process or jargon. Trust erodes fastest when people feel decisions were made about them rather than with their awareness. This connects to the empathy-accountability balance, which will be explored more in Chapter 6. Leaders can understand the difficulty a decision creates while still holding the line on expectations. Both matter.

We coached a CEO during an acquisition. She knew layoffs were coming, but waited weeks to communicate because she wanted all the details finalized. Her intentions were good. She wanted to provide complete information. The delay backfired. Rumors spread. Anxiety grew. By the time she announced the plan, employees had already heard versions of it through unofficial channels. They felt misled. She had not lied, but she had not been transparent. Trust was damaged, not by the layoffs, but by the lack of transparency.

Choosing Trust Over Convenience: The Barry-Wehmiller Example

During the early months of the pandemic, Barry-Wehmiller, a privately held manufacturing and engineering firm based in St. Louis, faced the same economic uncertainty as many industrial companies. Orders slowed. Revenue projections dropped. Pressure mounted to reduce costs quickly. Like many firms, leadership had options: lay off employees, cut benefits, reduce hours quietly, or communicate minimally. Instead, Barry-Wehmiller's leadership took a different approach.

They communicated early and often. They explained the financial reality clearly. They shared what they knew and what they did not. They asked leaders across the organization to help find alternatives to layoffs. They emphasized shared sacrifice rather than unilateral action. The result? Temporary salary reductions at senior levels, voluntary measures before forced ones, and a strong emphasis on transparency and dignity.

Not every employee loved the outcome, but trust was preserved. Why? Because people believed leadership was telling the truth, sharing the burden, and treating employees as professionals. Trust did not come from optimism. It came from honesty. We will learn more about this example in Chapter 7 on priorities and values. When leaders align their communication with stated values, even difficult decisions reinforce trust rather than erode it.

Listening for Understanding: The Most Underrated Trust Skill

Most leaders believe they listen well, but in reality, when under pressure, few listen as well as they think they do. Leaders often listen to confirm their thinking, move meetings along, identify flaws quickly, or respond efficiently. But trust is built when leaders listen to understand, not to control. Listening to understand is fundamentally different from listening to respond. People trust leaders who do not interrupt, ask follow-up questions, allow pauses, and resist the urge to correct immediately. Listening signals respect, and respect is where trust grows.

During a major HVAC installation, a technician approached his project manager and said quietly, "I don't think the new system is working the way it's supposed to." The manager's first reaction was defensive. The equipment had been carefully selected. The controls package was state-of-the-art. The system had been designed to integrate with multiple components: sensors, air handlers, variable-speed drives, and building controls. On paper, everything was right. But instead of shutting the conversation down, he paused and asked, "Walk me through what you're seeing. What isn't working?" That changed everything.

The technician explained that the equipment itself was performing as designed. The real challenge was the complexity of the installation and commissioning process. There were multiple steps, new diagnostics to interpret, and tighter tolerances than he had ever dealt with before. A single missed setting or incorrect sequence could throw off the entire system. He felt behind before the job even reached full startup.

What made it worse was the pressure. The install schedule was tight, and the customer was watching. Others were waiting for his work. He did not want to slow the project down or look like he did not know what he was doing by asking too many questions, but he felt stuck. The issue was not the equipment. It was not the design. It was not the technology. The real issue was confidence, training, and support in a world where HVAC installations are no longer simple mechanical work. Today's systems demand deeper technical understanding, better sequencing, and real-time problem solving under pressure.

Had the project manager stopped at the first communication, assuming resistance or incompetence, he would have missed the real problem entirely. By listening longer, he realized the fix was not a new tool or a tougher directive. There was a need for better training and guidance. People struggle when leaders underestimate how much has changed and how much real support their people need to keep up.

Consistency: The Quiet Builder and Destroyer of Trust

When discussing accountability, people forgive mistakes but struggle with inconsistency. Nothing erodes trust faster than shifting standards, uneven enforcement, exceptions without explanation, or changing priorities without context. Leaders often justify inconsistency as flexibility. Employees experience it as unfairness.

Consistency does not mean rigidity. It means predictability in values and expectations. People want to know what matters, what does not, what will be enforced, and what will not. When leaders are consistent, trust compounds, even when decisions are hard.

We worked with a manager who allowed one employee to leave early on Mondays because they had worked late the previous week. Her boss questioned the decision, then another, then another. The manager felt micromanaged. She believed her boss did not trust her. She stopped making decisions. From the boss's perspective, he was simply trying to understand how the team operated. He was asking questions to learn, not to criticize. Neither leader communicated their intent. Both assumed the worst. Trust broke down because of a lack of direct, honest communication.

> **CONSISTENCY DOES NOT MEAN RIGIDITY. IT MEANS PREDICTABILITY IN VALUES AND EXPECTATIONS.**

In remote work environments, consistency becomes even more

critical because employees cannot observe patterns as easily. When working from home, people notice if some team members receive faster responses than others, if certain requests get approved while similar ones do not, or if meeting attendance seems mandatory for some but optional for others. What might be explained away in an informal office conversation becomes evidence of favoritism when it happens at a distance. Remote leaders must be more intentional about explaining decisions and ensuring standards apply equally across the team.

HOW TO BUILD TRUST DELIBERATELY

Building trust is not accidental. It requires intentional daily actions. The following practices, when consistently applied, lay the foundation for lasting trust.

Do What You Say You Are Going to Do

This is the fastest path to trustworthiness. Following through on commitments builds credibility more than any other single action. If you tell someone you are going to do something, write it down. Put it on your calendar. Track it. Then do it. Consistently delivering what you promised, when you promised it, builds a reputation as a leader people can count on.

In virtual work settings, this becomes even more important. When you promise to send information after a meeting, send it that day. When you commit to a decision timeline, meet it. When face-to-face accountability is reduced, written commitments and visible follow-through become the primary signals of trust.

Go Beyond the Conventional Relationship

Leaders are expected to fulfill certain responsibilities. Completing performance evaluations is expected. Passing around a birthday card for someone in the department is not required, but it shows you care. When you do something extra, you go beyond the conventional relationship. That builds trust. This connects to what we discussed in Chapter 4 about courtesy as a strategic advantage. Small acts of consideration, remembering personal details, or acknowledging effort before it becomes a formal achievement all contribute to trust.

Practice the Concept of "No Surprises"

Keep surprises positive. Too many surprises are negative. Employees should not find out about policy changes from customers. Leaders should not learn about problems after they become crises. Eliminating negative surprises builds strong trust. This is especially challenging in distributed teams where leaders cannot overhear hallway conversations or read body language that signals brewing problems. Remote leaders must create explicit channels for early warning and make it psychologically safe to surface concerns before they escalate.

Communicate, Communicate, Communicate

The more open and honest your communication is, the more trust you build. The importance of frequent communication cannot be overstated. The more you communicate, the more opportunities you have to build trust. This does not mean flooding people with information. It means providing context, explaining reasoning, acknowledging uncertainty, and maintaining regular touchpoints even when there is no news to share.

Be Honest, Especially When It Costs You Something

Everyone agrees that honesty builds trust. What we want to emphasize is the power of honesty when it costs you something. You gain the most trust when being honest requires sacrifice. To say "I screwed up" or to tell your board, "Our team was responsible for this achievement, not me," seems to cost you something to be honest. In the long run, you are building trust and relationships with both the board and your team. As we discussed in Chapter 3, when examining decision-making, taking ownership of consequences builds credibility, while deflecting blame destroys it.

Determine Expectations Clearly

Clear expectations are critical to building trust. The more clarity you provide about what others can expect from you and what you expect from them, the easier it is to build trust. This connects directly to the accountability framework we will establish in Chapter 8. When expectations are vague, people interpret gaps as betrayal. When expectations are explicit, gaps become learning opportunities rather than trust violations.

Repairing Trust When It Is Broken

Trust repair is possible, but only with humility and action. We coached a highly trusted leader who, over a couple of months, lost the trust of almost everyone on his team. He had a new executive leader who raised performance expectations. This change impacted his confidence, causing him to question whether he was the right person for the job.

As a result, his behavior changed. Instead of giving credit to the team, he took credit for successes. When problems occurred, he publicly blamed individuals. He canceled meetings. He withdrew from communication. He lied about what he knew regarding organizational changes. He made promises he knew he could not keep.

He eventually recognized what he had done. He asked, "Is there any hope of rebuilding this trust?" The answer was direct. "The easiest thing for you to do is find another job. Then, every day, do what trustworthy leaders do." He did not want to leave. He asked, "What do I need to do?"

Effective trust repair includes acknowledging what happened, taking full responsibility, explaining what will change, and consistently demonstrating that change over time. Apologies without behavior change do nothing. Trust is restored when people see different patterns, not different words.

THE PROCESS OF REBUILDING TRUST

Rebuilding trust takes time. Here is how to do it:

Recognize That Rebuilding Trust Takes a Long Time

Most people, when burned by a leader, will not respond well to the leader's statement, "From this point forward, you can trust me." Trust is not rebuilt with words. It is rebuilt with consistent actions over an extended period. Expect the process to take at least as long as the period during which trust was damaged, often longer.

Tell the Truth, Even When Uncomfortable

Tell the truth, even when it may be uncomfortable, or the other person may not want to hear it. This shows people they can always trust you for an honest answer. Early in the rebuilding process, people will test whether your commitment to honesty is real. They will ask difficult questions. They will watch how you respond to bad news. Every truthful response, especially when lying would be easier, deposits trust back into the account.

Be Vulnerable

People find it easier to trust you when you are transparent. When you can say "I don't know the answer" or "I might be wrong," people know you are human. Leaders who defend wrong actions at all costs are not trusted. This vulnerability must be genuine, not performative. People can distinguish between a leader who is authentically uncertain and one who is using vulnerability as a tactic.

Help and Support Others Daily

Most people will go out of their way to help you when they see you are more interested in their success than your own. This is where the practices from Chapter 4 about working well with others become essential. Small acts of support, removing obstacles, providing resources, and advocating for your team all rebuild trust through demonstrated care rather than stated care.

LEADERSHIP WITHOUT TRUST IS AUTHORITY THAT DEPENDS ON POSITION.

Give Away the Credit, Claim the Blame

When your team is successful, give all the praise and recognition to your team. When there is failure, step up and state, "I take responsibility for ensuring this problem does not happen again." This pattern, maintained consistently, eventually overcomes even significant damage to trust.

Hold Team Members Equally Accountable

Great leaders do not have favorites. They hold all team members equally accountable to high performance standards, so no employee perceives the leader as having favorites. Trust is rebuilt through consistent expectations and behavior. Inconsistent accountability destroys trust faster than almost any other leadership failure. We will discuss this concept more in Chapter 8 on Accountability.

Follow Through on Commitments

Do what you say you will do when you say you will do it. Nothing builds trust faster. During the trust rebuilding process, this becomes especially critical. People are watching to see if you mean what you say. One missed commitment can undo weeks of progress.

Model the Behavior You Expect

If you want trust, demonstrate trustworthiness. If you want honesty, be honest. If you want accountability, hold yourself accountable first. This principle applies throughout leadership, as we have established throughout this book, but it becomes particularly important when trust is damaged. You cannot ask for what you are not willing to give.

Trust as a Daily Discipline

Trust is not built through grand gestures. It is built through showing up, following through, explaining decisions, listening carefully, and treating people with dignity. Every interaction either deposits or withdraws trust. Leaders decide daily what kind of balance they are building. Gaining and retaining trust is one of the most difficult things a leader can do. It can take weeks, months, and even years to build trust, but mere minutes to destroy it.

Leadership is nonexistent without the relationships you build with your employees. Without trust, you have no followers. And without followers, there is no leader.

WHY THIS CHAPTER MATTERS

Leadership is tough because trust is both the foundation on which everything else rests and the first thing that erodes when leaders are under pressure. Every discipline explored in this book, from making unpopular decisions in Chapter 3 to holding people accountable in Chapter 8, requires trust to function. Without it, decisions get questioned, accountability feels punitive, change initiatives stall, and the best people quietly start looking elsewhere. Trust is not built through grand gestures or inspiring speeches. It is built through showing up consistently, communicating honestly even when it costs something, following through on commitments, and treating people with dignity in the moments that feel too small to matter. Leaders who invest in trust daily find that every other aspect of leadership becomes more effective. Leaders who neglect it find that no amount of strategy, talent, or resources can compensate for what its absence destroys.

KEY TAKEAWAYS:

- **Trust is a leadership discipline, not a personality trait.** It requires intentional daily practice.

- **Self-trust precedes interpersonal trust.** Leaders who do not trust themselves cannot earn others' trust.

- **Communication is the primary trust vehicle.** Every message either builds or spends trust.

- **Small behaviors compound into large trust impacts.** Being late, withholding information, or gossiping may seem minor, but they cause significant damage over time.

- **Consistency builds credibility.** People forgive mistakes but struggle with inconsistency.

- **Distance magnifies trust gaps.** Remote and hybrid work require more intentional communication, not less.

- **Honesty, especially when costly, builds trust fastest.** Admitting mistakes and sharing credit demonstrates trustworthiness more than claiming perfection.

- **Listening to understand builds more trust than listening to**

respond. Genuine listening requires pausing, asking questions, and resisting the urge to correct immediately.

- **Trust can be repaired, but only through sustained action.** Apologies without behavior change accomplish nothing.

- **Leaders must model the trust they expect.** Organizations take cues from leadership behavior, not leadership language.

REFLECTION QUESTIONS:

1. Where might trust be weaker than I assume? What behaviors might people be interpreting differently than I intend?

2. How predictable am I in my leadership behavior? Would my team say my responses are consistent or that they depend on my mood?

3. What messages might I be sending unintentionally through small actions like punctuality, response times, or body language?

4. How do I respond when people challenge me? Does my reaction encourage or discourage honest dialogue?

5. Where might clearer communication build trust immediately? What information am I withholding because "the timing isn't right"?

6. Am I withholding information because I am genuinely protecting people, or because communicating is uncomfortable?

7. Do my actions consistently match my words? Where might there be gaps between what I say I value and what I actually prioritize?

8. When was the last time I admitted I was wrong? How did people respond?

9. How quickly do I communicate bad news? Do I wait for all the details or share what I know when I know it?

10. Where have I accidentally undermined trust in my team through inconsistency, gossip, or broken commitments?

CHAPTER 6

EMPATHY IS A DISCIPLINE
UNDERSTAND WITHOUT LOWERING THE BAR

Empathy has become one of the most misunderstood concepts in leadership. For some, it is considered nice. For others, it is a reason to avoid hard conversations. And for too many leaders, it feels incompatible with accountability, standards, and results. During COVID, many leaders felt they needed to be empathetic, but that somehow translated into not holding people accountable. That misunderstanding has cost organizations clarity, performance, and trust.

In Chapter 4, we explored how leaders treat people in daily interactions and why those moments matter more than most realize. Courtesy, respect, and intentionality are not soft skills, but strategic disciplines. This chapter goes deeper into the leadership quality of empathy that makes those interactions meaningful.

Here is what empathy is not: soft, agreement, or lowering the bar. Empathy is the discipline of understanding perspectives, pressures, and contexts so leaders can make better decisions. Like all leadership disciplines, empathy requires effort, intentionality, and restraint.

Research shows that leaders who demonstrate empathy have 32 percent higher team engagement scores and 28 percent lower turnover rates than leaders who do not. Empathy is not optional. It is strategic.

EMPATHY IS NOT SYMPATHY

Before we go further, we need to clarify what empathy is. Sympathy means you feel sorry for an individual. You acknowledge their emotion. "I am sorry to hear that your car was stolen." Empathy means understanding others' needs. With empathy, you can personally relate to what others are feeling or saying. "It must be awful that your car was stolen. It is a real hassle to be without wheels."

Being empathetic does not necessarily mean you agree with what is being said; it means you can understand and appreciate what others are going through. This distinction matters in leadership. Sympathy creates distance. You feel bad for someone from afar. Empathy creates connection. You step into their experience long enough to understand it.

We worked with a manager who constantly confused the two. When an employee struggled with a project, he said, "That's too bad. I hope it works out for you." The employee felt dismissed. The manager thought he was being supportive. Sympathy acknowledges. Empathy understands. Leaders need the latter.

EMPATHY IS NOT AGREEMENT

One of the most damaging leadership myths is that empathy requires agreement. It does not. Leaders can understand someone's position and still say no. They can acknowledge effort and still require improvement. They can appreciate difficulty and still hold the line. Empathy informs judgment. It does not replace it.

In fact, leaders who skip empathy often unintentionally lower standards by solving the wrong problem. Understanding the real issue allows leaders to apply accountability where it belongs. We coached a manager who struggled with this distinction. An employee missed a deadline. The manager empathized with the employee's workload and extended the deadline. The pattern repeated. The employee learned that missed deadlines were negotiable.

We worked with the manager to separate empathy from accountability. Next time, the conversation shifted. "I understand you are facing a heavy workload. That is real. The deadline is also real. Let me know what support you need to meet it, but the expectation stands." Empathy acknowledged the pressure. Accountability held the standard. Both were necessary.

This distinction becomes the foundation for everything that follows. Empathy is not about making things easier. It is about making decisions better. With that clarity established, the question becomes: why does empathy matter strategically?

THE STRATEGIC CASE FOR EMPATHY

According to Meg Bear, Oracle Group Vice President. "Empathy is the critical 21st century skill." Why? Because technology is replacing people in more roles every day. Manufacturing, healthcare, construction, financial institutions, and even fast food increasingly rely on automation, artificial intelligence, and robotics.

When Oxford Economics asked employers which critical workplace skills would be needed in the next five to ten years, the responses were surprising. The answers did not include business acumen, analysis, or profit-and-loss management. Instead, employers' top priorities included relationship-building, working well on a team, co-creativity, brainstorming, cultural sensitivity, and managing diverse employees.

It is becoming clear that the most effective groups are those whose members possess essential human qualities such as empathy, social sensitivity, storytelling, collaboration, problem-solving, and relationship-building. We are social beings, hardwired to relate to one another. In the past, to be successful at work, you had to be machine-like. If you did it with a focus on speed, quality, and efficiency, you were a good employee. Now, being a great performer is becoming less about what you know and more about who you are.

Organizations with empathetic cultures report higher innovation, stronger customer satisfaction, and better financial performance. Conversely, the cost of lacking empathy is measurable and expensive. Low engagement costs organizations billions in lost productivity. High turnover disrupts operations and drains resources. Poor leadership relationships drive talented people to competitors.

Empathy is not soft. It is a competitive advantage. But understanding why empathy matters strategically is only the beginning. The next question is: what does disciplined empathy actually look like in practice?

WHAT EMPATHY LOOKS LIKE IN LEADERSHIP

Empathy shows up most clearly in leaders who must make difficult decisions that affect people and who still choose to understand before they act. Contemporary business leaders provide powerful examples of how empathy strengthens rather than weakens leadership effectiveness.

GLENMARK PHARMACEUTICALS CULTURAL TRANSFORMATION

Glenmark Pharmaceuticals is a global pharmaceutical company founded in 1977 and headquartered in Mumbai, India. It specializes in the development, manufacturing, and marketing of branded and generic pharmaceutical products across various therapeutic areas.

In June 2024, Glenmark Pharmaceuticals USA initiated a voluntary nationwide recall of 114 batches of potassium chloride extended-release capsules after internal quality testing showed the medication failed dissolution specifications, meaning the drug may not release correctly in the body, which could affect safety and effectiveness.

Glen Saldanha, CEO of Glenmark Pharmaceuticals, immediately understood that this was not primarily a business or legal problem. It was a human problem. Saldanha's empathy for the victims and public safety drove every decision that followed, even when those decisions came at a high cost.

ACTIONS DEMONSTRATING ACCOUNTABILITY AND EMPATHY

- The company publicly disclosed the recall through an FDA safety notice and a press release, clearly listing the affected lot numbers and advising wholesalers, distributors, and pharmacies to remove them from distribution immediately.

- It provided specific instructions for patients to consult their healthcare providers before discontinuing use and offered contact information for returning the product or getting more details.

- The recall was initiated voluntarily, not just in response to regulatory pressure, signaling acceptance of responsibility for product quality issues even in the absence of reported serious harm.

Why this matters: Pharmaceutical recalls, especially at the batch or national level, have direct implications for patient health and continuity of care. A voluntary recall with transparent communication and patient guidance is stronger evidence of *corporate accountability* than simply reacting to a regulator's mandate. Including detailed recall information and patient-centric instructions helps patients feel informed and supported, which is an expression of *empathy* in practice.

Saldanha's empathy was not passive sympathy. It drove accountability. He held employees accountable, ranking responsibility to customers and the public above that of stakeholders. Saldanha understood that empathy without accountability is empty, and accountability without empathy is cruel. His leadership combined both: a deep understanding of human impact paired with decisive action to prevent future harm.

> **EMPATHY WITHOUT ACCOUNTABILITY IS EMPTY, AND ACCOUNTABILITY WITHOUT EMPATHY IS CRUEL.**

Saldanha's crisis leadership demonstrates that empathy and

accountability are not opposing forces. Empathy clarifies what matters most. Accountability ensures the response matches that understanding. Together, they build trust that endures long after the crisis.

HOWARD SCHULTZ AND PARTNER-CENTERED LEADERSHIP

Howard Schultz built Starbucks on a foundation of empathy, though he never used that language. He called Starbucks employees "partners" and backed that designation with benefits unusual in the retail industry: health insurance for part-time workers, stock options, and tuition reimbursement through the Starbucks College Achievement Plan, a partnership with Arizona State University.

These decisions were not altruistic gestures. They were strategic choices rooted in understanding. Schultz understood that baristas faced financial pressure, limited career mobility, and the challenge of being treated as disposable labor in an industry with notoriously high turnover. He understood that if Starbucks wanted to create a distinctive customer experience, it needed employees who felt valued and invested in the company's success.

When Schultz returned as CEO in 2008 during the financial crisis, he faced enormous pressure to cut costs. Board members and investors pushed him to reduce benefits and scale back partner programs. Schultz refused. Instead, he closed stores for retraining, invested in partner development, and maintained benefits even as the company struggled financially. His empathy for partners' challenges did not lower his expectations for performance. It informed his strategy for achieving it.

The result was one of the most successful turnarounds in retail history. Starbucks not only survived the recession but also emerged stronger. Employee engagement increased. Customer satisfaction improved. Financial performance recovered. Schultz's leadership demonstrated that understanding what people need and providing it is not soft management. It is strategic leadership.

These leaders share a common pattern. They saw people's challenges clearly. They understood constraints before setting expectations. They acknowledged difficulty while maintaining standards. They used empathy to inform decisions, not to avoid them. Their success came not despite empathy, but because of it.

THE FOUR DIMENSIONS OF DISCIPLINED EMPATHY

Empathy in leadership operates across four interconnected dimensions. Each dimension builds on the others, and together they create a framework for practicing empathy without sacrificing accountability, clarity, or results.

Dimension 1: Understanding Context

The first dimension of empathy is understanding the full context in which people operate. This means recognizing the pressures, constraints, resources, competing priorities, and personal circumstances that shape behavior and performance. Leaders who understand context make better decisions because they see the complete picture, not just the visible symptoms.

Empathy is not about feelings. It is about information. Leaders who practice disciplined empathy gather better data. They understand constraints before setting expectations. They recognize pressure points before systems break. They hear concerns that would otherwise remain hidden. They distinguish between resistance and confusion. That understanding leads to better decisions, not easier ones.

We coached a director who received feedback that his team felt he did not care about them. He was stunned. "I care deeply about results," he said. "That is how I show I care." We explained that care without understanding feels transactional. His team needed him to understand their constraints, their pressures, and their challenges before he pushed for more.

EMPATHY IS NOT ABOUT FEELINGS. IT IS ABOUT INFORMATION.

He started practicing empathy deliberately. He asked better questions. He listened longer. He acknowledged difficulties before jumping to solutions. Within three months, his team's engagement scores increased by 18 points. His team did not need him to lower standards. They needed him to understand what they were facing as they met those standards.

Understanding context prevents leaders from solving the wrong problem. It allows them to respond proportionately rather than emotionally. It prevents overcorrection, misdiagnosis, and unnecessary conflict. In short, empathy reduces leadership blind spots.

Dimension 2: Acknowledging Experience

The second dimension is acknowledgment. Understanding alone is not enough. People need to know they have been seen and heard. Acknowledgment creates psychological safety, builds trust, and opens pathways for honest conversation. Leaders who skip this step may understand the situation intellectually but fail to connect emotionally, which undermines their ability to influence and lead effectively.

Acknowledgment does not mean agreement. It means validation. When leaders acknowledge someone's experience, pressure, or emotion, they signal respect without surrendering judgment. This is particularly critical during difficult conversations, performance issues, or organizational change.

One manager told us about an employee who seemed disengaged. The manager assumed the employee was unmotivated. During a one-on-one, the manager asked, "You seem frustrated lately. What is going on?" The employee opened up. Her mother had just moved in with her after entering hospice, and juggling caregiving responsibilities was wearing her down. She was not disengaged. She was exhausted.

The manager temporarily adjusted expectations, provided flexibility, and checked in regularly. The employee stayed engaged and loyal because she felt understood. Acknowledging emotion does not solve problems, but it creates space for honest conversations that do.

A great way to demonstrate acknowledgment is to make an educated guess and name the emotion. For example, when someone talks about their children, try acknowledging them by saying, "It sounds like you are really proud of what your child has accomplished." When you acknowledge emotion, people feel seen. That connection builds trust.

Acknowledgment also shows up in recognizing effort, contributions, and strengths. Most people need to feel valued and appreciated. Leaders with strong emotional intelligence are quick to acknowledge others' successes, results, and contributions. Theodore Roosevelt is credited with saying, "No one cares how much you know, until they know how much you care." Acknowledgment is how leaders demonstrate care in ways that matter.

Dimension 3: Asking Questions

The third dimension of empathy is inquiry. Empathetic leaders ask questions that surface information, clarify understanding, and demonstrate genuine interest. Questions signal that the other person's perspective matters. They also prevent leaders from making assumptions, jumping to conclusions, or solving problems that do not actually exist.

Asking questions and listening help leaders show empathy and simultaneously improve decision quality. When you ask questions about what your counterpart is talking about, you show that you are interested and care. Asking questions also helps you determine exactly what your counterpart is feeling so that you can acknowledge their emotion appropriately.

Good questions include:

"What has been hardest about this situation?"
"What would help right now?"
"What am I missing?"
"How are you holding up?"
"What is your opinion on this?"
"If you were in my position, what would you do?"

These questions signal care. They also surface information that improves decision-making.

Often, what people say is not the real issue. Leaders who listen only to words miss concerns, fears, incentives, and context. Leaders who ask questions and listen beyond the first layer uncover what actually should be addressed.

WITHOUT EMPATHY, LEADERS TREAT SYMPTOMS RATHER THAN CAUSES, CREATING NEW PROBLEMS IN THE PROCESS.

Dimension 4: Taking Appropriate Action

The fourth dimension is action. Understanding, acknowledgment, and inquiry mean nothing without appropriate follow-through. Empathy must translate into decisions, support, adjustments, or clarity that address the situation in a way that balances understanding with accountability.

This is where empathy earns its place as a leadership discipline rather than a personality trait. Action requires judgment. Leaders must decide when to provide support, adjust expectations, hold the line, and remove obstacles. Empathy informs those decisions. It does not make them for you.

When you demonstrate empathy through appropriate action, you help employees continue to grow, learn, and further develop in their careers. Team members engage when they know their boss cares and follows through. You encourage creativity and risk-taking because people know they are working in a safe environment and will not be personally blamed when things do not work out. You cultivate loyalty to you and your team because empathetic leaders have higher employee retention. You resolve problems sooner because people are not afraid to bring up issues and address conflicts.

You also encourage empathetic team behavior. You are the role model. When you demonstrate empathy in difficult situations through your actions, team members observe how you handle them and understand what is expected of them. You foster a culture of open, genuine communication. These are not intangible benefits. They translate directly into performance, retention, and results.

One executive we worked with spent 90 percent of his time in his office with the door closed. When we asked his team how connected they felt to him, one person said, "I could quit, and I'm not sure he would notice for a week." That leader started walking the floor every morning. He stopped by the desks. He asked how people were doing. He listened. He acted on what he learned. Six months later, his team engagement scores jumped 22 points. Presence plus action equals impact.

These four dimensions work together. Understanding without acknowledgment feels cold. Acknowledgment without question feels superficial. Questions without action feel manipulative. But when all four dimensions operate together, empathy becomes a powerful leadership discipline that strengthens relationships, improves decisions, and drives results.

EMPATHY PREVENTS LAZY LEADERSHIP

Getting angry is easy. Avoiding conflict is easy. Issuing blanket rules is easy. Empathy is harder. It requires leaders to slow down long enough to diagnose the situation before reacting. It requires listening not to validate feelings, but to understand reality.

Lazy leadership reacts to behavior. Disciplined leadership investigates causes. Empathy allows leaders to distinguish between skill gaps and effort gaps, burnout and disengagement, resistance and lack of clarity, and inexperience and unwillingness. Without empathy, leaders treat symptoms rather than causes, creating new problems in the process.

One executive implemented a policy requiring all employees to respond to emails within one hour. The policy was a reaction to slow communication. The result? Employees stopped doing deep work because they were constantly checking their email. Productivity dropped.

Had the executive practiced empathy first, he would have discovered the real problem. People were overwhelmed with meeting overload and had no time for focused work. The solution was not faster email responses. It was reducing the number of meetings and protecting focus time. Empathy prevents leaders from solving the wrong problem loudly.

This is why empathy improves decision quality. It forces leaders to pause, gather information, and understand root causes before acting. That discipline produces better outcomes than reactive decision-making ever could.

PRACTICING EMPATHY: WHAT IT LOOKS LIKE DAILY

Empathy is not an abstract concept. It shows up in specific, observable behaviors that leaders can practice intentionally. These behaviors reflect the four dimensions and translate theory into daily practice.

Be Present

It is hard to show empathy if you do not show up. Periodically, get up from behind your desk and check in with your team. Find out how they are doing and ask what they need from you to be successful in their jobs. When someone on your team is facing a challenge, check back later to see if the issue has been resolved.

Leaders who greet people by name, make eye contact, and acknowledge their presence create an immediate connection. Leaders who rush past without acknowledgment communicate something entirely different. Presence signals that people matter. Absence signals the opposite.

Walk in Their Shoes

It is easier to demonstrate empathy when you ask yourself, "If I were in their situation, how would I feel?" Thinking about how you would feel in specific situations allows you to have a better understanding of how others most likely feel.

During a naval command, I watched a senior officer handle a difficult personnel issue. A junior person had made a significant mistake that required disciplinary action. Before issuing the reprimand, the senior officer said, "If I were 22 years old, facing the pressure you are facing, with your level of experience, I might have made the same decision. That does not excuse the mistake. But I understand how it happened."

That acknowledgment changed everything. The junior officer accepted accountability without becoming defensive. The correction landed because empathy came first.

Listen Actively and Completely

Spend more time listening than talking. We have two ears and one mouth, and should use them proportionately. Genuinely engage in a two-way conversation. Ask questions and listen to the whole message, including both the words and the body language, to better understand the complete message.

Leaders who want results often have a strong urge to solve the problem immediately and tell their counterpart what they need to do. Empathy is about listening first and trying to understand what the other person is thinking and feeling. Nelson Mandela learned the importance of listening from watching his father, Chief Jongintaba, interact with his tribe during court meetings. When Mandela conducted meetings, he listened first and spoke last.

We worked with a manager who interrupted constantly. He finished people's sentences and jumped to solutions before problems were fully explained. His team stopped bringing him issues. Why bother? He was not listening anyway. We coached him to practice a simple discipline: count to three after someone finishes speaking before responding. Use that pause to confirm understanding. 'Let me make sure I heard you correctly. You are saying...'

That small change transformed his relationships. People felt heard. Problems got solved faster because they were fully understood before solutions were proposed. Active listening is not passive. It requires intention, attention, and discipline.

Be Open to Ideas and Challenge

Your team will not remain successful by adhering to the status quo. Encourage your team to challenge assumptions, address tough issues, solve problems, and anticipate the future and the changes needed to ensure ongoing success. Be open to new ideas. Whenever possible, give employees permission to try out their ideas. Reward their efforts, not just their outcomes.

We worked with a CEO who shot down every new idea. His team stopped offering suggestions. Innovation died. We challenged him. "What message are you sending when you reject ideas without consideration?" He changed his approach. When someone proposed a new idea, he asked, "What problem are you trying to solve? What would success look like? What support would you need?"

Even when he ultimately said no, people felt heard. Innovation returned because empathy created psychological safety.

WHEN EMPATHY MATTERS MOST

While empathy should be a consistent leadership practice, there are specific contexts where its presence or absence has an outsized impact. These situations require leaders to practice empathy with even greater intentionality.

In Mentorship and Development

Mentorship without empathy becomes prescriptive. Development without empathy becomes misaligned. Mentors who lack empathy push too hard or not hard enough, misread readiness, offer advice that does not land, and confuse confidence with capability.

Empathy allows mentors to stretch people without breaking them. It ensures discomfort leads to growth, not disengagement. This is especially critical when developing future leaders. Empathy helps mentors calibrate pace, pressure, and expectations while still maintaining standards.

We worked with a mentor who relentlessly pushed his mentee. He believed his tough-love approach-built character. The mentee burned out and left the organization. The mentor was devastated. "I was trying to help him grow." We asked, "Did you ever ask him what pace felt sustainable? Did you understand his other pressures?" He had not. Empathy does not mean lowering expectations. It means understanding capacity so development is sustainable.

In Crisis

True leaders realize that during times of crisis, certain aspects of leadership need to shift. A crisis creates a sense of loss, fear, and scarcity. Leaders need to step up with better, more frequent communication, greater empathy, and greater flexibility. We also need more strategic leadership, focused action, and a calm plan with clear goals. As leaders, we need to help people take the correct action at the right time.

Fires, floods, natural disasters, and the recent pandemic underscore the need for leaders to analyze what to do in crisis situations. During any difficult situation, whether caused by Mother Nature, a hostile business takeover, or a company reorganization, the need for strong leadership is critical. A lack of leadership during a crisis is glaringly evident.

How can we best lead through a crisis? First, acknowledge the problem. Make sure that we, as the people in charge, understand the real issues and the true nature of the crisis. Once we are clear, we need to view the crisis from other perspectives. Sometimes we are so worried about our own role that we neglect how others feel, how they are affected, and how they view the issue.

When members of your team are fearful and stressed in uncertain times, the prescription most needed is for leaders to turn up the volume on empathy. President Ronald Reagan demonstrated this when he addressed the country after the Space Shuttle Challenger exploded on January 28, 1986. He said, "We will never forget them, nor the last time we saw them, this morning, as they prepared for their journey and waved goodbye, and slipped the surly bonds of earth to touch the face of God." His words honored the astronauts who lost their lives aboard the Challenger while providing comfort to a grieving nation. Empathy in crisis is a sign of strong leadership.

In Remote and Hybrid Work Settings

Remote work creates unique situations that require greater empathy because of the lack of physical proximity. Managers have to understand that employees not answering the phone on the first ring does not mean they are not working. Electronic communication can often be more ambiguous than face-to-face communication. Because so much of how and what we communicate is conveyed through our body language and eyes, it can be easy to misinterpret digital communications such as email and instant messaging.

Leaders who recognize this and practice empathy and patience, rather than jumping to conclusions about a person's tone or intention, help cultivate an environment of trust, openness, and improved performance. It can be easy for remote team members to feel like they are on an island. Working from a home office can leave employees feeling disconnected from their leadership team, coworkers, and overall shared mission.

The best virtual leaders combat this tendency through regular, meaningful communication, recognizing that keeping employees motivated and informed can lead to higher-quality work and increased productivity. This requires intentional effort to check in, ask questions, acknowledge challenges, and maintain connection across distance.

During Performance and Accountability Conversations

Empathy becomes particularly critical when leaders must address performance issues, deliver difficult feedback, or hold people accountable for results. These conversations often determine whether someone improves, disengages, or leaves. Leaders who practice empathy in these moments separate the person from the problem, understand contributing factors before assigning blame, and balance clarity about expectations with support for improvement.

Without empathy, accountability conversations feel punitive. People become defensive. They protect themselves rather than acknowledging the issue. With empathy, the same conversation can become a developmental one. People feel respected even when they disagree with the assessment. They are more likely to take ownership and commit to change.

During Organizational Change

Change creates uncertainty, fear, and resistance. Leaders who practice empathy during transitions help people process loss, understand the rationale for change, and see a path forward. They acknowledge that change is difficult even when necessary. They provide context that reduces speculation. They listen to concerns without becoming defensive.

Leaders who skip empathy during change create unnecessary resistance. People do not fight the change itself as much as they fight feeling unheard, disrespected, or blindsided. Empathy does not eliminate the difficulty of change, but it significantly improves how people experience and respond to it.

THE EMPATHY-ACCOUNTABILITY PARTNERSHIP

This brings us to one of the most critical dynamics in leadership: the relationship between empathy and accountability. These are not opposing forces. They are partners. Strong leaders use empathy to understand context and accountability to set expectations, reinforce standards, and drive improvement.

Empathy without accountability creates drift. Accountability without empathy creates fear. Neither produces sustainable performance alone. Together, they create trust.

We worked with a CEO who was excellent at empathy but terrible at accountability. He understood every excuse. He empathized with every challenge. Standards eroded because empathy became a justification for avoiding hard conversations. His team lost respect for him. High performers left because mediocrity was tolerated.

We coached him to separate understanding from expectation. "I understand this is hard. The expectation stands. How can I support you in meeting it?" That phrase changed everything. Empathy acknowledged reality. Accountability maintained standards. Both were necessary.

Conversely, we have seen leaders who are strong on accountability but lack empathy. They set high standards and hold people to them, but they do so without understanding constraints, pressures, or context. Their teams comply out of fear, not commitment. Turnover is high. Innovation is low. People do the minimum required because they do not feel valued or understood.

The most effective leaders master both. They understand deeply and expect clearly. They acknowledge difficulty and maintain standards. They provide support and require results. This balance is not easy, but it is essential.

THE EMPATHY TRAP LEADERS MUST AVOID

There is a trap on the far side of empathy. Leaders sometimes confuse understanding with exemption. Disciplined empathy never removes responsibility. It never excuses repeated failure. It never indefinitely shields people from consequences.

Empathy should clarify expectations, not blur them. When leaders use empathy to delay decisions, avoid conflict, or tolerate underperformance, they undermine both credibility and culture. That is not empathy. That is avoidance.

We coached a manager who kept a struggling employee for two years because she empathized with the employee's personal challenges. The employee never improved. The team suffered. Morale dropped. When we asked why she had not addressed the performance issue, she said, "I feel bad for her. She is going through a lot."

We responded, "Your empathy for one person is causing harm to the rest of your team. That is not compassionate leadership. That is misplaced empathy." She finally had the accountability conversation. The employee transitioned out. The team's performance improved immediately. Three team members thanked her for finally addressing the issue.

Empathy that protects one person at the expense of many is not leadership. It is favoritism. Leaders must guard against this trap by remembering that empathy informs decisions, not replaces them.

Understanding someone's situation does not mean exempting them from consequences. True empathy includes caring enough to hold people accountable for their growth and their impact on others.

FOR RESULTS-ORIENTED LEADERS: THE DISCIPLINE OF CONNECTION

RESULTS-ORIENTED LEADERS WHO MASTER EMPATHY BECOME MORE EFFECTIVE, NOT LESS, BECAUSE EMPATHY IMPROVES INFORMATION, REDUCES RESISTANCE, AND BUILDS TRUST.

Some leaders naturally lean toward empathy. Others must practice it more intentionally. Leaders who identify as competitive, direct, and results-focused often find empathy challenging because it requires slowing down, processing emotion, and prioritizing connection over speed.

For results-oriented leaders, empathy can feel inefficient. There is always another goal to achieve, another problem to solve, another metric to improve. Spending time understanding how someone feels can seem like a distraction from getting things done. This perspective, while understandable, misses a critical truth: empathy is not a distraction from results. It is a pathway to better results.

Results-oriented leaders who master empathy discover that it makes them more effective, not less. They make better decisions because they have better information. They experience less resistance because people feel understood. They retain talent because employees know their boss cares. They build teams that execute faster because trust eliminates friction.

Practicing empathy as a results-oriented leader requires intentional discipline. It means consciously slowing down conversations even when you want to jump to solutions. It means asking questions before giving answers. It means acknowledging emotions even when they feel awkward. It means investing time in connection, even when it feels inefficient.

Martin Seligman, one of the leading researchers on self-esteem, states that meaningful connections with others lead to better mental and physical health and faster recovery from illness. Encouraging your employees is valuable. But even better is taking the time to talk, socialize, and connect with others on your team. A few minutes spent with one of your team members today can be a valuable investment for years to come.

The question for results-oriented leaders is not whether empathy matters. The data is clear. The question is whether you are willing to practice it as a discipline even when your instincts push you toward speed and efficiency. For leaders who aspire to greatness and want to accomplish something more significant than they could alone, empathy is not optional. It is essential. Without the help of the people in both our professional and personal lives, we do not get very far. Empathy is a powerful tool, and the greatest leaders practice it often. It may not be easy, but it is well worth it.

WHY YOUR LEADERSHIP INSTINCTS ARE SOMETIMES WRONG

We once spoke with a dad who was struggling because he wanted to give his children a wonderful childhood while also raising them to be generous and to appreciate what they receive. He did not want to raise self-centered adults. He wanted his children to be successful now and in the future. He and his wife were arguing because they disagreed about how much the kids should be allowed to do on their own, and when, as parents, they should step in to make it easier for the kids and protect them from being hurt.

Do you give your kids the answers or encourage them to look things up? Do you help with homework by giving them the answers because it goes faster, or do you encourage them to work through the problems? Do you catch your kids every time they stumble, or do you let them fall so they can pick themselves back up?

Our instinct is to make it easier on those we care about. That might be exactly the wrong approach. Good leaders care about their employees. They do not want their people to experience challenges. But removing every obstacle does not build capability or resilience.

It builds dependency.

Empathy helps leaders understand when to support and when to step back. Both are acts of care. Sometimes, the most empathetic thing a leader can do is let someone struggle through a challenge, because that struggle builds the capacity they need for future success. Sometimes empathy means providing support. Sometimes it means providing space. Sometimes it means adjusting expectations. Sometimes it means holding the line. The discipline is knowing which response fits the situation.

This is why empathy is not soft. It is not about making things easier. It is about making things better. Empathy does not make leadership easier. It makes leadership fairer, clearer, and more effective. It improves judgment. When paired with accountability, it ensures execution. When practiced as a discipline rather than a feeling, it becomes one of the most powerful tools in a leader's arsenal.

WHY THIS CHAPTER MATTERS

Leadership is tough because empathy is consistently misunderstood as the discipline that makes leadership softer when it is actually the discipline that makes leadership sharper. Leaders who skip empathy do not become more decisive. They become more reactive, solving the wrong problems with confidence, tolerating performance issues they have misdiagnosed, and losing people they never understood well enough to retain. Trust is built through how leaders treat people in the moments that feel too small to matter. Empathy is what ensures leaders are actually paying attention in those moments rather than simply going through the motions. When paired with the accountability disciplines explored in Chapter 8, empathy becomes one of the most powerful tools a leader carries, not because it makes difficult conversations easier, but because it makes them more accurate, more fair, and more likely to produce the outcome the organization actually needs.

KEY TAKEAWAYS:

- **Empathy is a leadership discipline**, not a personality trait. It requires intention, restraint, and practice.

- **The Empathy Trap confuses understanding and with exemptions.** Sympathy feels bad for someone. Empathy understands their experience.

- **Empathy is not agreement.** Leaders can understand perspectives without surrendering standards or lowering expectations.

- **There are four dimensions of disciplined empathy.** They are: understanding context, acknowledging experience, asking questions, and taking appropriate action.

- **Empathy reduces blind spots.** Understanding context leads to better judgment, not softer leadership.

- **Empathy prevents lazy leadership.** It replaces reaction with diagnosis, ensuring leaders solve the right problems.

- **Empathy matters.** Especially in mentorship, crisis, remote work, performance conversations, and organizational change.

- **Empathy and accountability are partners, not opposites.** Empathy explains behavior while accountability changes it.

- **Empathy without accountability creates drift.** Accountability without empathy creates fear. Together, they create trust.

- **Leaders who demonstrate empathy are more effective.** They have significantly higher engagement scores and lower turnover rates.

- **The empathy trap is confusing understanding with exemption.** Empathy informs decisions but does not replace them.

REFLECTION QUESTIONS:

1. Where might I be making decisions without fully understanding the pressures or constraints others are facing?

2. How do I personally distinguish between empathy and agreement, and where might I blur that line?

3. When have I reacted quickly to behavior instead of diagnosing the underlying cause?

4. Which of the four dimensions of disciplined empathy (understanding, acknowledging, asking, acting) is my strongest? Which needs the most development?

5. How effectively do I balance understanding with expectation-setting in difficult conversations?

6. Where might empathy be missing in our mentorship or leadership development efforts?

7. Have I ever used empathy to delay accountability? What was the impact on the individual and the team?

8. What does disciplined empathy apply to the way I hold people accountable today?

9. Am I confusing understanding with exemption anywhere in my leadership?

10. How well do I practice empathy in remote, hybrid, or crisis situations where it matters most?

11. For results-oriented leaders: Where am I sacrificing connection for speed, and what is that costing me in trust, information, or retention?

CHAPTER 7

PRIORITIES AND VALUES

ALIGN PURPOSE WITH WHAT
ACTUALLY GETS DONE

The new CEO found the company's core value, Integrity, engraved on a marble slab in the lobby. Innovation. People First. Collaboration. She asked the head of HR how long those values had been there. "Since 2008," he said. "Do people actually live them?" she asked. He paused. "We talk about them a lot." That was not the question she asked.

Leadership reveals itself not in what we say matters, but in what we choose to prioritize, especially when time, money, and attention are limited. Every organization claims to have values. They are framed on walls, printed in annual reports, featured on websites, and referenced in speeches. Leaders speak passionately about purpose, mission, and culture. Boards approve values statements. Marketing teams refine the language.

And yet, inside many organizations, people quietly ask a different question: If these are truly our values, why don't our priorities reflect them?

This chapter is about that gap, the tension between stated values and

121

lived behavior, between declared purpose and daily decisions, between what leaders say matters and what actually receives time, resources, and protection. Leadership is revealed in the decisions we make, especially the unpopular ones. This chapter goes deeper into what guides those decisions when pressure mounts and competing priorities collide. Because in leadership, priorities are values in action.

> **THE REAL TEST OF VALUES OCCURS WHEN THEY COME INTO CONFLICT WITH PRESSURE.**

VALUES ARE ONLY REAL WHEN THEY COST YOU SOMETHING

Values are easy to affirm when they are convenient. Integrity is simple when telling the truth carries no consequence. Respect is effortless when everyone agrees. Accountability feels noble when outcomes are positive. The real test of values occurs when they come into conflict with pressure:

- When revenue targets clash with people's commitments
- When speed challenges quality
- When short-term wins threaten long-term trust
- When doing the right thing is harder than doing the expedient thing

That is where leadership becomes uncomfortable and honest. If values do not guide decisions under pressure, they are not values. They are aspirations, and organizations know the difference.

Research from the Ethics & Compliance Initiative shows that when employees perceive a gap between stated values and leadership behavior, organizational trust drops by 42 percent, engagement declines by 38 percent, and voluntary turnover increases by 27 percent. The cost of misalignment is not abstract. It is measurable and expensive.

We worked on an executive coaching project in which a senior executive directed one of his managers to lie about his whereabouts. The senior executive wanted his boss to think he was in client meetings when he was at the gym, home for long lunches, or golfing.

The senior executive started by asking his manager to "cover for him" once or twice a month, then that escalated to once or twice a week. The manager's career was on the line. He knew that lying would protect his job and his boss, and telling the truth would damage his relationship with the executive, and possibly the CEO.

When the CEO cornered the manager and asked him directly where the executive was, the manager told the truth.

The short-term outcome was brutal. The CEO didn't reassure the manager or back him up. The manager's executive blamed him for the resulting confrontation with his boss. Everyone found out about it, and working relationships were damaged. Teamwork and collaboration in the department eroded. In the long term, the manager maintained his integrity, but he left soon after.

THE QUIET EROSION OF ALIGNMENT

Misalignment rarely happens all at once. It begins subtly. A leader approves a decision that technically violates a stated value but justifies it as "temporary." A team is rewarded for hitting numbers, even though they burned people out to do it. A high performer behaves badly but is tolerated because "we need them right now." A value is invoked selectively to discipline some and is ignored for others.

None of these moments feels catastrophic in isolation. Over time, however, patterns form. People notice. Cynicism creeps in. Trust erodes, not because leaders are malicious, but because they are inconsistent. Eventually, employees stop asking whether values matter. They assume they don't. And once that happens, culture becomes transactional.

According to research from the Harvard Business Review, organizations where employees perceive leadership hypocrisy experience 55 percent lower discretionary effort. People do what is required, nothing more. Innovation slows. Problems stay hidden. The best people start looking elsewhere. The erosion happens quietly, but the damage is profound.

WHY LEADERS STRUGGLE TO ALIGN PRIORITIES AND VALUES

Senior leaders do not wake up intending to compromise their values. Most drift into misalignment because of three realities that make alignment harder than it appears.

Pressure Distorts Perspective

As leaders rise, the consequences of decisions multiply. Stakeholders increase. Visibility intensifies. Time compresses. Urgency becomes constant. Under sustained pressure, leaders begin to optimize for relief, making decisions that reduce immediate tension rather than decisions that reinforce long-term integrity.

The danger is not one poor choice. It is normalization. What was once an exception becomes precedent. The temporary compromise becomes standard practice. Leaders justify each decision individually without recognizing the pattern forming beneath their choices. Over time, the organization learns that values are negotiable under pressure, precisely when they matter most.

Success Can Mask Misalignment

Strong results can hide unhealthy behavior. Organizations hitting targets often overlook warning signs: high turnover in certain departments, burnout among top performers, silence in meetings, or reluctance to challenge decisions. Success delays reckoning. Leaders must learn to ask not only "Are we winning?" but "How are we winning?" because the cost of misalignment is often deferred, not avoided.

We have seen organizations celebrate record revenue while ignoring the fact that achieving those numbers required sustained overtime, sacrifice of development time, and erosion of team morale. The results looked excellent in quarterly reports. Eighteen months later, talent was gone, institutional knowledge had walked out the door, and the organization faced a rebuilding challenge that erased years of progress. Success without alignment is borrowed time.

Leaders Confuse Values With Intentions

Good intentions are not the same as aligned behavior. Leaders often believe that because they care about values, those values are being lived. They assume alignment because it exists in their head. But organizations do not experience leadership intentions. They experience leadership decisions.

This gap between intention and impact shows up everywhere. A leader believes they value collaboration but consistently make unilateral decisions. A leader claims to prioritize development but never protects time for it. A leader says respect matters, but tolerates incivility when it comes from high performers. The disconnect is invisible to the leader but obvious to everyone else.

Understanding why misalignment happens does not excuse it, but it does help leaders recognize the patterns and guard against them. The next question becomes: how do we know when alignment exists or when it has eroded?

Priorities Tell the Truth

If you want to understand an organization's real values, do not read its mission statement. Look at:

- What gets funded
- What gets rewarded
- What gets tolerated
- What gets corrected
- What gets ignored
- What gets people promoted, coached, or fired

Those choices tell the truth. If collaboration is a value but bonuses reward individual performance above all else, collaboration is optional. If innovation is valued but failure is punished, innovation becomes a significant risk. If respect is a value but incivility from high performers is excused, respect is conditional. People are not confused by this. They are observant. They align their behavior accordingly.

This diagnosis is simple but revealing. Leaders should regularly audit their own decisions through this lens. Over the past quarter, what actually received time, money, and attention? What was protected when resources were scarce? What was sacrificed first? What behavior was rewarded in practice, regardless of what was praised in theory? The answers reveal operating values that may differ significantly from the stated ones.

UNDERSTANDING THE VALUES SPECTRUM: NOT ALL VALUES ARE CREATED EQUAL

One reason leaders struggle with alignment is that they treat all values as equally important and equally rigid. In reality, values exist on a spectrum, and understanding that spectrum helps leaders navigate the inevitable tensions that arise.

Core Values: Non-Negotiable Standards

These are the values you will not compromise regardless of pressure, cost, or consequence. They define who you are as a leader and what the organization stands for. Examples include integrity, safety, legal compliance, or respect for human dignity. Core values are bright lines. When you cross them, you damage something essential. A great example of a non-negotiable core value is honesty. If you steal something or if you lie, you will be terminated. Leaders must identify these in advance and communicate them clearly. When pressure mounts, there is no debate. Core values are protected, period.

Balanced Values: Context-Dependent Priorities

These values are important but must sometimes be balanced against competing needs. Speed and quality both matter, but sometimes you emphasize one over the other depending on the situation. Transparency and discretion are both valuable, but context determines which takes precedence. Empathy and accountability are partners, as we explored in Chapter 6, but the balance between them shifts based on circumstances.

The mistake leaders make is treating balanced values like core values, insisting on perfection in all dimensions simultaneously, or treating them like preferences, negotiating them away whenever convenient. The discipline is knowing when each value takes priority and explaining that reasoning clearly.

Aspirational Values: Direction, Not Destination

These are values you are working toward, but have not fully embodied. They represent the culture you are building, not necessarily the culture you have today. Aspirational values matter because they set direction, but pretending you have already arrived creates cynicism. Leaders who conflate aspiration with reality lose credibility. Better to say, "We are not there yet, but here is what we are doing to move toward it."

Understanding this spectrum allows leaders to make values-based decisions without falling into rigid perfectionism or convenient relativism. It also helps communicate tradeoffs more honestly when priorities conflict.

The Leader's Role: Choosing What Not to Do

One of the hardest leadership disciplines is deciding what not to prioritize. Every "yes" consumes resources. Every initiative competes for attention. Every goal dilutes focus. Leaders who attempt to honor every priority end up honoring none. Alignment requires subtraction.

It requires leaders to say:

- "This matters more than that."
- "We are not doing this, even though it is tempting."
- "This decision aligns with our values, even if it costs us."

These moments are uncomfortable. They are also defining. When leaders clearly articulate what will not be prioritized and why, they create clarity that cascades through the organization. People understand where to invest energy, what tradeoffs are acceptable, and how to make decisions when leadership is not in the room. Strategic subtraction is not about doing less. It is about doing what matters most with the full weight of organizational focus and resources behind it.

A technology company executive was interviewing a senior software engineer from their largest competitor. Everyone on the team was excited that an engineer from the competitor wanted to join their team. He was not only a solid engineer but also had extensive leadership experience, having built strong teams. Everyone, including the CEO, agreed that landing this engineer would be a huge win. Everything in the interview was going well until the engineer candidate told the senior leader and the CEO that he could bring proprietary information from his current employer that would greatly benefit their company's software. At the end of the interview, the CEO told the senior executive that they would not be hiring this engineer. The CEO believed that if the engineer was willing to steal intellectual property from his current employer, he would most likely be willing to steal from them. The CEO made the tough decision not to bring on a candidate who would significantly benefit the software design team but, in the long term, would undermine the company's values.

Patagonia: When Values Actually Mean Something

Most companies post values on their walls. Patagonia built an entire business model around theirs. Founded by climber Yvon Chouinard in 1973, Patagonia didn't start with a mission to save the planet. They started by making better climbing gear. But over time, something shifted. The company realized that the outdoor industry, the very industry that depended on pristine wilderness, was contributing to its destruction.

That realization could have been filed away as an uncomfortable truth. Instead, it became the foundation of everything Patagonia does. Here's what makes Patagonia different: they don't just talk about environmental responsibility in annual reports and marketing materials. They consistently and repeatedly make decisions that cost them money, complicate their operations, and slow their growth, all because those decisions align with their stated values. That level of commitment is rare. And it matters.

THE DECISIONS THAT PROVED IT

In 2011, Patagonia ran a full-page ad in The New York Times on Black Friday, the biggest shopping day of the year. The headline read: "Don't Buy This Jacket." The ad explained the environmental cost of producing one of their bestselling fleece jackets. It detailed the water used, the emissions created, and the waste generated. Then it asked customers to think twice before buying anything they didn't absolutely need.

Most companies spend Black Friday trying to sell as much as possible. Patagonia spent it telling customers to buy less. Why? Because their stated value is environmental responsibility. And if you value the environment, encouraging mindless consumption contradicts everything you claim to stand for.

Did it hurt sales? In the short term, possibly. In the long term, it built something more valuable than a temporary revenue spike. It built trust. Employees watched that decision. They saw leadership put values ahead of revenue when the two conflicted. Customers saw it too. The campaign strengthened brand loyalty among people who shared those values and attracted talent who wanted to work for a company that meant what it said.

But Patagonia didn't stop there. They launched the Worn Wear program, which repairs damaged clothing to extend its life rather than encouraging customers to buy new items. They committed 1% of sales to environmental causes, not 1% of profits, meaning they give even in years when profits are minimal. They transitioned to 100 percent organic cotton despite the cost and complexity. They became a certified B Corporation, legally committing to consider environmental and social impact alongside profit.

In 2022, Yvon Chouinard took the ultimate step. Rather than selling the company or taking it public, he transferred ownership to a trust and nonprofit organization dedicated to fighting climate change. The company's profits, rather than enriching the founder or shareholders, now fund environmental protection. This decision ensured that Patagonia's values would outlast its founder.

Every one of these decisions carried cost: financial cost, operational complexity, slower growth, or reduced personal wealth. But every decision reinforced the same message: these values are not negotiable. They are not marketing. They are who we are. Employees don't wonder what Patagonia stands for. Customers don't question whether the company means what it says. The alignment between stated values and actual priorities is visible, consistent, and costly. That is what makes it credible.

Patagonia demonstrates a critical truth: values become real when they cost you something. Words are cheap. Decisions are expensive. Leadership is revealed in which expenses you are willing to bear.

PROTECTING FOCUS AND VALUES UNDER PUBLIC PRESSURE

Basecamp is a privately held software company best known for its project-management platform. At the time of its most controversial values decision, the company had about 50 to 60 employees, making it firmly a small organization, not a corporate giant. Basecamp's leadership, co-founders Jason Fried and David Heinemeier Hansson, had long articulated core values centered on focused work, calm and sustainable productivity, respectful collaboration, and avoiding performative corporate behavior.

In 2021, during a period of intense national and workplace tensions about social and political issues, Basecamp made a decision that immediately put those values to the test. Leadership announced that political and societal debates would no longer take place on internal company channels, stating that these discussions were harming trust, focus, and collaboration. At the same time, they reinforced commitments to fair pay, benefits, and respectful treatment, but drew a clear boundary around how work time and internal communication would be used.

This decision came at a cost. Public backlash was swift. Many employees resigned. Media criticism was intense. The company was accused of being out of step with broader cultural expectations.

From a popularity standpoint, the decision was painful. From a values-alignment standpoint, it was consistent. Basecamp leadership did not claim neutrality out of convenience. They argued that protecting focus, psychological safety, and productive collaboration were central to their company's purpose. They openly acknowledged the tradeoffs and accepted the consequences rather than walking back the decision to regain approval.

VALUES THAT ARE NEGOTIATED IN THE MOMENT RARELY SURVIVE THE MOMENT.

What were the outcomes of Basecamp's new internal communication policy? On the negative side, there were large-scale employee departures. About one-third of Basecamp's workforce left after the announcement. Roughly 20 out of 57 employees opted for voluntary severance rather than remain under the new policy. This included senior staff, such as heads of design, marketing, and customer support.

Many employees expressed frustration and disagreement with the policy, viewing it as a restriction on open dialogue and employee voice. Some publicly criticized the decision and the leadership's approach on platforms like Twitter and blogs. This included disputes over how the policy was communicated and interpreted, which were seen as discouraging discussion of important issues, including diversity, equity, and inclusion. The decision also attracted widespread media scrutiny and sparked debate in the tech industry about workplace freedom of speech.

There were also positive benefits. Basecamp's CEO, Jason Fried, framed the ban as a way to refocus the company on its core mission, building software, rather than debating divisive issues on internal channels, which he felt took energy away from productive work.

Even after the initial upheaval, Basecamp leadership stood by the policy despite apologizing for how it was communicated and for underestimating the internal cultural fallout. They argued it was the right decision for the company in the long term, even if the short-term effects were painful.

Deciding in Advance: The Discipline That Protects Values

Leaders often ask, "How do I protect values without losing momentum?" The answer is simple but not easy: you decide in advance what you will not compromise. Values that are negotiated in the moment rarely survive the moment.

This means doing the hard work of clarity before pressure arrives. It means identifying your core values, the non-negotiables, and explicitly naming them. It means discussing with your leadership team which tradeoffs are acceptable and which are not. It means communicating to the organization what will be protected, even when it costs something. This advance decision-making creates what psychologists call a "precommitment," a choice made in a calm state that governs behavior in a heated one.

Here is what deciding in advance looks like in practice. A leadership team sits down and works through scenarios: If revenue drops 20 percent, what gets cut first, and what gets protected? If a star performer violates our values, what happens? If we face pressure to compromise quality for speed, what is our line in the sand? If stakeholders demand something that contradicts our stated priorities, how do we respond?

These conversations are uncomfortable because they force specificity. Leaders can no longer hide behind vague commitments to "balance" or "do our best." They must choose. But that discomfort is precisely the point. Making those choices in advance, when emotions are calm and stakes are theoretical, protects leaders from making reactive choices under pressure when emotions are high and stakes are immediate.

When pressure arrives, and it will, leaders who have decided in advance do not need to relitigate the question. The decision has already been made. Their job is simply to execute it. This does not eliminate difficulty, but it eliminates doubt. The organization watches leaders honor precommitments and learns that values are not situational. That credibility becomes the foundation for trust, autonomy, and cultural strength.

VALUES MUST BE OPERATIONALIZED THROUGH SYSTEMS

Organizations often treat values as slogans rather than standards. Real alignment requires translation. Leaders must answer questions like: What does this value look like in decision-making? How does it affect hiring, promotion, and termination? How does it influence budgeting? How does it shape how conflict is handled? Without this translation, values remain abstract and therefore optional.

Values are reinforced or undermined by systems such as performance evaluations, compensation structures, promotion criteria, meeting norms, and decision rights. If systems reward behavior that contradicts values, values lose. Leaders must regularly audit alignment by asking whether their incentives reinforce what they say matters, whether their processes reward the behavior they claim to value, and whether their leaders model the trade-offs they expect others to make. Alignment is not a one-time exercise. It is a discipline.

One organization claimed "people first" as a core value. During a downturn, leadership cut development budgets and froze communication while maintaining executive perks. The message was not lost. Contrast that with another organization facing similar pressure. Leadership reduced executive compensation, preserved training, and communicated transparently about tradeoffs. Same environment. Different values in action. The difference was not in what leaders said. It was in what systems reinforced.

Practical steps for operationalizing values include embedding them in hiring criteria so that values alignment is assessed alongside skills and experience, building them into performance reviews so that how people achieve results matters as much as what results they achieve, tying compensation to values-aligned behavior rather than outcomes alone, using values as decision filters in strategy discussions, and celebrating examples of values-based decisions publicly to reinforce what the organization honors. When systems and values align, culture becomes self-reinforcing. When they conflict, words lose meaning.

WHEN PRIORITIES CONFLICT, AND THEY WILL

Every leader eventually faces value conflict:

- Efficiency versus empathy
- Growth versus sustainability
- Speed versus stewardship
- Transparency versus discretion

These are not signs of failure. They are the reality of leadership. The question is not whether conflict exists. It is whether leaders confront it openly. Strong leaders name the tension. They explain tradeoffs. They articulate why one priority must temporarily outweigh another without pretending the cost does not exist. People can accept hard decisions when they understand the reasoning and trust that the choice is principled rather than convenient.

We have worked with several executives who have decided to hire their friend as a direct report. This decision is not a problem if the friend is truly a friend. A true friend works harder than the average team member, produces extraordinary results, and makes their boss look like a leadership hero. The problem arises when the friend is a mediocre performer or a poor collaborator, and the boss lacks the courage to hold that direct report to the same standards as all others because they value the friendship and do not want to give feedback that would undermine the relationship. When this happens, the outcomes include lower team morale, a lack of respect for the boss, and the best team members leaving for an organization that truly values fairness and accountability.

The key is consistency over time. When leaders make tradeoffs transparently and apply the same reasoning across situations, people learn the organization's actual hierarchy of values. They understand that transparency usually wins, but discretion takes precedence in specific circumstances. They see that speed matters, but not at the expense of safety. That pattern recognition enables employees to make better independent decisions because they understand how the organization thinks.

TEACHING THE ORGANIZATION HOW TO DECIDE

Perhaps the most overlooked benefit of alignment is this: leaders who consistently align priorities with values teach their organizations how to make decisions without them. Over time, people learn what matters, how tradeoffs are evaluated, what will be supported, and what will not be tolerated. That is leadership at scale.

When leaders fail to align priorities and values, decision-making becomes personality-driven. People wait for direction. They hedge. They protect themselves. They escalate decisions that should be handled locally because they do not trust their own judgment about what the organization values. This creates bottlenecks, slows execution, and prevents the organization from scaling effectively.

Alignment creates autonomy. When people understand the values hierarchy and see it consistently applied, they can make decisions confidently. They know that choosing quality over speed in certain contexts will be supported. They understand that protecting people sometimes takes precedence over hitting short-term targets. They recognize that transparency is valued except in specific circumstances where confidentiality is required. This clarity allows decisions to be made faster, closer to the problem, and with less leadership involvement.

The practical impact is significant. Organizations with strong value alignment experience faster decision-making, higher employee engagement, better risk management because people understand which risks are acceptable, stronger innovation because people know which boundaries are firm and which are flexible, and greater leadership bench strength because future leaders are learning to lead by watching current leaders make principled decisions.

This is how leadership outlasts leaders. When values are embedded in decision-making, they persist beyond any individual's tenure. The organization develops muscle memory for principled decision-making that continues regardless of who sits in the leadership role.

WHEN LEADERS' VALUES COLLIDE — AND THEY GET IT WRONG

When leaders mishandle a values conflict, trust drops first, and it drops fast.

People rarely leave because of a single decision. They leave because of what that decision signals. When a values clash is poorly handled, employees begin asking quieter, more dangerous questions: *Do they actually understand us? Am I safe here if I disagree? What else might they get wrong?* Once that doubt takes root, every future decision is filtered through suspicion. The leader may believe the issue has passed. The organization knows it has not.

One of the most common accelerants of damage is the intent-versus-impact divide. Leaders often try to explain what they meant, believing clarity will fix the problem. But when leaders prioritize intent over impact, they unintentionally communicate something far more damaging: *Your experience matters less than my reasoning.* That's the moment conflict widens into a breach. What could have been a disagreement becomes distrust.

Value conflicts are rarely just about differing opinions. They frequently touch identity, dignity, and belonging. When people feel their lived experience was minimized, their concerns treated as distractions, or their voice framed as the problem itself, the organization begins to shift. It no longer feels like a community. It feels transactional. And once people feel reduced to transactions, commitment erodes.

Worse still, mishandled value conflicts rarely stay contained. Internal tension spills outward. Exits become public narratives. Slack debates become headlines. Silence is interpreted as indifference. Leaders may still be technically within their rights, but they have lost control of the story. And in leadership, perception shapes reality far more than technical correctness ever will.

HOW LEADERS RECOVER

Recovery is possible, but it requires leaders to understand that value errors are not logic failures; they are trust failures. You cannot reason your way out of a trust deficit. You must repair it.

The first step is naming the harm. This is where many leaders stumble because they feel compelled to defend the decision before acknowledging its consequences. Effective leaders resist that instinct. They say, plainly, "We underestimated the emotional impact of this." Or, "We caused people to feel unheard." Or even, "Our process failed, even if our goals were reasonable." There are no qualifiers attached. No "but." The absence of defensiveness signals moral seriousness. It tells people this is not about saving face; it is about restoring integrity.

The next step is separating the value from the execution. Strong leaders do not abandon core values simply because they were applied poorly. Instead, they examine how those values were enforced. A commitment to focus, collaboration, or accountability may still be the right choice. But if the enforcement erased voice or diminished dignity, that application was wrong. Credibility returns when leaders can say, "The value still matters. The way we implemented it did not."

After a rupture, restoring voice matters more than restoring policy. People need to be heard before they need answers. That may require structured listening sessions, neutral facilitators, visible feedback loops, and public acknowledgment that dissent is legitimate. If leaders rush to "move on," they compound the damage. Healing cannot be accelerated by decree.

Trust also rebuilds only when people see leaders pay something. Repair is not theoretical; it is costly. The cost might come in reputation, ego, control, time, or comfort. It may require reversing part of a policy, changing decision rights, pausing enforcement, or publicly owning the mistake. If recovery costs leadership nothing, it will feel cosmetic to everyone else.

Finally, values must be re-anchored in behavior. Abstract principles are not enough. People need clarity. What is encouraged? What is protected? What is off-limits? Who decides? When values are translated into concrete expectations, safety begins to return. Clarity is reassurance.

WHAT DOESN'T WORK

Leaders sometimes try shortcuts. They say, "We hear you," without making a change. They apologize while simultaneously justifying. They blame misinterpretation or social media. They wait for people to forget. They treat departures as proof that the policy was right all along.

None of these strategies rebuilds trust. They deepen cynicism by preserving authority at the expense of accountability.

THE HARD TRUTH

Many leaders double down when challenged. They defend why the decision was technically correct, even when others experience it as harmful. They argue from principle when what is required is humility.

The leaders who recover are different. They are willing to say, "I was wrong." They are willing to admit, "I made a bad decision." And they are courageous enough to add, "I want to work with you so we can make this right." That is not a weakness. It is strength under discipline.

THE PERSONAL COST OF MISALIGNMENT

Misalignment affects leaders personally, whether they admit it or not. Leaders who consistently act against their values experience moral fatigue, a loss of confidence, a lack of clarity, and quiet disengagement. They may remain successful externally while becoming conflicted internally. That internal tension is unsustainable.

Leaders who align priorities with values, even imperfectly, experience something different: greater clarity, stronger credibility, deeper trust, and greater resilience under pressure. Alignment does not remove difficulty; it gives difficulty meaning. When leaders know their decisions reflect their values, they can defend those decisions with conviction. When employees trust that leadership acts from principle rather than convenience, they extend greater patience during difficult periods. When stakeholders see consistency between words and actions, they place trust in organizations that carry them through challenges.

The personal benefit is not just external credibility. It is internal coherence. Leaders who align priorities and values sleep better, lead longer, and finish stronger because they are not carrying the weight of unacknowledged contradictions. This is not about perfection. It is about integrity, the integration of stated belief and lived behavior.

WHY THIS CHAPTER MATTERS

Leadership is tough because values are tested daily, not annually. As we explored in Chapter 1, leadership is revealed under pressure. As Chapter 3 demonstrated, the hardest decisions often involve choosing between competing goods or accepting short-term pain for long-term integrity. Leadership is tough because alignment requires courage, clarity, and consistency, especially when no one is applauding.

> **LEADERSHIP INTEGRITY IS BUILT ONE DECISION AT A TIME. LEGACY IS THE CUMULATIVE RESULT OF WHEN THESE DECISIONS REFLECT VALUES.**

But leadership is also meaningful because alignment creates organizations that people trust, cultures people commit to, and legacies leaders can stand behind. At the end of your career, people will not remember your strategic plans in detail. They will remember whether you meant what you said. They will remember whether your priorities reflected your values or contradicted them. They will remember whether you led with integrity or convenience. That memory will be your legacy.

KEY TAKEAWAYS:

- **Priorities reveal values more clearly than words.** What receives time, money, and attention shows what actually matters.

- **Values that do not guide decisions under pressure are not values.** They are aspirations.

- **Not all values are equal.** Core values are non-negotiable. Balanced values are context-dependent. Aspirational values set direction.

- **Alignment requires leaders to choose what not to prioritize.** Strategic subtraction creates focus.

- **Core values that are negotiated in the moment rarely survive the moment.** Leaders must decide in advance what they will not compromise.

- **Systems reinforce values more powerfully than speeches.** Compensation, promotion, and accountability structures teach what the organization truly values.

- **Misalignment costs trust, clarity, and long-term performance.** The damage is often deferred but never avoided.

- **Strong leaders name value conflicts openly.** They explain tradeoffs rather than pretending they do not exist. If your values never conflict, then you have no values.

- **Alignment teaches organizations how to decide without the leader present.** This creates autonomy, speed, and scalability.

- **Correction matters more than perfection.** Leaders who acknowledge misalignment and course-correct preserve credibility.

- **Leadership integrity is built one decision at a time.** Legacy is the cumulative result when these decisions reflect values.

REFLECTION QUESTIONS:

1. Where might my stated values and actual priorities be misaligned? What receives time, money, and attention regardless of what I say matters?

2. What decisions am I currently justifying as "temporary" that are becoming permanent patterns?

3. Which behaviors are being rewarded in practice that contradict our stated values?

4. What are my core values, the ones I will not compromise regardless of pressure? Have I communicated them clearly?

5. Where have I avoided a difficult decision that values alignment requires?

6. How do our systems, compensation, promotion criteria, and performance reviews reinforce or undermine our stated purpose?

7. What values would others say guide my decisions when pressure is high, and no one is watching?

8. Have I decided in advance what I will not compromise, or am I making those decisions reactively under pressure?

9. Where might success be masking unhealthy behavior or misalignment in my organization?

10. If I left tomorrow, what priorities would continue and why? What does that reveal about whether values are embedded or personality-dependent?

11. What is one decision I need to revisit through a values lens?

12. How well do I explain value conflicts and tradeoffs when priorities compete?

CHAPTER 8

ACCOUNTABILITY
HOLD THE LINE WITHOUT BREAKING TRUST

The executive team sat in uncomfortable silence. For the third consecutive quarter, the sales VP had missed his numbers. Everyone in the room knew it. Everyone also knew he was the CEO's college roommate. The CFO finally spoke: "We can't keep pretending this isn't a problem." The CEO's response would define the culture for years to come.

Accountability is one of the most talked-about leadership concepts and one of the least consistently practiced. Most leaders say they value accountability, include it in value statements, reference it in performance reviews, and talk about "owning results" and "holding people responsible."

And yet, accountability often breaks down precisely when it matters most. It breaks down when relationships are at stake, when the person involved is talented or powerful, when leaders are tired, stretched thin, or unsure of themselves, and when holding the line feels harder than letting it slide.

This chapter is about accountability as a discipline. As we explored in Chapter 6, empathy and accountability work as partners: empathy without accountability creates drift, while accountability without empathy creates fear. This chapter focuses specifically on the discipline of accountability itself: what it is, why leaders avoid it, and how to practice it without breaking trust. Because real accountability does not weaken relationships. Avoiding accountability does.

WHY ACCOUNTABILITY IS SO OFTEN AVOIDED

Leaders rarely avoid accountability because they are lazy or indifferent. They avoid it because accountability feels personal. Holding someone accountable risks discomfort, conflict, and being disliked. It risks discovering that the leader may have been unclear, inconsistent, or complicit. Many leaders convince themselves they are being kind by letting things go.

"I don't want to damage the relationship."
"They're under a lot of pressure."
"This isn't the right time."
"I'll address it later."

Avoidance masquerades as empathy. But over time, the cost becomes visible. When leaders do not hold people accountable, they quietly shift the burden to others. Strong performers compensate. Standards erode. Resentment grows, not toward the underperformer, but toward the leader who allowed it.

We worked with a manager whose employee consistently missed deadlines. The manager justified it. "She's going through a tough time. I don't want to add more stress." Six months later, three team members quit. When we asked why, one said, "We were tired of covering for someone who never delivered. And we were tired of a manager who wouldn't address it."

The manager thought she was being compassionate. Her team experienced it as unfair. Accountability delayed is accountability denied.

We work with a healthcare organization that has a highly respected surgeon on staff. His clinical outcomes are excellent, and his procedures generate significant revenue for the organization. Hospital

ACCOUNTABILITY DELAYED IS ACCOUNTABILITY DENIED.

leadership frequently points to his service line as a financial cornerstone.

Inside the operating room, however, this doctor is known for harsh behavior. He regularly speaks to nurses and technicians in a demeaning tone, dismisses questions, and reacts angrily to delays. Several staff members report feeling intimidated and reluctant to raise concerns during his cases. Over time, multiple complaints are submitted to management and human resources. Turnover in the surgical unit increases, and exit interviews cite working with this surgeon as a key reason for staff leaving.

Senior leaders are aware of the situation but choose not to address it directly. They worry that confronting the surgeon could prompt him to leave for another hospital, resulting in lost revenue and prestige. Instead, leaders encourage staff to "work around" the issue, quietly reassign personnel, and frame the behavior as the cost of working with a high performer. No formal feedback or corrective action is taken. This surgeon continues to operate without accountability, and staff learn that professional conduct expectations are unevenly enforced.

Over time, trust in leadership erodes, psychological safety declines, and the hospital's stated values of respect and teamwork are undermined by inaction.

THE COST OF LOW-ACCOUNTABILITY CULTURES

Low-accountability cultures are rarely loud or chaotic. They are quiet. People stop speaking up because it does not change anything. High performers stop going the extra mile because it feels unfair. Mediocrity becomes normalized, not because people lack capability, but because expectations lack enforcement.

In these environments, deadlines are flexible for some and rigid for others. Behavior standards are applied selectively. Feedback is vague. Consequences are inconsistent. People notice who gets away with what.

Over our combined decades of consulting and military leadership, one finding stands out consistently. When employees perceive accountability as inconsistent, trust in leadership drops by an average of 28 points. That is not a small number. That is a leadership crisis. Over time, leaders lose moral authority, not because they lack vision, but because they lack follow-through. Trust erodes not from harshness, but from inconsistency.

Understanding why accountability breaks down and what it costs is essential. But equally important is understanding what accountability actually is, because many leaders operate under damaging misconceptions.

WHAT LEADERS GET WRONG ABOUT ACCOUNTABILITY

Before leaders can practice accountability effectively, they must dismantle several persistent misconceptions that undermine their efforts.

Misconception #1: Accountability Is Mean

Many leaders believe that holding people accountable is harsh, unkind, or incompatible with being a supportive leader. This belief causes them to soften expectations, delay difficult conversations, or avoid consequences altogether. The truth is that accountability is an act of respect. It signals that you believe someone is capable of meeting standards and that their contribution matters enough to require excellence. What feels mean is allowing someone to fail repeatedly without clear feedback or support. Avoidance is not kindness. It is neglect.

Misconception #2: Accountability Means Catching People Doing Things Wrong

Some leaders treat accountability as a policing function, constantly watching for mistakes to correct. This creates a culture of fear and compliance rather than ownership and initiative. Real accountability focuses on clarity upfront and evaluation afterward. It defines success, provides support, and then measures outcomes. The goal is not to catch failure but to enable success and address gaps when they occur.

> **POPULARITY IS NOT A METRIC OF LEADERSHIP. RESPECT IS.**

Misconception #3: Nice Leaders Don't Hold People Accountable

Leaders who pride themselves on being approachable, empathetic, or supportive sometimes believe that accountability contradicts those qualities. They confuse being liked with being respected. Popularity is not a metric of leadership. Respect is. People respect leaders who care enough to hold them to high standards. They lose respect for leaders who tolerate mediocrity to avoid discomfort. Nice leaders who avoid accountability are not preserving relationships. They are slowly eroding them.

Misconception #4: Accountability Is the Same as Micromanagement

This is one of the most damaging misconceptions. Leaders who fear being seen as micromanagers often swing too far in the opposite direction, providing little clarity and even less follow-up. But accountability and micromanagement are not the same thing:

- Micromanagement is about control. Accountability is about clarity.

- Micromanagement watches effort. Accountability measures outcomes and behavior.

- Micromanagement intrudes. Accountability defines expectations and checks results.

When accountability is weak, leaders often compensate by hovering, asking for constant updates, inserting themselves unnecessarily, or redoing work themselves. This does not create accountability. It creates dependence. Strong accountability reduces the need for control because expectations are clear and consequences are predictable. When people know what success looks like, who owns it, and when it will be evaluated, leaders can step back without losing standards.

One director we coached struggled with this distinction. She hovered over every project, checking in multiple times daily. Her team resented it. We asked, "What would happen if you clarified expectations upfront, set checkpoints, and then stepped back?" She tried it. Within three weeks, her team's productivity increased. They stopped waiting for her approval on every decision. They took ownership. Clarity creates space. Micromanagement suffocates it.

With these misconceptions addressed, leaders can approach accountability more effectively. But before they can credibly hold others accountable, they must confront a harder truth about themselves.

THE FOUR LEVELS OF ACCOUNTABILITY

Accountability operates at multiple levels within organizations, and understanding these levels helps leaders diagnose where breakdowns occur and where to focus their efforts.

Level 1: Self-Accountability

This is the foundation. Leaders who do not hold themselves accountable cannot credibly hold others accountable. Leaders model what they expect, and organizations take cues from leadership behavior, not leadership language. Self-accountability means publicly owning missed deadlines, acknowledging when decisions caused unintended consequences, admitting when clarity was lacking, and correcting course visibly.

During a command assignment, I watched a senior officer reprimand a junior officer for being late to a briefing. The junior officer was five minutes late. The senior officer was routinely 15 minutes late for his own meetings. The message? Accountability applies to you, not to me. That double standard destroyed credibility faster than any performance issue could.

ORGANIZATIONAL ACCOUNTABILITY IS EMBEDDED IN SYSTEMS, PROCESSES, AND CULTURE RATHER THAN DEPENDENT ON INDIVIDUAL LEADERS.

Before leaders can move to any other level of accountability, they must master this one. When leaders fail to model accountability, they unintentionally teach people that commitments are flexible, deadlines are suggestions, and responsibility is negotiable.

Level 2: Direct Report Accountability

This is where most leaders focus their accountability efforts: holding the people who report directly to them accountable for results and behavior. This level requires clear expectations, consistent follow-through, and timely conversations when gaps appear. It is the most visible form of accountability and the one that most directly impacts team performance. We will explore the practical elements of this level in depth throughout this chapter.

Level 3: Peer Accountability

Accountability often breaks down at this level. Peers hesitate to challenge one another. Senior leaders avoid conflict. Everyone assumes someone else will address the issue. This is where CEOs and organizational leaders must set the tone. Peer accountability does not require positional authority. It requires norms, permission, and modeling.

In one executive team we worked with, the CEO implemented a simple practice. At the end of each meeting, each leader made one commitment and asked the team to hold them accountable. The following week, the meeting started with each leader reporting on that commitment. It felt awkward initially. Within three months, accountability improved across the entire organization. Silence at the top teaches avoidance everywhere else.

Level 4: Organizational Accountability

This is accountability embedded in systems, processes, and culture rather than dependent on individual leaders. It includes performance management systems, transparent metrics, regular review cadences, and predictable consequences. When accountability reaches this level, it becomes self-sustaining. People know what is expected, how performance is measured, and what happens when standards are not met, regardless of who their manager is. Building organizational accountability is the ultimate goal because it creates consistency, fairness, and scalability.

Understanding these four levels helps leaders diagnose where accountability is strong and where it is weak. Most leaders discover they are stronger at some levels than in others. The key is to build deliberately across all four, starting with self-accountability and expanding outward.

Clear Expectations: The Cornerstone of Accountability

You cannot enforce what you have not defined. Many accountability failures are not performance failures. They are clarity failures. Leaders assume alignment because expectations feel obvious to them, forgetting that experience, context, and perspective shape understanding.

We coached a CEO who was frustrated that his team was not executing his vision. When we asked him to describe what success looked like, he said, "They should know. We talked about it." We asked his team the same question. Five people gave five different answers. The problem was not effort. It was clarity.

Clear accountability requires four essential elements, each of which must be explicitly defined:

1. What does success look like?
Describe the outcome in specific, measurable terms. Not "improve customer service." Instead, "reduce customer complaints by 15 percent within 90 days."

2. Who owns it?
Assign one person primary responsibility. Shared accountability often becomes no accountability.

3. When is it due?
Set clear deadlines. "Soon" and "as soon as possible" are not deadlines.

4. What authority do they have?
Clarify decision rights. Can they approve spending? Reassign resources? Change the approach?

When these four elements are clear, accountability becomes straightforward. Vague expectations create unfair accountability. If success has not been articulated in observable terms, holding someone accountable feels arbitrary, even when the leader is right. Clarity is an act of respect.

Once expectations are clear, the next challenge is to have conversations that reinforce them when gaps arise.

THE ACCOUNTABILITY CONVERSATION FRAMEWORK

Accountability conversations do not have to be dramatic. In fact, the most effective ones are calm, factual, and timely. They focus on what was expected, what occurred, the impact, and what happens next. They avoid character judgments and emotional escalation.

Language matters:
"There's a gap between what we agreed to and what happened."
"Here's the standard. Here's where we missed it."
"This needs to change."

A firm approach does not require harshness. People can handle high standards. They struggle with ambiguity, surprise, and delayed confrontation. We worked with a manager who waited six months to address a performance issue. When she finally had the conversation, the employee said, "Why didn't you tell me this six months ago? I thought I was doing fine." The delay did not protect the relationship. It damaged it. When accountability is timely and consistent, trust grows, even when conversations are uncomfortable.

Here is a framework that keeps accountability conversations productive and trust-preserving:

Step 1: State the gap directly
"We agreed you would deliver the report by Friday. It's now Monday, and I haven't received it."

Step 2: Ask for their perspective
"What happened?"

Listen without interrupting. Sometimes there are legitimate reasons. Sometimes there are not. Either way, you need to understand, and that requires listening to their full explanation before responding.

Step 3: Clarify the impact
"When the report is late, the client presentation gets delayed. That affects our credibility."

Step 4: Reset expectations
"Going forward, if you realize you'll miss a deadline, I need you to tell me at least 48 hours in advance so we can adjust."

Step 5: Confirm understanding
"What questions do you have?"

This framework keeps the conversation focused on behavior and outcomes, not character or intent. It preserves dignity while maintaining standards. It connects back to the empathy-accountability balance we explored in Chapter 6: understanding context while holding the line on expectations.

While this framework works well for most accountability situations, there is one scenario that tests leaders more than any other: dealing with high performers who violate behavioral standards.

THE HIGH PERFORMER ACCOUNTABILITY TRAP: EXPANDED GUIDANCE

One of the most damaging leadership mistakes is tolerating poor behavior from high performers. This is also one of the most common accountability failures we see in organizations. Leaders rationalize it in predictable ways:

"They deliver results."
"We can't afford to lose them."
"That's just how they are."
"Everyone has flaws."
"The business needs them right now."

The message to everyone else is clear: performance excuses behavior.

This creates a two-tier culture in which values are applied selectively. High performers receive latitude. Others absorb the cost.

WHY LEADERS RATIONALIZE

The rationalization is understandable. High performers often generate significant revenue, solve complex problems, or possess skills that are hard to replace. Leaders fear that addressing behavioral issues will cause these individuals to leave, taking their contributions with them. The short-term cost of confrontation feels greater than the long-term cost of tolerance. This calculation is almost always wrong.

THE HIDDEN COSTS

What leaders fail to see is the damage occurring beneath the surface. Ironically, tolerating poor behavior from high performers often drives away the very people leaders want to keep: the steady, values-aligned contributors who refuse to compete with toxicity.

The costs accumulate in predictable ways:

- **Trust in leadership erodes.** When employees see leaders excuse bad behavior because someone hits their numbers, they conclude that values are negotiable and leadership is inconsistent.

- **Team morale drops.** People resent having to work with someone who treats them poorly or fails to do their job, while leadership does nothing. The burden falls on everyone else to compensate, accommodate, or endure.

- **Good people leave.** Not immediately, but over time. High-integrity performers who have options elsewhere choose to use them. They leave not for more money but for healthier cultures where behavior matters.

- **Standards decline.** If poor behavior is tolerated at the top of the performance curve, it signals that results justify means. Others begin testing boundaries, and the culture shifts toward ends-justify-means thinking.

- **The toxic performer's contribution decreases.** Without accountability, even high performers plateau or decline because they receive no feedback, face no consequences, and have no incentive to improve.

We coached an executive team where one leader consistently undermined colleagues in meetings. He was brilliant strategically. He was also destructive culturally. The CEO tolerated it for two years. During that time, three senior leaders left, not for better compensation but for healthier cultures. When the CEO finally addressed it, the damage was done. The toxic leader left. But so had the trust.

HOW TO ADDRESS IT

Addressing high performer behavioral issues requires the same framework as any other accountability conversation, but with additional considerations:

1. Separate performance from behavior explicitly.
Acknowledge the strong performance while making clear that behavior is non-negotiable. "You consistently exceed your targets, and that matters. The way you speak to colleagues in meetings is unacceptable, and that also matters. Both are true."

2. Make the standard clear.
Do not hint. Do not soften. State the behavioral expectation directly and explain why it matters. Reference organizational values if applicable. "Respect is a core value here. Dismissing others' ideas publicly violates that standard."

3. Explain the consequences.
Be specific about what will happen if behavior does not change. "If this pattern continues, you will not be eligible for promotion, regardless of your performance numbers. If it escalates, your role here will be at risk."

4. Provide support for change.
Offer coaching, feedback, or resources. Make it clear you want them to succeed, but that success requires behavior change. "I'm willing

to invest in your development. Here's what support looks like. But the accountability is yours."

5. *Follow through.*

This is where most leaders fail. They have the conversation, see a temporary improvement, and then relax. When behavior regresses, they avoid re-engaging. Follow-through is what makes accountability credible. If you said there would be consequences and behavior does not change, consequences must follow.

THE OUTCOME

In our experience, one of three things happens when leaders finally hold high performers accountable for behavior:

Option 1: The person changes. They realize that the behavior will no longer be tolerated, receive clear feedback, and adjust accordingly. They remain a high performer and become a positive cultural influence. This happens more often than leaders expect.

Option 2: The person leaves. They decide they do not want to work in an environment with behavioral expectations. While this feels like a loss, it is often a net positive for the

> **HIGH PERFORMANCE DOES NOT EXEMPT ANYONE FROM ACCOUNTABILITY.**

organization. The disruption they caused outweighed their contribution.

Option 3: The leader realizes they must make a change. The person does not improve, and the leader transitions them out. This is difficult but necessary. As we discussed in Chapter 3, delayed decisions are decisions, and allowing misalignment to persist communicates acceptance regardless of intent.

In every scenario we have observed, teams respond with relief when leaders finally address behavioral issues from high performers. People were waiting for leadership to hold the line. When it happens, respect for leadership increases, not decreases.

High performance does not exempt anyone from accountability. In fact, the higher the role, the higher the standard must be, because the impact of poor behavior multiplies with influence and visibility.

Addressing high performers is challenging, but it is not the only level where accountability requires intentional effort. Peer and senior-level accountability present unique challenges that require different approaches.

BUILDING ACCOUNTABILITY INTO ORGANIZATIONAL SYSTEMS

Accountability cannot rely solely on individual courage or willpower. It must be reinforced by systems that make expectations visible, track progress, and make consequences predictable. When systems support accountability, leaders do not have to chase it. The infrastructure does the work.

Organizations in our Best of the Best Benchmark consistently score 20 points higher on accountability than other organizations. Why? They have built systems that make accountability visible and routine. Here is how they do it:

1. Track commitments publicly.
Use shared documents, dashboards, or project management tools where everyone can see who owns what and when it is due. Transparency creates natural accountability because people do not want to be visibly behind.

2. Schedule regular check-ins.
Weekly or bi-weekly reviews where progress is discussed openly. Not to micromanage, but to surface obstacles early and keep commitments front of mind. Consistency matters more than the format.

3. Celebrate accountability.
Recognize people who deliver consistently. Make accountability a positive cultural norm, not just a corrective measure. Publicly acknowledge those who meet commitments, especially when it was difficult.

4. Address gaps immediately.
When someone misses a commitment, address it within 48 hours. The longer you wait, the weaker the signal becomes. Immediate

follow-up reinforces that commitments matter.

5. Build accountability into performance reviews.

Evaluate not just what people accomplish but how consistently they deliver on commitments. Make follow-through a formal part of the performance assessment and reward system.

6. Create shared visibility at the leadership level.

Executive teams should model transparency by openly sharing their own commitments and progress. When senior leaders hold each other accountable visibly, it cascades through the organization.

These systems do not replace leadership judgment; they create conditions in which accountability becomes routine rather than episodic. Consistency matters more than severity. People respond to fairness and predictability, not punishment.

Even with strong systems, there are moments when accountability reaches a breaking point, and leaders must make the hard call.

WHEN ACCOUNTABILITY FAILS: MAKING THE HARD CALL

Not every accountability issue can be coached away. Patterns matter. When expectations are clear, support has been provided, and behavior does not change, leaders face a harder responsibility. As we discussed in Chapter 3, tough decisions rarely get easier with time. The same is true for accountability decisions.

Delayed decisions are decisions. Allowing misalignment to persist communicates acceptance, regardless of intent. Strong leaders act before damage spreads.

One manager came to us frustrated. "I've had six conversations with this employee. Nothing changes. What else can I do?" We asked, "What message are you sending by keeping them?" She paused. "That I don't really mean what I say." Two weeks later she decided to transition the employee out. The team's response? Relief. They had been waiting for the manager to hold the line.

THE COST OF AVOIDING HARD DECISIONS

When leaders avoid terminating poor performers or fail to address persistent behavioral issues, several predictable things happen:

- **Strong performers lose respect for leadership.** They wonder why they work so hard when others face no consequences for failing to meet basic standards.

- **Team morale drops.** People resent having to cover for someone who does not carry their weight or tolerate someone who creates unnecessary conflict.

- **Standards erode.** If poor performance or bad behavior is tolerated long enough, it becomes the new normal. Others adjust their effort downward to match what is actually enforced rather than what is stated.

- **The leader's credibility suffers.** People stop believing commitments matter. They stop taking performance conversations seriously because they have learned that consequences do not follow.

Making the hard call is not cruel. Avoiding it is. The kindest thing a leader can do for someone who is persistently misaligned is to help them find a better fit elsewhere, rather than allow them to fail slowly in a role they cannot or will not meet the standards for.

SELF-DIAGNOSTIC: EVALUATING YOUR ACCOUNTABILITY PRACTICE

Before you can strengthen accountability in your organization, you need an honest assessment of where you currently stand. Use these diagnostic questions to evaluate your own accountability discipline:

On Clarity:

- Can each person on my team articulate what success looks like in their role using specific, measurable terms?

- Have I explicitly stated who owns each major outcome and when results are due?

- Do people know what authority they have to make decisions and spend resources?

On Consistency:

- Do I apply standards equally regardless of who is involved, or do I make exceptions based on performance, relationships, or convenience?

- When I set expectations, do I follow up predictably, or do commitments fade into the background?

- Would my team say accountability is fair here, or would they point to inconsistencies?

On Timeliness:

- When gaps appear, do I address them within 48 hours, or do I delay uncomfortable conversations, hoping things will improve?

- How many accountability issues am I currently avoiding that I know need to be addressed?

- Do people receive feedback in real-time, or do problems accumulate until they become crises?

On Self-Accountability:

- Do I publicly own my mistakes and missed commitments, or do I deflect, justify, or stay silent?

- Do I hold myself to the same standards I expect from others?

- Would my team say I model accountability, or would they point to gaps between what I expect and what I do?

On Follow-Through:

- When I say there will be consequences, do they actually occur, or do I back down when tested?

- Do I celebrate and recognize consistent performers, or do I take reliability for granted?

- Have I made hard calls when patterns do not change, or am

I tolerating ongoing misalignment?

These questions are not meant to generate guilt. They are meant to generate clarity. Most leaders discover they are strong in some areas and weaker in others. The goal is not perfection. The goal is honest assessment followed by intentional improvement.

REBUILDING ACCOUNTABILITY AFTER AVOIDANCE

If you are reading this chapter and recognizing that accountability has eroded within your team or organization, you are not alone. Many leaders realize too late that avoidance has become a pattern. The question is not whether you have avoided accountability in the past. The question is: what do you do next?

> **REBUILDING ACCOUNTABILITY AFTER A PERIOD OF AVOIDANCE REQUIRES HONESTY, RESET, AND CONSISTENCY.**

Step 1: Acknowledge the Gap

Do not pretend it has not happened. If accountability has been weak, people know it. Pretending otherwise damages credibility further. Instead, acknowledge it directly. "I have not been holding us to the standards we agreed to. That changes now." Own it without over-explaining or making excuses.

Step 2: Clarify Expectations Going Forward

Restate what success looks like, who owns what, and when outcomes are due. Be explicit about standards for both results and behavior. Do not assume people remember previous expectations. Treat this as a reset and communicate accordingly.

Step 3: Explain What Accountability Will Look Like

Let people know how you will check progress, how often you will review commitments, and what will happen when gaps appear. Transparency reduces anxiety. People can handle high standards if they know what to expect.

Step 4: Start Immediately

Do not wait for the perfect moment. Begin holding people accountable right away using the framework outlined earlier in this chapter. The first few conversations will feel awkward. That is normal. Consistency will rebuild credibility faster than any explanation.

Step 5: Be Consistent

The temptation will be to relax once you see initial improvement. Do not. Rebuilding accountability requires sustained consistency. People are watching to see if this is real or temporary. Prove it is real through repeated follow-through.

Step 6: Acknowledge Progress

When people meet commitments, recognize it. Rebuilding accountability is not just about addressing gaps. It is about reinforcing success. Celebrate those who step up and meet the new standard. Make accountability feel positive, not just punitive.

Rebuilding accountability takes time, but it is possible. Leaders who commit to this process often find that teams respond with relief rather than resistance. People want clear expectations and consistent follow-through. When leaders finally provide it, performance and trust improve quickly.

In our careers, we have worked with many managers who were hired to lead a team or inherited one in which accountability was not a strength of the prior manager. In most instances, the new managers were not welcomed by the team members who lacked accountability. There are common themes we see when new managers arrive and bring accountability. Some of the themes include resentment toward the new manager; team members unwilling to accept feedback; a lack of collaboration and teamwork; an unwillingness to share what work they're doing and how they spend their day; and poor results. Among the managers who successfully turned their departments around, where accountability was focused and valued, they used one or more of the suggestions below.

BUILDING AN ACCOUNTABILITY CULTURE FROM THE GROUND UP

For leaders who have the opportunity to build accountability into a team or organization from the beginning, or for those rebuilding after significant turnover or restructuring, here is how to establish a culture where accountability is the norm rather than the exception.

1. Hire for accountability.

In interviews, ask candidates about times they missed a commitment, how they handled it, and what they learned. Listen for ownership versus blame. Probe for examples of holding others accountable. People who value accountability reveal it in how they talk about past experiences.

2. Set the tone immediately.

In onboarding, make expectations explicit. Explain how accountability works here: how commitments are tracked, how progress is reviewed, and what happens when gaps occur. Do not wait for someone to fail before explaining the standards.

3. Model it visibly.

As we have established, leaders teach accountability by practicing it themselves. Share your commitments publicly. Report on your progress. Own your misses. Show what accountability looks like in action, especially when it is uncomfortable.

4. Create early wins.

Start with small, clear commitments that people can meet successfully. Build momentum and confidence. Let people experience the satisfaction of delivering on what they said they would do. Celebrate those wins publicly.

5. Address gaps immediately and consistently.

The first time someone misses a commitment, address it within 48 hours. Not harshly, but clearly. Establish the pattern that gaps get discussed, not ignored. Consistency in the early months sets the cultural expectation for years. What happens when you address the performance gaps and it does not work? We encourage you to coach and counsel the employee. Document your conversations with the employee and involve Human Resources to ensure they are aligned with how you are handling this difficult situation. When coaching, counseling, and documentation do not work, we recommend sharing this difficult employee with your best competitor.

6. Build systems that reinforce accountability.

Implement the tracking, review, and recognition systems discussed earlier in this chapter. Make accountability visible and routine rather than personality-dependent.

7. Protect the culture.

When new people join or when pressure mounts, the temptation will be to relax standards to accommodate or to avoid conflict. Resist it. Protecting accountability during challenging times is what makes it a culture rather than a temporary initiative.

Building an accountability culture does not happen overnight, but it does happen predictably when leaders are intentional, consistent, and willing to hold the line even when it is difficult.

WHY ACCOUNTABILITY MATTERS

Leadership is tough because accountability requires courage. It requires leaders to risk discomfort, popularity, and ease in the service of clarity and fairness. It requires leaders to look inward before looking outward, as we explored in Chapter 4 when we discussed how leaders are always being watched and must model what they expect. And it requires consistency, especially when no one is watching.

But accountability, done well, does not break trust. It builds it. People trust leaders who hold them accountable far more than leaders who avoid difficult conversations. Why? Because accountability signals that the leader cares enough to invest in their success, believes they are capable of meeting high standards, and respects them enough to tell the truth.

Avoidance signals the opposite. It signals indifference, low expectations, or a lack of courage. None of those builds the trust required for leadership at any level.

As you consider your own accountability practice, remember this:

the goal is not perfection. The goal is consistency, clarity, and courage. The goal is to hold the line without breaking trust, enforce standards without creating fear, and build a culture where people know what is expected and trust that commitments matter.

That is accountability. And that is what separates leaders who build lasting, high-performing cultures from those who wonder why talented people leave and standards slowly erode.

The question is not whether accountability is hard. It is. The question is whether you are willing to practice it, even when it is uncomfortable, unpopular, or inconvenient. Because that is when accountability matters most. That is when it defines culture. And that is when leadership is revealed.

KEY TAKEAWAYS

- **Accountability is clarity, not control.** It requires defining what success looks like, who owns it, when it is due, and what authority exists.

- **As established in Chapter 6, accountability and empathy work as partners.** Accountability without empathy creates fear. Empathy without accountability creates drift.

- **Leaders must model accountability first.** Organizations take cues from leadership behavior, not leadership language.

- **Avoiding accountability erodes trust faster than tough conversations.** People respect leaders who hold the line, even when it is uncomfortable.

- **High performers are not exempt from behavioral standards.** Tolerating poor behavior because someone delivers results creates a two-tier culture that drives good people away.

- **Accountability operates at four levels: yourself, direct reports, peers, and organizational systems.** Strength at all four levels creates sustainable accountability.

- **Clear expectations are the foundation of fair accountability.**

You cannot enforce what you have not defined.

- **Timely conversations preserve relationships.** Delayed accountability damages trust and makes problems worse.

- **Consistency builds credibility more than severity.** People respond to fairness and predictability, not punishment.

- **Systems support accountability better than willpower alone.** Tracking, review cadences, and visible consequences make accountability routine.

- **Patterns matter more than single incidents.** When behavior does not change despite clear expectations and support, leaders must make the hard call.

- **Rebuilding accountability after avoidance is possible through acknowledgment, reset, and sustained consistency.**

REFLECTION QUESTIONS:

1. Where am I avoiding accountability right now, and why? What is the real reason I am delaying this conversation or decision?

2. What behavior am I tolerating that contradicts our stated values or standards?

3. How consistently do I hold myself accountable in visible ways? Would my team say I model what I expect?

4. Who is carrying the burden because I am not holding the line? What is the cost to strong performers when I tolerate mediocrity?

5. Where have I allowed performance to excuse behavior? What message does that send to the rest of the team?

6. What expectations need to be clarified before accountability can improve? Am I assuming alignment that does not actually exist?

7. Using the four elements of clear expectations, where have I

failed to define success adequately?

8. What hard decision am I postponing? What will it cost if I continue to delay?

9. Am I confusing kindness with avoidance? Where might delayed accountability actually be causing more harm than a difficult conversation would?

10. What message am I sending by what I tolerate? If someone new joined the team tomorrow, what would they learn about what really matters here based on what I enforce versus what I ignore?

CHAPTER 9

LEADERSHIP GETS LONELY

LEAD YOURSELF WHEN YOU'RE THE ONE IN CHARGE

There is a quiet truth about leadership that few people honestly discuss. Leadership can be lonely. Not the dramatic, cinematic kind of loneliness. The quieter kind. The kind that settles in gradually as responsibility increases and candor decreases. The kind that shows up when decisions get heavier, conversations get guarded, and the number of people you can speak to freely shrinks.

Leadership has always carried inherent isolation, but the rise of remote and hybrid work has fundamentally changed how loneliness shows up, both for leaders and for the people they lead. What was once a personal challenge for those at the top has become a systemic risk affecting entire organizations. Leaders today face a dual responsibility: managing their own isolation while preventing it from spreading through their teams.

This chapter is about naming that reality without self-pity, managing it without denial, and leading through it with discipline. Because the truth is this: you cannot effectively address isolation in your organization while drowning in your own. Both require intentional practice. Both shape leadership effectiveness. And both have become more dangerous in a world where distance has replaced proximity as the default.

THE LONELINESS NO ONE TELLS YOU ABOUT

Most leaders are prepared for pressure. Few are prepared for isolation. Early in your career, leadership feels collaborative. Ideas bounce freely. Mistakes are shared. Decisions are debated openly. There is safety in proximity. As responsibility grows, so does distance.

You become the one who sets direction rather than seeks it. You hold information others should not carry. You absorb anxiety so others do not have to. You make decisions that will disappoint people you respect. Over time, leaders learn, sometimes unconsciously, to self-edit. They stop voicing uncertainty, stop venting, stop asking questions that might undermine confidence, and stop sharing half-formed thoughts. Not because they are dishonest, but because they are responsible.

Leaders carry an invisible burden that others do not see. Part of that burden is the isolation that comes with responsibility. You are always being watched, which means you are rarely unguarded. That constant visibility creates a paradox: you are surrounded by people, yet increasingly alone in your experience.

We coached an executive who described this perfectly. "I used to have lunch with my team every day," she said. "We'd talk about everything. Work problems, family stuff, and what frustrated us about the company. Then I got promoted. Now, when I walk into the break room, conversations stop. People are polite, but it's different. I'm not one of them anymore." She paused. "I didn't realize how much I'd miss that."

That shift is real. Leadership changes the dynamic. Your presence changes what people feel safe saying. Your title creates distance you did not ask for.

WHY LEADERSHIP ISOLATION IS SO DANGEROUS

Loneliness is not just emotional discomfort. It is a leadership risk. Isolated leaders are more likely to overthink decisions, delay hard conversations, seek affirmation instead of truth, confuse silence with agreement, and drift from values without realizing it.

Isolation narrows perspective. When leaders lack trusted sounding boards, judgment suffers, not because leaders become careless, but because they become inward. Isolated leaders are more likely to drift from stated values without realizing it. Without trusted advisors to surface the gap between intention and action, misalignment grows quietly until it becomes visible to everyone else first.

The connection to accountability is equally significant. As we saw in Chapter 8, accountability requires consistency, honesty, and the courage to have difficult conversations. But isolated leaders struggle to maintain that consistency because they lack the feedback loops that keep them grounded. They may avoid accountability conversations because they feel disconnected from their teams, or they may overcorrect by being harsh because they have no one to help them calibrate their responses.

We have seen this repeatedly. A CEO stops testing ideas before making them public. A director avoids feedback because it feels like criticism. A manager makes decisions alone because involving others takes too long. Each choice makes sense in the moment. Collectively, they erode leadership effectiveness.

One senior leader we worked with made a strategic decision that blindsided his team. When we asked why he had not consulted anyone, he said, "I didn't want to burden them with something I should be able to figure out myself." His team did not feel protected. They felt excluded. Six months later, three of his best people left. Not because the decision was wrong, but because they no longer felt like partners.

These same dangers apply not only to isolated leaders but to isolated employees.

> **ISOLATION DOES NOT MAKE YOU TOUGH. IT MAKES YOU VULNERABLE TO BLIND SPOTS.**

When team members feel disconnected, they disengage, withhold ideas, stop taking initiative, and eventually leave. The costs are identical whether the isolated person sits in the corner office or works remotely from home. Leadership is not meant to be solitary. It is meant to be anchored.

THE BUSINESS CASE FOR CONNECTION

Some leaders dismiss isolation as a personal problem. "I'm paid to make tough calls," they say. "I don't need to be popular." That is true. Leaders are not selected to be liked. But isolation is not about popularity. It is about effectiveness.

Research consistently shows that leaders who maintain strong relationships make better decisions, retain talent longer, and navigate crises more successfully than those who operate in isolation. In our work across multiple industries, we have found that leaders who regularly engage with their teams, peers, and mentors demonstrate higher strategic clarity, faster problem resolution, and stronger organizational alignment.

The same holds true for employees. According to Cigna research, loneliness costs U.S. employers over $154 billion annually in lost productivity, absenteeism, and turnover. Remote workers report loneliness at rates 20 percent higher than their in-office counterparts. Gallup research shows that employees who feel isolated are 12 times more likely to be disengaged and twice as likely to leave within six months.

Isolation does not make you tough. It makes you vulnerable to blind spots. Connection is not a weakness. It is a strategic discipline that affects performance at every level of the organization.

LEADING YOURSELF THROUGH ISOLATION

Before leaders can address loneliness in their organizations, they must lead themselves through it. Self-leadership begins with acknowledgment. That does not mean complaining or being dramatic. It means acknowledging the reality of the situation: "I am carrying more than

I can bear. I do not have as many places to be unguarded. I need intentional support, not sympathy."

Leaders who pretend they are unaffected by isolation often become brittle. Leaders who acknowledge it can better manage it.

During my Navy career, I learned this lesson clearly. The higher I advanced, the fewer people I could speak candidly with about the weight of certain decisions. That isolation was real. Pretending it did not exist made it worse. What helped was naming it. Not to complain, but to recognize that managing isolation was part of the job. Once I acknowledged it, I could address it systematically.

THE DIFFERENCE BETWEEN PRIVACY AND ISOLATION

Strong leaders understand the difference between discretion and disconnection. Some information must remain private. Some decisions must be made alone. Some burdens belong to the leader by design. That is not isolation.

Isolation occurs when leaders have no place to process, test, reflect, or be honestly challenged. Privacy is intentional. Isolation is accidental, and accidental isolation is where leadership judgment quietly erodes.

A CFO we coached understood this distinction well. "There are things I can't share with my team," he said. "Budget cuts coming. Merger discussions. Board concerns. But I have three people outside this organization I can talk to. One of them is my executive advisor. They help me think through what I can't process internally." He was private without being isolated. That is the balance leaders must maintain.

Build a Small Circle of Truth

Every leader needs a small, carefully chosen circle, not a crowd. This may include one peer outside the organization, a mentor who has already walked this road, an advisor who can challenge thinking without consequence, or a trusted partner who understands the weight, not the details.

This circle is not for decision-making authority. It is for perspective.

Leaders who confuse isolation with independence deprive themselves of wisdom.

One executive we worked with initially resisted this idea. "I don't need a sounding board," he said. "I can figure things out." We asked, "What happens when you can't?" He did not have an answer. Six months later, after a costly misstep, he reached out. "I should have listened," he said. "I convinced myself that asking for input was weak. Now I realize it was arrogant." He built his circle. He hired an executive advisor. His decision-making improved immediately.

Schedule Reflection Like a Responsibility

Loneliness grows in leaders who never slow down. When every moment is reactive, leaders lose the ability to process. Reflection becomes optional until judgment falters. Reflection is not indulgent. It is strategic.

Leaders who build time to think make fewer reactive decisions, regulate emotions better, notice misalignment earlier, and lead with greater steadiness. Quiet is not empty. Quiet is where leadership clarity lives.

We recommend that leaders schedule at least 30 minutes of uninterrupted reflection weekly. Not for email. Not for planning. For thinking. What decisions am I avoiding? What patterns am I noticing? Where am I feeling stuck? What feedback have I been dismissing? These questions surface truths that reactive leadership buries.

Watch for the Warning Signs

Leadership isolation rarely announces itself. It shows up as irritability, overcontrol, withdrawal, cynicism, and emotional fatigue. A sense of carrying everything alone. These are not moral failures. They are signals. Leaders who pay attention early can recalibrate. Leaders who ignore the warning signs often burn out quietly or become disconnected from the people they lead.

One director clearly described the warning signs. "I started snapping at people over small things," she said. "I stopped attending social events. I convinced myself I was just busy. Looking back, I was isolated and didn't realize it."

She course-corrected by reconnecting with her team, scheduling regular one-on-ones, and rebuilding relationships that had eroded during a difficult quarter. The isolation did not disappear immediately. But acknowledging it stopped the downward spiral.

The Leader's Emotional Load

One of the most misunderstood aspects of leadership is emotional labor. Leaders hold uncertainty for others, contain fear during crises, project steadiness during volatility, and absorb frustration without passing it down. This is real, emotional work, and when unacknowledged, it becomes even more exhausting. Leaders must permit themselves to recognize the weight they carry without becoming defined by it.

In our consulting work, we have observed leaders carry extraordinary emotional burdens while maintaining composure in public. A CEO managing layoffs while reassuring remaining employees. A VP navigating a merger while protecting team morale. A director holding space for grief after a colleague's sudden death. A healthcare CEO is changing strategy and making decisions in response to threats to federal funding.

ISOLATED LEADERS CREATE ISOLATED TEAMS.

These moments require emotional strength that goes unseen and often unacknowledged. Leaders who ignore their own emotional load eventually crack. Not because they are weak, but because they are human.

THE MYTH OF THE SELF-SUFFICIENT LEADER

Many leaders carry an unspoken belief: "I should be able to handle this." That belief isolates leaders faster than any workload. Leadership is not a test of endurance. It is a practice of stewardship. Seeking perspective, support, and connection is not a failure. It is a responsibility.

One senior leader resisted coaching for years. "I didn't want to admit

I needed help," he said. Finally, facing burnout, he reached out. "I thought asking for help meant I wasn't good at my job," he said. "Now I realize that refusing help is what made me ineffective."

Strength is not self-sufficiency. Strength is self-awareness.

WHY YOU MUST ADDRESS BOTH: YOUR ISOLATION AND THEIRS

Here is the uncomfortable truth many leaders miss: you cannot effectively address isolation in your team while drowning in your own. The two are connected, and the connection runs deeper than most realize.

Isolated leaders create isolated teams. When you withdraw, your people notice. When you stop being present, accessible, or emotionally available, they mirror that behavior. The distance you feel becomes the distance they experience. Your isolation becomes their isolation, multiplied across every person who reports to you.

This is not about blame. It is about cause and effect. Leaders set the emotional tone. Your energy, presence, and availability signal what is normal, acceptable, and expected. When leaders operate in isolation, they unconsciously teach their teams that isolation is how work gets done here.

We worked with a senior director who was deeply isolated. She rarely left her office, and her door was frequently closed. She declined social invitations. She skipped team events. She told herself she was protecting her time for strategic thinking. What she did not see was that her entire department had become equally isolated. People worked in silos. Collaboration stopped. Cross-functional projects stalled. When we asked her team what the culture felt like, one person said, "Everyone just does their own thing. No one really connects."

The director was stunned. She had not realized her behavior was contagious. Once she understood the pattern, she made changes. She started having lunch with her team twice a week. She attended team events. She scheduled walking meetings. Within three months, the culture shifted. People started collaborating again. Energy returned. Problems got solved faster.

The discipline required here is dual management. You must simultaneously tend to your own need for connection while creating conditions that prevent others' isolation. This is not easy. It requires self-awareness, intentionality, and sustained effort. But it is non-negotiable.

Leaders who manage only their own isolation become better decision-makers but fail to build healthy cultures. Leaders who focus only on team connection while neglecting their own needs eventually burn out and lose effectiveness. Both must be addressed. The question is not which one matters more. Both matter equally, and both require different practices.

HOW REMOTE AND HYBRID WORK CHANGED EVERYTHING

The shift to remote and hybrid work did not create loneliness. People have always experienced isolation. But remote work created conditions in which isolation became normalized, invisible, and therefore more dangerous. Distance magnifies every challenge we have discussed so far.

Before remote work became widespread, physical proximity provided natural safeguards against isolation. Hallways created an informal connection. Coffee breaks allowed casual check-ins. Body language signaled when someone was struggling. Silence was noticeable. Now, in a world of scheduled video calls and asynchronous communication, those safeguards have disappeared.

Remote Work and Increased Loneliness

Several large, recent studies show that workers who are fully remote (especially those working 3+ days per week) tend to report higher levels of loneliness than workers who are on-site or in hybrid roles. We see this in several studies that conclude people working remotely 3–4 days per week and those working remotely 5+ days per week had higher odds of reporting loneliness than non-remote workers, even after adjusting for demographics and social isolation factors. In some cases, remote workers were nearly twice as likely to report frequently feeling lonely and to experience other negative emotions, such as sadness and anger, compared with their office or 1-2 days-a-week hybrid-working peers.

A leading explanation is that remote work reduces casual, spontaneous social interactions, things like water-cooler chats, taking a walk, eating lunch together, and informal office conversations, which contribute significantly to social well-being.

The relationship between remote work and loneliness isn't uniform: Those working remotely only 1–2 days per week do not have significantly higher odds of loneliness than onsite workers. This suggests that a moderate hybrid schedule may help maintain social connections while preserving flexibility.

So, the frequency and intensity of remote work matter. A little remote flexibility may not harm social well-being, but extended periods alone appear linked to greater isolation.

For leaders, remote work intensifies isolation in specific ways. You lose the informal feedback that proximity provided. You cannot read the room anymore. You cannot gauge energy levels through casual observation. You make decisions with less information about how people are actually doing. The distance creates a barrier between you and the truth.

One manager described the challenge clearly. "When we were all in the office, I could read the room," he said. "I knew who was struggling. I could see body language, hear tone, and notice when someone was off. Now? Everyone's fine in their Zoom box. But I'm not sure they actually are." He was right to be concerned. Remote work hides what proximity reveals.

The Hidden Cost of Distributed Teams

Remote and hybrid models offer flexibility, broader talent pools, and cost savings. They also create conditions that foster isolation at scale. People working from home may go days without meaningful human interaction. They may feel invisible, forgotten, or disconnected from the mission. They may not say anything because virtual environments normalize silence.

In one organization we worked with, employee engagement scores dropped 16 points in 18 months after the shift to remote work. When we asked why, the consistent theme was clear. "I feel like I'm working alone," one employee said. "I complete my tasks. I attend meetings. But I don't feel connected to anyone."

Another said, "My manager never checks in unless something's wrong. I could disappear, and I'm not sure anyone would notice."

That sense of invisibility is dangerous. It erodes engagement, productivity, and loyalty. And because it happens quietly, behind closed doors and muted microphones, leaders often miss it until people start leaving.

WHY PEOPLE DON'T SAY THEY'RE LONELY

Most people don't announce loneliness. They say "I'm fine," "I'm busy," or "Everything's okay." Loneliness is often disguised as disengagement. Remote employees may speak less in meetings, avoid collaboration, avoid discussing concerns or problems, deliver work but withdraw emotionally, or stop offering ideas.

Leaders who mistake quiet compliance for engagement miss the warning signs. The relationship-building principles we explored in Chapter 4 remain essential, but remote work requires adapting those practices because the signals are harder to read. You cannot sense the energy in a virtual room.

We coached a leader whose team seemed fine. Deadlines were met. Work quality remained high. But when we conducted interviews, the feedback was revealing. "I feel like a cog in a machine." "No one asks how I'm doing." "I deliver my work and disappear."

The leader was stunned. "I had no idea," she said. "They never said anything." We asked, "Did you ever ask?" She had not.

RECOGNIZING ISOLATION IN YOUR TEAM

Leaders must watch for isolation in others, especially in remote and hybrid environments. The empathy we discussed in Chapter 6 becomes even more critical when you cannot read body language in hallways or notice energy shifts in real-time. You must look for subtler signals.

Pay attention to changes in engagement: someone who used to participate actively goes silent, reduced collaboration where people work in silos rather than reaching out, missed signals where questions go unanswered, or feedback is ignored, and silence from previously vocal contributors.

Sometimes the most important leadership move is simply noticing.

CREATING CONNECTION WITHOUT MICROMANAGING

Connection does not require constant meetings. It requires intentional leadership behavior. Effective leaders check in without an agenda, ask questions they actually want answered, listen without rushing to solve, and create space for informal connection. These principles remain foundational, but remote work requires adapting them for distance.

The relationship disciplines we explored in Chapter 4 remain foundational: courtesy, presence, active listening, and acknowledging people's contributions. But remote work requires adapting these practices because the environmental cues that made them natural have disappeared. You cannot greet someone by name when passing in the hall when there are no halls. You cannot read body language when the cameras are off. You must be more intentional.

Simple questions still matter, perhaps more than ever:

"How are you really doing?"
"What's been harder lately?"
"What feels isolating right now?"

These are not therapy sessions. They are leadership moments that apply the "check in without agenda" principle from Chapter 4 in a context where check-ins require scheduling rather than happening organically.

One executive started every one-on-one with a simple question: "What's one thing going well and one thing that's challenging?" The question took 90 seconds to answer. It created space for honesty without forcing vulnerability. Over time, people started opening up. Problems surfaced earlier. Trust deepened. Engagement improved. The investment was minimal. The return was significant.

Here are specific strategies that create connections across distance:

Use Video Strategically

Not every meeting needs video, but some do. Video creates presence. It allows leaders to read body language, notice energy, and connect beyond words. This extends the "be present" discipline from Chapter 4 into virtual spaces where presence must be created intentionally rather than assumed.

One leader implemented "Video Fridays." Every Friday, the team met on camera for 30 minutes. No slides. No agenda. Just faces. People shared what they were working on, what was challenging them, and occasionally what was happening in their personal lives. It became the most valued meeting of the week because it recreated the informal connections that office environments naturally foster.

The key is balance. Too much video creates fatigue. Too little creates distance. Leaders must calibrate based on team needs and work rhythms.

Encourage Informal Communication

Create channels for non-work conversations. Slack channels for hobbies, pets, or random thoughts. Virtual water coolers where people can connect casually. These spaces matter. They replace the hallway conversations that remote work eliminates.

This builds on the "courtesy and simple words" principle from Chapter 4. When you cannot casually say "good morning" in person, you need structures that allow for casual human interaction. One team created a "#random" channel where people shared anything unrelated to work. Initially, engagement was low. The leader modeled it by sharing first. Gradually, others joined. Within two months, it became the most active channel, and team cohesion measurably improved.

The risk is creating spaces that feel forced or artificial. The solution is giving people permission to be human without mandating participation. Informal channels work when they are optional, leader-modeled, and genuinely casual.

Rotate Meeting Facilitators

Give different team members the chance to lead meetings. It builds visibility, confidence, and connection. People who facilitate meetings feel more invested. People who see their peers leading feel more connected to them.

This distributes leadership presence rather than concentrating it in one person. It also surfaces different perspectives and styles, which help combat the monotony that can develop in remote work.

One director rotated meeting facilitation monthly. Each person chose the format, set the agenda, and led the discussion. The meetings became more dynamic. People paid more attention because the format kept changing. Collaboration increased because everyone had ownership.

Over-Communicate Temporarily

During times of uncertainty, leaders should communicate more than they feel necessary. Daily updates. Weekly check-ins. Transparent sharing about what is known and what is not. Over-communication builds trust. Under-communication breeds fear and speculation.

This applies the "clarity over comfort" principle from Chapter 3 in a remote context where silence is more easily misinterpreted. When people cannot see you or gauge your mood through casual interaction, they fill the gaps with assumptions. Over-communication reduces those gaps.

One CEO we worked with during the pandemic sent a brief video message to the entire company every Monday morning. Sometimes it was 90 seconds. Sometimes five minutes. He shared what he knew, what he did not know, and what he was thinking about. Employees consistently cited those videos as the reason they stayed engaged during uncertainty. "At least we knew he was still here," one person said. "We knew he hadn't forgotten about us."

The key is temporary. Over-communication is unsustainable long-term. But during crises, transitions, or periods of high uncertainty, it is essential.

Create Mentorship Opportunities

Pair remote employees with mentors, either within or outside their immediate teams. Mentorship reduces isolation by creating structured relationships that develop over time.

This is especially important for newer employees who joined remotely and have never experienced the organization's culture in person. They lack the informal networks that develop naturally through proximity. Formal mentorship creates what proximity once provided automatically.

One organization implemented a "remote onboarding buddy" program. Every new hire was paired with someone outside their direct team for monthly check-ins during their first year. The program reduced first-year turnover by 31 percent. Exit interview data showed that people who left felt isolated. People who stayed cited their mentorship relationship as a key factor in feeling connected.

THE ROLE OF PSYCHOLOGICAL SAFETY

Isolation grows where people do not feel safe being honest. If people believe that speaking up has consequences, that vulnerability signals weakness, or that disagreement is risky, they will withdraw. Psychological safety is not comfort. It is permission. Permission to ask questions, admit uncertainty, say "I don't know," and express concern.

Leaders set this tone by modeling it themselves.

In one team meeting, a director admitted, "I'm struggling with this decision. I need your input because I'm not sure I'm seeing it clearly." The room shifted. People leaned in. Ideas flowed. The decision improved. One team member later said, "That was the first time I felt like my opinion actually mattered."

Leaders' vulnerability creates safety for everyone else. When you admit you don't have all the answers, you give others permission to do the same. That permission is what breaks through isolation.

LEADERS AS CONNECTORS, NOT ENTERTAINERS

Leaders are not responsible for eliminating loneliness. They are responsible for reducing unnecessary isolation. This means connecting people to one another, encouraging collaboration across silos, avoiding over-reliance on email for everything, and creating moments of human interaction that feel natural rather than forced.

Connection does not require forced fun or mandatory team-building exercises that make people groan. Connection requires a thoughtful structure that removes barriers to relationship-building. One executive we advise told us his CEO decided to do a team-building activity with the senior team. The CEO told everyone to come prepared with two truths and a lie about themselves. The executive commented to us that he wanted to shoot himself.

We worked with a remote team that felt disconnected. The leader tried virtual happy hours. Attendance was low. People were exhausted from Zoom fatigue and had no interest in more screen time.

So, she tried something different. She paired people randomly for 15-minute "coffee chats" once a month. No agenda. No requirements. Just an invitation to connect. It worked. People started building relationships outside their immediate teams. Collaboration improved across functions. Engagement scores rose 12 points in six months. The structure was simple. The impact was real because it removed the awkwardness of reaching out cold while giving people permission to connect.

CREATING RITUALS OF CONNECTION

Geographically dispersed teams need rituals that create predictable moments of connection. Daily check-ins. Weekly team meetings. Monthly all-hands. Quarterly off-sites. These rituals matter, not because they are fun, but because they are consistent. Consistency builds trust. Trust reduces isolation. This builds on the "consistency that builds trust" principle from Chapter 1, applied to team cadences rather than individual behavior.

One organization we worked with implemented "Monday Morning Check-Ins." Every Monday at 9 a.m., teams gathered virtually for 15 minutes. No formal agenda. No slides. Just presence. People shared weekend highlights, upcoming challenges, or random thoughts. It was informal. Unscripted. Human.

That simple ritual reduced turnover by 18 percent in one year. When we asked departing employees from other departments why they were leaving, many cited feeling disconnected. When we asked people who stayed in the Monday check-in department what made the difference, they consistently mentioned those 15 minutes. "It made me feel like I was part of something," one person said. "Like people actually knew I existed."

Rituals work because they create expectation. People know a connection is coming. They show up prepared to engage. Over time, those small moments compound into genuine relationships.

WHEN LEADERS FEEL LONELY, SO DO THEIR TEAMS

Isolation is contagious. Leaders who withdraw unintentionally signal distance. Teams respond by pulling back further. This creates a reinforcing loop: the leader feels isolated, becomes less available, the team disengages, the leader feels more isolated, and the cycle accelerates in the wrong direction.

Breaking the cycle requires intentional presence, not perfection. Sometimes that means being visible even when tired, naming uncertainty rather than hiding it, and reaching out rather than retreating.

One leader we coached admitted, "I was so overwhelmed that I stopped showing up to team meetings. I thought I was protecting them from my stress. Instead, they assumed I didn't care." When he explained what had been happening and committed to reconnecting, the team responded immediately. "We just needed to know you were still with us," one person said.

Presence matters more than perfection. Your team does not need you to be flawless. They need you to be present, engaged, and accessible.

LEADING WITH STEADINESS, NOT STOICISM

There is a difference between strength and silence. Stoicism without connection becomes emotional absence. Steady leadership allows appropriate transparency, human acknowledgment, and emotional regulation, not suppression.

Leaders do not need to share everything. They need to share enough to remain human. During a particularly difficult period, a CEO sent a company-wide message. "I know this year has been hard," he wrote. "It's been hard for me, too. I don't have all the answers. But I'm committed to figuring this out with you."

The response was overwhelming. Employees appreciated the honesty. They did not expect him to have all the answers. They needed to know he was still engaged. That single message rebuilt trust across the entire organization by acknowledging a shared reality without pretending to be invulnerable.

Steadiness is not about hiding your humanity. It is about managing it responsibly so your emotions inform your leadership rather than driving it reactively.

REBUILDING CONNECTION TAKES TIME

Isolation rarely resolves with one conversation. Connection is rebuilt through consistency, presence, follow-through, and trust. Leaders who treat connection as episodic struggle. Leaders who treat it as a discipline succeed.

One organization we worked with had severe engagement problems after two years of fully remote work. Employees felt disconnected, undervalued, and isolated. The turnaround took 18 months. It required daily attention from leadership, consistent communication across all levels, visible commitment to connection initiatives, and sustained investment even when results were slow to come.

But it worked. Engagement scores climbed from 42 percent to 71 percent. Turnover dropped from 28 percent annually to 11 percent. Productivity improved by 19 percent. The organization became an employer of choice in their industry, specifically because of their culture of connection.

Connection is not a quick fix. It is a long-term investment that compounds over time. The leaders who succeed are those who commit to the discipline even when progress feels slow.

DISTANCE CAN BE LONELY

Leadership is tough because responsibility creates distance. The higher you rise, the fewer people you can speak to freely. The more you carry, the less you can share. That reality will not change. But leadership is also meaningful because connection can be rebuilt, intentionally, thoughtfully, and honestly.

You do not have to be isolated to be strong. You do not have to be silent to be steady. You do not have to carry everything alone to lead well.

The most effective leaders first learn to lead themselves through isolation. They build small circles of truth. They schedule reflection as a responsibility. They watch for warning signs and course-correct before burnout arrives. They acknowledge the emotional load they carry without being defined by it.

Then, and only then, can they effectively address isolation in their teams. They recognize the signs. They create connections without micromanaging. They build psychological safety through vulnerability.

They establish rituals that combat distance. They lead with steadiness rather than stoicism.

Both require discipline. Both require intention. Both require sustained effort over time. That balance is not easy. It is necessary. Because isolation at any level weakens leadership effectiveness, and in a world of remote and hybrid work, the risk has never been higher.

The question is not whether leadership feels lonely. It does. The question is whether you will manage that loneliness with discipline or let it erode your judgment and organization. That choice belongs to you. That is why leadership is tough.

WHY THIS CHAPTER MATTERS

Leadership is tough because isolation is not a personal weakness to manage privately. It is an organizational risk that compounds quietly until it becomes visible in the decisions leaders make, the talent they lose, and the cultures they unintentionally create. Leaders are always being watched, and the emotional tone they set cascades through every level of the organization. When that tone is one of withdrawal, distance, and disconnection, teams mirror it whether they realize it or not. The accountability disciplines of Chapter 8 require leaders who are grounded and connected enough to hold the line consistently. The trust foundations of Chapter 5 require leaders who are present enough to notice when that trust is eroding. The empathy we explored in Chapter 6 requires leaders who have not become so isolated that they have lost the ability to read what their people actually need. Isolation does not just hurt the leader. It quietly degrades every other leadership discipline this book has built.

KEY TAKEAWAYS:

- **Isolation is real.** Leadership isolation is real, cumulative, and amplified by remote work for both leaders and employees.

- **Leaders need feedback.** Isolated leaders make worse decisions, delay accountability, and drift from values without realizing it.

- **Privacy is not the same as disconnection.** Leaders need places to process without being completely isolated.

- **Remote and hybrid work breeds isolationism.** Remote and hybrid work changed how isolation shows up, making it more normalized, invisible, and dangerous.

- **Connection requires intention, not micromanagement.** Simple questions and consistent presence matter more than elaborate programs.

- **Leaders set the emotional tone.** Psychological safety reduces isolation by permitting people to be honest about their struggles.

- **Build a small circle of truth.** Seeking support is a leadership responsibility, not a personal weakness.

- **Ask better questions.** Questions create meaningful connections: "How are you really doing with everything going on?" matters more in remote work than ever.

- **Consistency builds trust over time.** Rituals of connection combat isolation in distributed teams.

- **Connecting with people is critical.** Rebuilding a connection after isolation takes sustained effort, not quick fixes. Treat it as a discipline, not an event.

REFLECTION QUESTIONS:

1. Where am I experiencing isolation in my leadership role right now? What am I carrying alone that needs a sounding board?

2. Who is in my trusted circle, and is it sufficient? Do I have people outside my organization who can challenge my thinking without consequence?

3. How intentional am I about reflection and processing? When was the last time I had 30 uninterrupted minutes to think?

4. What signals of isolation might I be missing on my team? Who has suddenly gotten quieter? Who seems disconnected?

5. How do I model a connection without oversharing? Where is the line between appropriate transparency and burdening others?

6. What one action could reduce unnecessary isolation this month, either for myself or my team?

7. Where might my own withdrawal be affecting others? Have I pulled back from team interactions while telling myself I'm just busy?

8. Am I creating psychological safety for my team to be honest about struggle? Would people feel comfortable telling me they're lonely or overwhelmed?

9. What rituals of connection exist in my organization? Are they working, or have they become performative?

10. When was the last time I asked someone how they were really doing and then actually listened to the answer?

11. How has remote or hybrid work changed isolation patterns on my team? What worked in person that I haven't been able to replicate virtually?

12. If I'm honest, am I treating isolation as a personal problem to tough out, or am I addressing it as a leadership discipline? What needs to change?

CHAPTER 10

RESILIENCE IS EARNED
DEVELOP CAPACITY, WITHSTAND PRESSURE, AVOID BURNOUT

Resilience is one of the most misunderstood concepts in leadership. It is often framed as an attitude, as positivity, as the ability to "stay strong" or "bounce back." Leaders are encouraged to be optimistic, encouraging, and upbeat, even when conditions are overwhelming, relentless, and stressful. That framing is incomplete. What leaders need is to develop the capacity to withstand stress and pressure without burning out.

Real resilience is not just cheerfulness under pressure. It is the capacity to absorb stress, make sound decisions while depleted, recover deliberately, and resume work without becoming brittle, cynical, or exhausted. Leadership is not a sprint but an endurance event, and, as we explored in that opening chapter, resilience is the capacity to carry that weight sustainably over the long term. Resilience is not something leaders talk about; it is something leaders build. And it is built the same way strength is built anywhere else: through controlled exposure, disciplined recovery, and consistent practice.

This chapter is about how senior leaders intentionally develop resilience, manage stress without denial, and avoid burnout, not by retreating from responsibility but by leading themselves with the same rigor they lead others. How leaders deliberately allocate time and energy as strategic resources is addressed in Chapter 11. This chapter focuses on the foundation that makes that allocation possible: the capacity to absorb pressure without breaking. True resilience is proactive. It's about building systems and strategies that expect change, embrace opportunity, and pivot with purpose.

WHY RESILIENCE MATTERS MORE AT THE TOP

Stress is not evenly distributed in organizations. As leaders rise, the nature of stress changes. It becomes less visible, more persistent, more cognitive than physical, and more isolating. Senior leaders carry strategic uncertainty, financial risk, human consequences, reputational exposure, and long-term accountability. Much of this pressure cannot be shared.

The danger is not stress itself. Stress is inherent to leadership. The danger is unmanaged stress, stress that accumulates without recovery, perspective, or recalibration. As we explored in Chapter 2, when discussing how the brain responds to uncertainty and change, unmanaged stress degrades judgment before it damages health. Leaders begin to narrow options, default to control, avoid difficult conversations, delay decisions, and confuse urgency with importance. Here, the focus is on building the internal capacity to manage stress when it arrives, as it inevitably will.

Burnout does not usually arrive suddenly. It shows up slowly, eroding ability and capacity. We have seen this pattern repeatedly. The executive who used to make decisions confidently now second-guesses everything. The manager who once energized teams now barely engages. The leader who handled crises calmly now reacts defensively to minor issues. These are not personality changes. These are capacity problems.

THE MYTH OF THE RESILIENT PERSONALITY

Many leaders believe resilience is innate. "You either have it, or you don't." "They're just tougher than most." "She handles pressure well." These beliefs are comforting and false.

BURNOUT DOES NOT USUALLY ARRIVE SUDDENLY. IT SHOWS UP SLOWLY, ERODING ABILITY AND CAPACITY.

Resilience is not a personality trait. It is a trained response. What looks like natural toughness is usually the result of experience with adversity, learned recovery habits, emotional regulation skills, and perspective gained through failure. Leaders who appear resilient have usually earned it.

During my naval career, I watched junior officers struggle with stress that senior commanders handled easily. The difference was not genetics or intelligence; it was experience. Senior leaders had been through multiple deployments, equipment failures, personnel crises, and mission pivots. They had learned what mattered and what did not. They had developed systems for managing stress that newer leaders had not yet put in place.

The same pattern holds in business. Leaders who report high resilience consistently share several characteristics. They have faced significant adversity, practice deliberate recovery, maintain perspective through reflection, and have support systems in place. Resilience is earned through practice, not something we are born with. Leaders who have practiced making difficult calls with incomplete information develop the capacity to do it repeatedly without depleting themselves in the process.

STRESS IS NOT THE ENEMY. ACCUMULATION IS.

Stress is a signal. It mobilizes attention, sharpens focus, and prepares leaders to act. The problem is not stress exposure. The problem is chronic stress without release. Burnout occurs when leaders stay in high-alert mode indefinitely, eliminate recovery in the name of productivity, replace reflection with distraction, and normalize exhaustion as commitment.

Resilient leaders do not avoid stress; they cycle it. They understand when to push and when to recover.

We worked with a CEO who prided himself on working 80-hour weeks. He saw it as dedication. His board saw it as unsustainable. When we asked him about recovery, he said, "I'll rest when the business stabilizes." The business never stabilized. Markets shift. Competitors emerge. Problems arise. Waiting for stability is waiting for retirement.

Within 18 months, his performance declined visibly. Decisions took longer. His patience evaporated. He became defensive in meetings. His team started avoiding him. He was not weak. He was depleted. Recovery is not weakness. It is maintenance. As we explore in Chapter 11, the discipline of protecting recovery time within a structured schedule is one of the most important time management decisions a leader can make. But that discipline only works when the leader has first built the internal resilience to recognize when recovery is needed.

BUILDING RESILIENCE THROUGH ORGANIZATIONAL DISCIPLINE

Before exploring personal resilience practices, it is critical to understand that resilience cannot be built by individuals alone when organizational systems work against them. Leaders who tell people to "be resilient" while creating chaotic, unpredictable environments are shifting responsibility downward without providing the conditions that enable resilience.

Garrett Motion, a global turbocharger and automotive technology firm, faced significant operational pressure amid industry disruption and restructuring. Rather than framing resilience as morale management, leadership focused on operational discipline. They clarified non-negotiable priorities, reduced initiative overload, created clear decision rights, established predictable communication rhythms, and protected recovery time during intense cycles.

They did not ask people to "be resilient." They designed resilience into the system. Performance stabilized. Engagement improved, not because conditions were easy, but because leaders reduced unnecessary stressors and focused energy where it mattered. Resilience improved because leadership behavior changed. This illustrates what we explored in Chapter 7 about aligning priorities with values.

> **YOU CANNOT ASK PEOPLE TO BE RESILIENT IN A SYSTEM THAT PUNISHES HONESTY.**

When leaders protect what they say matters, systems reinforce resilience rather than undermine it.

When Alan Mulally arrived at Ford as CEO in 2006, the company was on the brink of collapse. Ford was facing deep financial trouble, declining product quality, falling sales, and a dysfunctional, ego-driven corporate culture that had eroded employee morale. The previous culture had been built on fear and secrecy, where admitting a problem was a career risk and executives showed up to meetings with nothing but positive information, even when major projects were failing badly. Mulally understood immediately that you cannot ask people to be resilient in a system that punishes honesty. Rather than telling leaders to toughen up or work harder, he changed the system.

He introduced a weekly Business Plan Review in which every executive had to present a color-coded scorecard, green for on track, yellow for at risk, and red for off-plan. The cultural turning point came when one executive, Mark Fields, Ford's Chief Operating Officer at the time, finally turned a slide red to flag a serious production problem. Instead of reprimanding Fields, Mulally clapped and said, "Thank you for the transparency, Mark. Now, what can we all do to help?" The following week, more red slides appeared across the entire team. The system had changed, so the behavior changed with it.

The results were both human and financial. When Mulally joined Ford, employee engagement was below 40 percent. When he left eight years later, it had leapt to 92 percent. By 2013, Ford had gone from a $17 billion loss to 11 consecutive quarters of profitability, while its Detroit competitors accepted government bailouts during the 2008 financial crisis, Ford did not.

The lesson that runs through Ford's story is one every leader needs to hear: resilience is not a personality trait you can demand in a broken or fearful system. It is something that emerges naturally when the structures, processes, and culture give people the safety to speak up, ask for help, and trust that the organization has their back. Mulally did not make Ford's people more resilient by talking about resilience. He made them more resilient by creating the conditions in which resilience could actually grow.

Telling people to be resilient without changing the factors that drain them is irresponsible. It shifts responsibility downward without giving them the tools they need to cope properly. Leaders build resilience by reducing unnecessary complexity, clarifying expectations, eliminating low-value work, creating predictability, and modeling recovery. Resilience is a system outcome, not a motivational slogan.

RESILIENCE BEGINS WITH SELF-LEADERSHIP

Leaders cannot delegate resilience. They must practice it personally before expecting it at the organizational level. Self-leadership under stress requires three disciplines: awareness, regulation, and recovery. Without these, leaders rely on adrenaline, and that always comes at a cost.

Be Aware and Know Your Stress Signals

Resilient leaders recognize stress early. They notice shortened patience, rigid thinking, emotional detachment, increased control behaviors, and difficulty sleeping or focusing. These are not failures. They are indicators.

Leaders who ignore them often rationalize: "This is just a busy season." "I'll rest later." "This is what leadership requires." Busy seasons end. Patterns do not. One executive we coached had no idea he was burning out, but it was obvious to his team. They watched him become increasingly irritable, micromanaging, and dismissive of input he used to welcome. When we showed him feedback from his 360-degree assessment, he was stunned. "I thought I was handling it well," he said. He was not. He had stopped noticing his own behavior.

Awareness is the first line of defense against burnout. If you do not notice the signals, you cannot address them. This connects to what we explored in Chapter 6 about empathy. Leaders who lack self-awareness struggle to read others accurately because they are not reading themselves accurately first. The same attentiveness that empathetic leaders bring to understanding others must be directed inward to recognize when personal capacity is approaching its limits.

Regulation: Staying Effective Under Pressure

Emotional regulation while stressed is not about suppressing what you feel or projecting calm you do not have. It is about remaining functional and thoughtful even when your nervous system is activated. In practice, it means noticing the physical signs that stress is rising, a tightening in the chest, a quickening of the breath, a shift toward defensive or reactive thinking, and pausing before responding rather than reacting from that activated state.

In real situations, emotional regulation often looks ordinary from the outside, which is partly the point. It looks like a leader who receives bad news and says, "Let me sit with that for a moment" rather than immediately assigning blame. It looks like someone who strongly disagrees but stays genuinely curious about the other person's perspective, rather than closing down. It looks like acknowledging uncertainty out loud rather than performing false confidence, because performing confidence you do not feel is itself a form of emotional dysregulation.

Regulation is the ability to function well while stressed. It includes pausing before reacting, separating urgency from importance, managing tone deliberately, and avoiding emotional spillover. Regulation does not mean suppressing emotion. It means controlling expression. Leaders who regulate well make fewer reactive decisions, preserve trust during tension, and maintain credibility under strain. This is not a personality trait; it is a practiced discipline.

Travis Kalanick co-founded Uber and turned it into a company valued at $70 billion, operating across 70 countries. What he could not do was manage his own emotional state under pressure, and that failure ultimately cost him his company.

Kalanick operated from what observers described as a "win at all costs" mindset. Under stress, he became reactive, dismissive, and aggressive, and those behaviors set the tone for everyone below him. When an Uber driver confronted him about pay cuts during a ride in 2017, Kalanick exploded on camera, telling the driver that people like him refused to take responsibility for their own problems. The footage went viral. It was not a one-off moment; it was a window into a culture that had been building for years. Employees reported harassment going unaddressed, dissent being silenced, and a leadership team that rewarded results while ignoring how those results were achieved.

When the full picture became public, the fallout was swift: over 20 senior executives left the company, the board commissioned an independent investigation, and Kalanick himself resigned. In his own words, he needed to "fundamentally change as a leader and grow up." His successor, Dara Khosrowshahi, spent years rebuilding the trust that reactive leadership had quietly destroyed.

Emotional regulation is not about avoiding hard conversations. It is about having them effectively when you are thinking clearly and objectively and can make good decisions. Regulation ensures leaders treat people with dignity even under pressure.

Recovery: The Most Ignored Skill in Leadership

Recovery is not time off; it is intentional restoration. Recovery can include physical movement, mental disengagement, perspective shifts, and short periods of genuine rest, such as engaging in a hobby unrelated to work. Leaders who skip recovery eventually pay for it in health, judgment, relationships, and performance.

Resilience is not built by pushing harder; it is built by recovering better. Chapter 11 addresses the practical mechanics of protecting recovery time within a structured

RECOVERY IS NOT TIME OFF; IT IS INTENTIONAL RESTORATION.

schedule and managing energy as a strategic resource. Here, the focus is on understanding why recovery is not optional and what happens to leaders who treat it as though it were.

One manager told us, "I don't have time to recover. I have too much to do." We asked, "How much time do you lose to poor decisions made while exhausted?" He paused. He had not considered that. Recovery is not time away from productivity. It is what makes productivity sustainable.

In remote and hybrid work environments, recovery becomes even more critical and more difficult. Without the natural boundaries that physical offices provide, work bleeds into evenings, weekends, and early mornings. Leaders working from home often find themselves checking email at 10 p.m. or joining calls during what used to be family time. The lack of commute, which initially seemed like a time-saver, eliminated one of the few transition periods that allowed mental separation between work and home. Remote leaders must deliberately create recovery boundaries because the environment no longer does so automatically.

WHAT BURNOUT LOOKS LIKE AT WORK

Burnout in senior leaders rarely looks dramatic. It looks like emotional flatness, irritability, withdrawal, loss of curiosity, reduced empathy, and increased cynicism. Leaders still perform. They still deliver, but they are running on depletion.

Burnout is dangerous because it can feel normal until it is not. We discovered that when leaders burn out, team engagement drops by an average of 31 points. Not because leaders are mean or bad people, but because they have become disconnected. Burned-out leaders make decisions more slowly, communicate less effectively, and disengage emotionally from their teams. Employees notice. They respond by disengaging themselves.

And most worrisome, burnout is contagious. António Horta-Osório arrived as CEO of Lloyds Banking Group in March 2011 with an enormous mandate: to turn around a bank still reeling from the financial crisis and a government bailout. He was brilliant, driven, and, by his own admission, believed that less sleep and more work were simply the price of leadership. Within eight months, that belief nearly broke him.

The warning signs were visible long before the breaking point. He stopped being able to sleep. He returned from family holidays more exhausted than when he had left, consumed by guilt for being away and unable to mentally disconnect from the bank. He pushed himself past fatigue into a state where, as he later described it, he would wake up exhausted, force himself through the day, and then lie awake knowing the same thing would happen tomorrow. The behaviors that colleagues and boards so often miss in burned-out leaders were all present: an obsessive, all-consuming focus on work that left no room for recovery, an inability to delegate or to trust that things would continue without his direct involvement, and a growing isolation because, as he put it, he had always understood the CEO role to be a lonely one where people need leadership from you, not the other way around.

In November 2011, he was admitted to a clinic to prevent a nervous breakdown. He took eight weeks of medical leave, which was described at the time as the most high-profile sick leave in the City of London.

What makes this example so valuable for leaders is what António Horta-Osório said afterwards. He had thought he was Superman. He had confused relentlessness with strength. When he returned to work, he committed to boundaries he had previously dismissed as weakness: working calls and emails only between 7 am and 7 pm, ongoing therapy, and a structured resilience program that he eventually extended to 200 of his senior executives.

The lesson he carried from that period was not that ambition was wrong, but that a leader who cannot recover cannot lead sustainably, and that asking for help is not a failure of leadership. It is what leadership actually requires.

If you do not stop burnout in yourself, it will spread through your organization.

RESILIENCE THROUGH STRATEGIC CONSTRAINT

Cascade Engineering, a privately held Michigan manufacturing company, faced significant cost pressures during economic downturns. Instead of pushing harder, leadership imposed strategic constraints.

Fewer priorities. Clearer decision criteria. Reduced meeting load. Explicit boundaries on availability. They treated personal energy as a finite resource. Resilience improved not because people were more motivated, but because leadership respected capacity.

This approach mirrors what we discussed in Chapter 2 about leading through change. When leaders reduce competing priorities during periods of high stress, they protect people's cognitive capacity to handle complexity without becoming overwhelmed. The discipline of deciding what to stop doing is as important as deciding what to start.

THE ROLE OF ADVERSITY IN BUILDING RESILIENCE

Resilience is learned and practiced over time. Leaders who have never faced adversity are the people who struggle most under pressure. Adversity is a gift. Adversity teaches perspective, endurance, emotional control, clarity of decision-making, and humility. But adversity only builds resilience when leaders extract learning from it. Pain alone does not create strength. Learning creates strength.

During my time in the Navy, we trained constantly for scenarios we hoped would never happen: equipment failures, medical emergencies, combat situations, security breaches. That training did not eliminate stress. It built our capacity to manage stress and situations more effectively. The first time something goes wrong is not the time to figure out how to respond. Resilience is built in advance through preparation, practice, and reflection.

PEOPLE GROW STRONGER THROUGH SUPPORTED CHALLENGES, NOT AVOIDANCE.

MANAGING STRESS THROUGH STRATEGIC LEADERSHIP

Managing stress does not mean eliminating it. It means choosing where to invest energy, saying no without guilt, letting go of control where appropriate, and delegating authority, not just tasks. Senior leaders burn out when they act as bottlenecks. Resilient leaders build redundancy, not dependency. As we established in Chapter 8 on accountability, leaders who take responsibility for every decision and own every outcome do not build strong organizations. They build fragile ones that depend entirely on their own capacity, which is always finite.

When Bob Chapek became CEO of The Walt Disney Company in February 2020, he inherited one of the most storied leadership legacies in corporate America. His predecessor, Bob Iger, had spent 15 years deliberately building a senior team, empowering division heads, and creating the conditions for creativity to flourish. Chapek took a different path, and the contrast revealed itself quickly.

Rather than distributing authority across his leadership team, Chapek consolidated power. He narrowed the circle of executives he trusted to a small handful of loyalists, which left other senior leaders feeling sidelined and underutilized. When crises emerged, as they did with Florida's controversial education legislation and a public dispute with actress Scarlett Johansson over film compensation, there was no deep bench of confident, empowered leaders to draw on.

Chapek handled both situations poorly, in part because the culture he had built did not encourage candid advice or shared accountability. A former Imagineer described the difference directly: under Iger, he said, a creative conversation felt collaborative, with the CEO leaning in and shaping the idea together. Under Chapek, the same conversation felt transactional, as if creativity was simply an input to a financial output.

Disney lost roughly 36% of its value in 2022, and shares rose 9% on the day his departure was announced, a signal from the market that confidence in the leadership itself had become the problem. That is not leadership. That is a single point of failure.

When Iger returned, one of his first public commitments was to restore what Chapek had quietly dismantled: a structure that empowered creative leaders to lead.

LEADING OTHERS THROUGH STRESS WITHOUT CODDLING

Resilient leaders do not remove all the challenges their people face. That is impossible and unrealistic. Great leaders provide clarity, reduce ambiguity, maintain standards, and offer support without lowering expectations. People grow stronger through supported challenges, not avoidance.

We worked with a team facing a significant workload during a product launch. The pressure was real. The deadlines were non-negotiable. The leader did not pretend it was easy. She said, "This is going to be hard. Here is why it matters. Here is what success looks like. Here is how I am supporting you. Here is where this intense period ends." The team delivered. Engagement stayed high. Why? Because the leader acknowledged reality, provided clarity, and gave them a finish line. Resilience is not built by denying difficulty. It is built by leading through it with realistic expectations and honest communication. This connects directly to what we explored in Chapter 5 about trust. Leaders who communicate honestly, even when the message is difficult, build the trust that allows teams to sustain effort over extended periods.

In distributed work environments, this clarity becomes even more important. Remote teams cannot see the leader's body language or gauge stress levels through hallway conversations. They need explicit communication about expectations, the support available, and when the intense period will end. Without that clarity, remote workers often assume the pressure will never relent and begin to disengage to protect themselves.

DAILY PRACTICES THAT BUILD RESILIENCE

Resilience is not built during annual retreats. It is built daily through small, consistent actions.

Protect Sleep

Leaders who sacrifice sleep also sacrifice their best judgment. Research consistently shows that sleep deprivation impairs cognitive function as significantly as alcohol intoxication. One CEO we worked with prided himself on sleeping four hours a night. His team dreaded his decision-making in the afternoons. He was irritable, reactive, and inconsistent. We challenged him to get 6 hours of sleep each night for 2 weeks. Just two weeks. He tried it, and his team noticed immediately. Decisions improved. Patience returned. Energy stabilized. Sleep is not optional. It is foundational.

Move Your Body

Physical activity reduces cortisol, improves mood, and enhances cognitive function. Leaders who exercise regularly report higher stress tolerance and better decision-making. This does not require marathons. A 20-minute walk works. Stretching works. Taking the stairs works. Movement matters. For remote workers, this becomes even more critical because the natural movement that occurred in physical offices, walking to meetings, moving between floors, and standing at someone's desk, disappears entirely. Remote leaders must deliberately build movement into their schedules.

> **THE ONES WHO ENDURE AND SUCCEED OVER TIME ARE NOT THE LOUDEST OR THE TOUGHEST. THEY ARE THE MOST DISCIPLINED.**

Build Margins Into Your Schedule

Back-to-back meetings eliminate recovery. Leaders who schedule realistic margins between commitments make better decisions and maintain energy longer. Between meetings, take five minutes. Walk. Breathe. Think. Do not check email. Just reset. Those five minutes compound throughout the day. The practical discipline of protecting that time within a structured schedule is addressed more fully in Chapter 11. The point here is simpler: margins are not inefficiency. They are the space where judgment recovers.

Practice Reflection

Resilient leaders reflect regularly. Not for hours, but for just a few minutes each day. What went well? What drained me? What would I do differently? Reflection creates learning. Learning builds capacity. Leaders who skip reflection may survive the day but miss the lesson it contains.

RESILIENCE IS A LONG GAME

Resilience compounds. Leaders who reflect regularly, recover intentionally, learn from adversity, and regulate under pressure build endurance over time. We have worked with leaders for decades. The ones who endure and succeed over time are not the loudest or the toughest. They are the most disciplined. They know when to push and when to restore.

This connects to everything we have explored throughout this book. The empathy from Chapter 6 requires emotional capacity. The accountability from Chapter 8 requires sustained energy. The decision-making in Chapter 3 requires clear thinking, which only comes with adequate rest. The trust-building from Chapter 5 requires consistency that depleted leaders cannot maintain. Resilience is not separate from effective leadership. It is the foundation that makes every other leadership discipline sustainable.

WHY THIS CHAPTER MATTERS

Leadership is tough because it requires sustained performance under pressure. Not bursts. Not sprints. Endurance.

The challenges we have explored throughout this book, making unpopular decisions, holding people accountable, leading through change, building trust, and aligning priorities with values, require capacity that does not replenish automatically. Leaders who do not deliberately build resilience eventually lose the ability to do these hard things well. They begin to avoid difficult conversations because they lack the energy for conflict. They delay decisions because they cannot think clearly. They become inconsistent because regulation requires resources they have depleted.

Leadership is tough because the work never stops, and the demands rarely decrease. Markets keep shifting. People keep struggling. Crises keep emerging. Leaders who treat resilience as optional discover, too late, that everything else discussed in this book requires the capacity resilience provides. The best leaders are not the ones who avoid stress. They are the ones who deliberately manage it, systematically recover, and lead themselves with the same rigor they lead others. Resilience is earned daily through the choices leaders make about where they invest energy, how they recover, and what they model for those around them.

KEY TAKEAWAYS:

- **Resilience is a capacity, not an attitude.** Leadership requires endurance, and resilience makes it possible.

- **Stress is inevitable; burnout is not.** The difference lies in how leaders manage accumulation and recovery before capacity is exhausted.

- **Recovery is a leadership responsibility, not a luxury.** Leaders who skip recovery eventually pay for it in judgment, health, and performance.

- **Resilience must be designed into systems, not demanded from individuals.** Leaders cannot expect outcomes without building capacity.

- **Leaders model resilience whether they intend to or not.** People watch leadership behavior constantly and adjust their own accordingly.

- **Awareness, regulation, and recovery are the three disciplines of resilient leadership.** All three require intentional practice, not just good intentions.

- **Adversity builds resilience only when leaders extract learning from it.** Pain alone does not create strength; reflection does.

- **Endurance is built through discipline and reflection, not toughness alone.** Sustainable leadership requires sustainable practices.

- **Remote work accelerates burnout without intentional boundaries.** Distance eliminates the natural recovery moments that office environments provide.

- **Leading through difficulty requires honesty, not false optimism.** Trust is built through transparency, especially when conditions are hard.

REFLECTION QUESTIONS:

1. Where am I absorbing unnecessary stress that could be eliminated through better systems or clearer priorities?

2. What signals tell me I am approaching depletion, and am I noticing them early or ignoring them until capacity is gone?

3. How intentional am I about recovery? Do I treat it as optional or as strategic maintenance?

4. Where might my leadership behavior be increasing stress for others rather than reducing it?

5. What one change would immediately improve my endurance without sacrificing results?

6. How do I model resilience for my team, and what patterns are they learning from watching me?

7. What adversity has shaped my leadership most, and what did I learn from it that I can apply now?

8. Am I treating energy as infinite or finite, and where does my behavior reveal the true answer?

9. What recovery habit have I neglected most, and what is that neglect costing me in performance and relationships?

10. Where am I acting as a bottleneck instead of building redundancy and developing others' capacity?

CHAPTER 11

MANAGING TIME AND ENERGY
ACHIEVE THE MOST IMPORTANT RESULTS

Time is the one resource leaders cannot create. Money can be raised. Talent can be hired. Strategy can be changed. Technology can be upgraded. But time, once spent, is gone forever. And yet, time is the resource leaders often manage most poorly. Not because they are careless, but because they confuse activity with progress, urgency with importance, and intention with execution.

This chapter is about reclaiming control of time and energy as strategic leadership disciplines, not through apps or productivity hacks, but through deliberate decisions about where attention goes and what gets protected. Resilience provides the capacity to absorb pressure. This chapter addresses how disciplined time and energy management prevents that pressure from accumulating unnecessarily in the first place. Managing time is not just a personal productivity issue; it is a leadership responsibility.

THE HARD TRUTH ABOUT TIME AND LEADERSHIP

Leaders do not suffer from a lack of time. You have exactly as much time as Satya Nadella, Elon Musk, and Jensen Huang all have. Leaders

207

today suffer from too many priorities, too many interruptions, too many self-imposed obligations, too much emotional labor, and too little discipline around decision-making. Feeling like there is never enough time is often a symptom, not the problem. The real issue is avoidance.

Leaders delay decisions they do not want to make. They hold onto work they should release. They tolerate inefficiencies because fixing them requires uncomfortable conversations. And they tell themselves they will deal with it "when things slow down." When exploring how priorities reveal values, how leaders spend their time is the most honest reflection of what they actually believe matters. The calendar does not lie. The people we coach who complain most about a lack of time are often the same ones who refuse to delegate, cannot say no, or continue doing low-value work out of habit. The issue is not time. It is discipline.

THE 168-HOUR REALITY

Every person, regardless of position or power, has exactly 168 hours per week. Not one hour more. Wealthy people cannot buy more. Forgetful people cannot lose it. Scientists cannot invent more. When it comes to time, there is true equality.

The question is not where to find more time. You cannot. The real question is how to invest the 168 hours available with intention. Consider a typical breakdown of how essential activities consume time each week: work at nine hours per day accounts for 45 hours, one hour of daily commuting adds five hours, two hours of daily meals accounts for 14 hours, seven hours of sleep per night accounts for 49 hours, and one hour for bathing and dressing adds seven hours. That totals 120 hours, leaving 48 hours for everything else: family, leisure, personal growth, faith, children's activities, errands, and rest.

If this breakdown reflects your reality, you have 48 hours per week beyond work, sleep, and basic maintenance. The question is not whether you have time. The question is how intentionally you are spending what you have.

TIME IS A GIFT

At the United States Naval Academy, time is treated as a gift. Midshipmen learn quickly that one minute matters. In one minute, you can dust the room, review a checklist, prepare for inspection, make the bed, or review facts for the next training session. There is no waiting to "feel ready." There is no indulgence in procrastination. The mission does not pause for motivation. That lesson carries directly into leadership. Waiting until you feel like doing something is not a strategy. It is avoidance dressed up as self-awareness. Leaders act because the situation requires action, not because the mood is right.

DON'T WAIT UNTIL YOU FEEL LIKE IT

This is one of the most destructive myths in modern leadership culture. "I'll do it when I'm in the right headspace." "I'll write that report when I'm in the mood." "I'll have that conversation when the time is right." That perfect time rarely comes, and waiting for it is not self-awareness. It is avoidance with a more palatable name.

The work that matters most, difficult conversations, strategic decisions, delegation, and development, often feels uncomfortable. That discomfort does not resolve itself through delay. It compounds. We coached a leader who kept postponing a difficult performance conversation with an underperforming employee. Every week, she said, "I'm not in the right frame of mind yet. I'll do it next week." Six months later, the conversation still had not happened. The employee's performance had worsened. The team's morale had declined. Two strong performers left because they were tired of covering for someone who was not held accountable.

When we finally pressed her, she admitted, "I'll never feel ready for that conversation. It's always going to be uncomfortable." Exactly. Which is why waiting for the perfect emotional state guarantees inaction. As we explored in Chapter 3 on strategic decision-making, the cost of delay often exceeds the cost of an imperfect decision made on time. Leaders who wait to act until they feel 100 percent ready lose time, credibility, and momentum. Disciplined leaders act despite resistance, not after it disappears.

TIME MANAGEMENT IS ENERGY MANAGEMENT

Not all hours are equal. An exhausted leader with a full calendar is less effective than a rested leader with fewer commitments and clearer priorities. Energy determines decision quality, emotional regulation, communication clarity, patience, and judgment. Burned-out leaders do not just waste time; they waste talent. Resilience is the foundation for sustained performance. This chapter addresses the complementary discipline: structuring time so that energy is protected rather than depleted by avoidable demands.

We worked with an executive who scheduled back-to-back meetings from 7 a.m. to 6 p.m. every day. By 3 p.m., he was visibly depleted. His decisions slowed. His patience evaporated. His communication became curt. The resilience dimension of this pattern, the burnout risk and recovery deficit it created, is addressed in Chapter 10. The time management dimension is equally important. His schedule had no architecture. Everything was treated as equally urgent. Nothing was protected. When we challenged his assumption that every meeting required his presence, he resisted. Then he tried blocking 90 minutes each afternoon for focused work. No meetings. No interruptions. Just time to think, process, and prioritize. Within three weeks, his effectiveness improved visibly. Decisions became clearer. His team noticed the difference. He began leaving the office at 5 p.m. instead of 7 p.m. The change was not about working less. It was about working with intention.

Managing energy requires leaders to identify where they add the most value, protect that time aggressively, eliminate low-value demands, and stop rewarding busyness as a proxy for productivity. Izabela Lungberg, an entrepreneur mentor, stated it best: "Protect your energy like a strategic asset. Because it is." This quote highlights that managing personal energy is not just self-care, but a critical, deliberate leadership practice necessary for high-level leadership performance. Great leaders conserve energy strategica ly by focusing on high-value activities rather than working longer hours.

THE LEADERSHIP TRIAGE FRAMEWORK: DECIDE, DO, DELEGATE, DEVELOP, DELETE

Every task, request, and obligation falls into one of five categories. Leaders who fail to triage their time end up doing everything, which means doing nothing particularly well. This framework is not about working less. It is about working on the right things at the right level.

Decide

Some things require a decision now. Indecision consumes more energy than action, and delayed decisions create confusion, stress, and rework for everyone waiting on direction. Leaders procrastinate on decisions because they want more information, fear consecuences, seek consensus, or hope the issue resolves itself. It rarely does. As we explored in Chapter 3, the cost of decision delay often exceeds the cost of an imperfect decision based on the available information.

Decide when the cost of waiting exceeds the risk of acting, when the decision is reversible, or when the organization needs direction to move forward. Clarity saves time even when the decision is not perfect. One CEO we worked with delayed a strategic pivot for nine months, repeatedly saying, "I need more data."

Boeing's story is one of the most striking examples in recent business history of what happens when leaders delay doing the right thing. After the first crash of a Boeing 737 MAX in October 2018, which killed 189 people, Boeing's CEO Dennis Muilenburg chose not to ground the aircraft or immediately acknowledge the severity of the design flaw in its flight control system, known as MCAS. Five months later, a second 737 MAX crashed in Ethiopia, killing 157 more people. Critics and legal experts have argued that, had Boeing grounded the plane after the first crash and acted swiftly to fix the problem, the second tragedy could have been entirely prevented. Instead, leadership delayed, minimized the issue publicly, and misled investors and regulators, which ultimately led to criminal fraud charges and a settlement of over $2.5 billion with the U.S. Department of Justice.

The financial and human cost of that delay cascaded far beyond the settlement. Boeing faced more than $20 billion in fines, compensation, and legal fees, as well as the cancellation of over 1,200 aircraft orders. By late 2024, the company was carrying $58 billion in debt and burning through roughly $1 billion a month. The leadership that followed under CEO Dave Calhoun, who took over in early 2020, continued to struggle with the same cultural issues: whistleblowers were silenced, safety concerns went unaddressed, and in January 2024, a door panel blew off an Alaska Airlines 737 MAX mid-flight. Calhoun eventually announced his resignation later that year.

What makes Boeing's story so important for leaders is that the delay was not due to ignorance but to priority. The company had shifted from an engineering-led culture to one driven by financial performance, where speed to market and stock price took precedence over safety. Engineers tried to raise concerns and were told, in the words of one quality inspector, to shut up. The lesson is clear and sobering: when leaders avoid a difficult decision to protect short-term results, they rarely avoid the consequences. They only defer them, and in doing so, they almost always make them worse.

Do

Leaders should personally execute work that requires their unique authority, uses expertise that cannot be transferred, carries strategic impact, or cannot be delegated without significant loss of quality or credibility. This category is often smaller than leaders assume. High-performing leaders are ruthless about what they personally execute because they understand that their most valuable contribution is judgment, not output.

A director once told us, "I have to review every client proposal before it goes out." We asked why. "Because I'm the only one who knows what quality looks like." It is not. That belief made him the bottleneck. Every proposal waited for his review. His team stopped developing their own judgment. His schedule is filled with work that others could do with the right guidance. We challenged him to define quality standards explicitly, review three proposals together with his team as a teaching exercise, and then release proposals without his approval. He resisted. Then he tried it. Within two months, proposals moved faster. Quality remained high. His team's confidence grew. He reclaimed 10 hours per week and redirected that time to client relationships and strategic work only he could do.

As Garry Ridge, former CEO and Chairman of WD-40, shared with us, "I cannot be the person who holds up my tribe members from doing their jobs. My job is to create an environment where people can make their best contributions, and I can be a great coach." Leaders who insist on doing what others could do are not demonstrating commitment. They are limiting their organization's capacity to grow.

Delegate

Delegation is not dumping. It is the intentional transfer of a task and the authority to complete it. Leaders often fail at delegation because they do not want to take the time to explain, do not trust outcomes, fear mistakes, or have built their identity around being needed. But delegation is not about convenience. It is about scale. If someone else can learn to do something, your job is to develop them to do it, not to keep doing it yourself.

One manager complained about spending hours each week creating reports. When we asked if anyone else could create them, she said, "Yes, but it's faster if I do it myself." Short-term, perhaps. Long-term, absolutely not. If you spend one hour each week on a task, that is 52 hours per year. If you spend three hours training someone else to do it, you save 49 hours in the first year alone. Every year after, you save the full 52 hours. The math is straightforward. Yet leaders resist because delegation requires an upfront investment of time and trust. That investment must be made.

Delegation without clear expectations and follow-through is not delegation. It is abdication. The difference is in the clarity of what is being transferred, the support provided during the transition, and the accountability maintained for the outcome.

Develop

Some tasks should be assigned intentionally for development rather than efficiency. Development takes time up front and creates capacity over time. Leaders who skip development become bottlenecks. Leaders who invest in it build organizations that can function and grow without depending on any single person.

We worked with a senior leader who personally handled all budget variance reports. When we suggested developing someone on his team to take over for him, he said, "But they don't know how." Exactly. Which is why this is a development opportunity, not a reason to keep doing it himself. He trained one team member for over 3 months. That team member now handles all variance reports independently. The senior leader reclaimed six hours per month. The team member gained new skills that ultimately led to a promotion. The development investment paid returns that efficiency never would have.

Henry Ford, the founder of Ford Motor Company, understood the importance of training and developing your people. He said it best, "The only thing worse than training your people and having them leave, is not training them and having them stay."

Delete

This is where most leaders struggle the most. They keep doing things because "we've always done it," because someone expects it, because it once mattered, or because no one has questioned it.

We even have an acronym for this: SDS. Stop Doing Stupid. Stop doing things that do not matter so that you can focus on the things that do. Delete work that no longer aligns with strategy, produces little value, exists purely out of habit, or drains energy disproportionate to its return. Deleting work is not laziness. It is leadership courage.

A major U.S. bank, ranked among the country's top 30, found itself buried under its own reporting. Risk analysts were spending the bulk of their time tracking down data and manually compiling spreadsheets rather than generating insights and doing the work that actually mattered. The bank had more than 100 recurring reports, many of which had grown outdated over time, and the situation had become serious enough to raise regulatory compliance concerns with the Office of the Comptroller of the Currency.

Rather than simply updating the reports and moving on, the bank brought in outside consultants to conduct a full review and assess which reports were genuinely necessary and which were simply the product of organizational habit. The review involved sitting down with credit officers and business leaders across the bank to evaluate each report based on its relevance, complexity, and actual use.

What they found was striking. Overlapping metrics and redundant reports had accumulated across product lines, and once they were identified and eliminated, the bank reduced its total number of reports and metrics by up to 70 percent. Analyst time previously consumed by preparation and validation was redirected to higher-value work, and the remaining reports were automated so that new data triggered updates without manual effort.

The lesson for any organization is clear: reports are rarely designed with an expiration date, and they tend to multiply over time without anyone stopping to ask whether they still serve a purpose. This bank's willingness to conduct that honest review freed its people to think rather than compile, which is exactly what leadership requires.

THE TIME AUDIT: WHERE DOES YOUR TIME ACTUALLY GO?

Most leaders have no idea how they actually spend their time. They think they know, and they are usually wrong. A time audit reveals the truth. For one week, track your time in 15-minute increments. Record everything: meetings, emails, phone calls, interruptions, social media, unplanned conversations, and transitions between tasks. At the end of the week, total the time spent advancing your top priorities versus the time spent on work that could be delegated, eliminated, or shortened.

We coached an executive who was convinced she had no time. We had her complete a time audit. The results shocked her. She spent three hours in meetings each day. She spent 40 minutes listening to one employee complain repeatedly about the same issues. She spent time on proposals that could have been easily delegated with better planning. We estimated that she lost 2 hours per day due to poor time management. Two hours per day equals 66 full eight-hour days of lost productivity per year. That is months of productivity wasted. The question is not whether you have time. The question is where and how you spend it.

Remember: how you choose to spend your time is a mirror of your priorities. The time audit makes what is true visible.

A COMPANY THAT MASTERED TIME DISCIPLINE

SRC Holdings, an employee-owned manufacturing company, faced operational complexity as it grew. Leadership noticed a pattern. Talented people were drowning in meetings and competing initiatives. Instead of asking people to manage time better, SRC leadership reduced initiative overload, forced prioritization at the executive level, clarified decision rights, and eliminated low-value meetings. Time discipline improved because leaders changed the system, not because employees worked harder. Productivity increased. Engagement improved. Turnover dropped. Time management became a leadership practice rather than an individual burden.

This mirrors what we explored in Chapter 10 about organizational resilience. Leaders cannot demand better time management from individuals while building systems that make it impossible. The system must support the discipline.

PROCRASTINATION IS A LEADERSHIP PROBLEM

Procrastination is often not laziness. It is avoidance of discomfort, fear of consequences, perfectionism, or decision anxiety. Senior leaders procrastinate on performance conversations, succession planning, strategic pivots, and delegation. The cost of delaying decisions compounds. Delayed decisions create confusion, rework, and distrust. The core principle is straightforward: action precedes motivation. Leaders do not wait to feel motivated. They act, and motivation follows from momentum.

Tried-and-true ways leaders stop procrastinating include starting smaller than seems necessary, committing to completing one paragraph of the report, or simply dialing the number before deciding whether to proceed. Time-boxing decisions by setting a deadline and committing to decide by that date, regardless of whether perfect clarity has arrived, also works. Separating thinking from doing matters because overthinking is not progress.

Analysis paralysis stops more leaders than bad decisions ever will. Making public commitments drives action because accountability to others creates urgency that internal intention rarely matches. And identifying immediate next actions converts vague goals into concrete steps. "Improve team communication" becomes "Send the team a weekly update every Friday at 3 p.m." Procrastination thrives in ambiguity. Action thrives in structure.

MANAGE MEETINGS RUTHLESSLY

Meetings consume time faster than almost any other activity in organizational life. Employees consistently identify meetings as the single greatest source of wasted time at work. Before scheduling or accepting any meeting, leaders must ask: Why is this meeting necessary? Can this be accomplished more efficiently through email or a brief written update? Who actually needs to be present? What specific decision will this meeting produce? What happens if we cancel it entirely?

We coached a rising executive who was frustrated by a weekly meeting that never had an agenda, produced no decisions, and served no clear purpose. After a year of dutiful attendance, she asked her supervisor directly, "Why do we have to be at these meetings?" Her boss replied, "Because it is on the schedule. If it is scheduled, we go." She resigned a month later. "I just couldn't work with people who couldn't see that this was a problem," she told us. We understood completely.

Another organization faced the same problem and made a different choice. A leadership team held a weekly two-hour status meeting: same format, same people, same complaints about wasted time. When we asked what would happen if they eliminated it, one VP said, "Honestly? Nothing. Everyone could just email their updates." They eliminated the meeting. Not a single negative consequence occurred. Everyone reclaimed two hours per week. Morale improved. Meetings without decisions are discussions. Discussions without purpose are distractions.

ENERGY LEAKS LEADERS COMMONLY IGNORE

Common energy drains include rehashing the same unresolved issues, unclear priorities that require constant re-explanation, emotional labor without appropriate boundaries, constant availability as a cultural expectation, and doing work that others should own. Resilience is built through managing what depletes capacity. Here, the focus is on identifying the specific drains that time discipline can close.

One executive realized she was spending hours each week in one-on-one meetings with an employee who constantly needed reassurance. Every week, the same conversation. The same reassurance is required. She structured those conversations differently. "I can meet with you once a week for 30 minutes. Before we meet, send me the three things you need help with. We will address those three things." The employee adapted. The meetings became productive. The executive reclaimed hours every month and redirected that energy toward higher-value leadership work.

Resilient leaders aggressively close energy leaks, not because they are unwilling to support their teams, but because energy invested poorly is energy unavailable when it matters most.

LEADING OTHERS TO MANAGE TIME AND ENERGY

Leaders model time behavior whether they intend to or not. People watch how leaders spend their time and draw conclusions about what is expected of them. If you reward responsiveness over results, praise long hours, and celebrate busyness, your team will burn out trying to mirror those standards. If you protect focus time, enforce priorities, and normalize recovery, your team will sustain performance over time.

One manager sent emails at 11 p.m. and expected responses. His team interpreted that as a signal that constant availability was required. Engagement scores dropped. Turnover increased. Exit interviews revealed the same theme: people felt they could never disconnect. When we showed him the data, he immediately changed his behavior. He stopped sending late-night emails. He explicitly told his team, "Do not respond to emails after 6 p.m. or on weekends unless it is a genuine emergency." Small behavioral signals carry large messages. His team's engagement improved within one quarter, not because conditions changed dramatically, but because one clear boundary communicated that their time and recovery mattered.

WORK YOUR ENERGY

Each person has a unique energy cycle. Some leaders are at their best early in the morning: focused, clear, and ready to engage with complexity. Others get off to a slow start and peak later in the afternoon or evening. Neither pattern is wrong. Both require awareness and intentional scheduling.

Save tasks that require your deepest focus and best judgment for your peak energy hours, regardless of when that is. Just because a task is high priority does not mean it should be scheduled based on calendar availability. One leader realized she had been scheduling all her strategic thinking sessions in the morning because that was when her calendar had openings. Her actual peak creative time was between 2 p.m. and 4 p.m. She flipped her schedule, protecting that window for strategic work and moving routine meetings to mornings. Her output on complex work improved significantly.

Hao Lam, founder of Best-in-Class Education Center, articulates this point well. "When I protect my energy and direct it toward activities that truly move the needle in my personal and professional life, everything flows better. My focus, creativity, and relationships."

PUTTING MORE TIME BACK IN YOUR DAY: THE POWER OF SMALL HABITS

Small habits compound into significant time savings over months and years. Leaders who build consistent placement habits, knowing exactly where files are stored, where physical items live, and where to find information quickly, eliminate the accumulation of small searches and delays that quietly consume hours every week.

LEADERS WHO MASTER TIME AND ENERGY DO NOT WORK LESS. THEY WORK BETTER, DECIDE FASTER, AND DELEGATE MORE.

It is estimated that the average person spends six months of their life looking for lost, misplaced, or disorganized items. This equates to about 10-15 minutes a day. Creating placement habits is not about personal tidiness. It is about eliminating friction that interrupts focus and wastes leadership capacity. Your phone goes in the same spot. Your key files are organized in the same system. Your meeting notes live in the same place. Small habits practiced consistently create the organizational infrastructure that prevents time from disappearing into search-and-recovery.

Throughout your day, step back briefly and ask yourself three grounding questions: Is what I am doing right now absolutely necessary? If not, reprioritize. Am I working as efficiently as I can on this? If not, adjust my approach. Am I doing something a team member could do more effectively? If so, delegate it now rather than later. These questions interrupt automatic behavior and redirect attention toward high-value work before time is lost rather than after.

MANAGING TIME WELL REQUIRES DISCIPLINE

Time does not reward intention. It rewards decision-making and action. Leaders who master time and energy do not work less. They work better. They decide faster. They delegate more. They develop intentionally. They delete ruthlessly.

WHY THIS CHAPTER MATTERS

Time management requires saying no to work people expect you to do, eliminating meetings people have grown accustomed to attending, and holding boundaries when pressure mounts and everything feels urgent. It requires discipline to protect what matters when everything is competing for the same finite hours. But leaders who master time and energy build the systems, habits, and disciplines required for sustainable high performance, not just short-term results that exhaust everyone involved.

Resilience provides the capacity to absorb pressure. This chapter provides the discipline to prevent unnecessary pressure from accumulating in the first place. Together, they form the foundation for leadership that endures: not because the work gets easier, but because the leader gets smarter about where their irreplaceable time and energy go.

KEY TAKEAWAYS:

- **Time management is a leadership responsibility, not a personal preference**. How you spend it reveals what you actually value.

- **Never wait until you feel like it to take the right action.** Discomfort does not resolve through delay. It compounds.

- **Energy management determines decision quality.** Depleted leaders make poor decisions regardless of how much time they have.

- **Triage work deliberately using the Decide, Do, Delegate, Develop, Delete framework.** Every task belongs in one category.

- **Procrastination is a leadership risk, not a personality flaw.** Its costs accumulate at the organizational level, not just at the personal level.

- **Deleting work requires courage.** Eliminating what once mattered but no longer does is one of the hardest and most important leadership disciplines.

- **Leaders model time discipline for their teams, whether they intend to or not.** A leader's behavior is always more instructive than stated expectations.

- **Track your time honestly through a time audit.** Most leaders are surprised by what the data reveals.

- **Protect your peak energy hours.** Know when you need to schedule your highest-value work, regardless of where those hours fall in the day.

- **Question every recurring meeting ruthlessly.** Meetings without decisions waste the organization's most finite resource.

- **Small habits compound into massive time savings.** Leaders who create clear systems for where things live eliminate the friction that slowly drains their team's capacity.

REFLECTION QUESTIONS:

1. Where am I waiting to "feel ready" instead of acting on something I already know needs to be done?

2. What work should I stop doing immediately, and what is preventing me from stopping?

3. Where am I the bottleneck, and what would I need to change to remove myself from that position?

4. What decisions am I avoiding, and what is the true cost of continued delay?

5. How does my time behavior affect my team's ability to work and recover effectively?

6. What would disciplined triage change about my next 30 days if I applied it consistently?

7. When is my peak energy time, and am I protecting it for my most important work?

8. Which meetings could I eliminate or transform with no negative consequences to the work?

9. Where am I modeling busyness instead of productivity, and what message does that send?

10. What one thing could I delete today that would free up meaningful hours every week?

CHAPTER 12

SUCCESSION PLANNING
BUILD YOUR BENCH AND FUTURE-PROOF THE ORGANIZATION

Leadership transitions are inevitable. What is not inevitable is whether your organization is ready for them.

Every organization will face the moment when a key leader departs, whether through retirement, illness, a better opportunity, or circumstances no one anticipated. The question is not whether that moment will come. The question is whether the organization will absorb the transition smoothly or spend the next two to three years recovering from it. Organizations that plan for leadership continuity treat succession as a strategic discipline. Organizations that avoid it treat succession as an emergency. The difference between those two approaches shows up in performance, culture, and the careers of everyone who remains.

Succession planning is one of the most avoided responsibilities in senior leadership. Not because leaders do not understand its importance. Not because they lack intelligence or experience. But, because succession planning forces leaders to confront uncomfortable realities about vulnerability, continuity, control, and identity. It requires leaders to think beyond their own tenure, admit that no one is permanent, and prepare others for roles they may never personally hold. That is precisely why succession

ORGANIZATIONS DO NOT FAIL WHEN LEADERS LEAVE; THEY FAIL WHEN NO ONE IS READY.

planning matters, and precisely why so few leaders do it well.

We worked with a large credit union that created and facilitated a year-long senior executive and VP development program. The leaders in each cohort met weekly, worked through extensive case studies, and participated in facilitated group discussions that pushed their thinking beyond their current roles. The program culminated with VP-level leaders building the organization's strategic plan, which was ultimately presented to the executive team and board. Although these development programs required significant time and preparation from everyone involved, every participant said the experience had meaningfully strengthened them as leaders. The credit union did not stumble into that outcome. They planned for it deliberately, years before any transition occurred.

This chapter is about doing the same: deliberately building bench strength, planning for inevitable transitions, and creating organizations that remain strong long after current leaders have moved on. It is not about replacement charts or emergency binders. It is about readiness, stewardship, and future-proofing. Organizations do not fail when leaders leave; they fail when no one is ready.

THE LEADERSHIP FAILURE NO ONE ADMITS

Most organizations do not lack talent. They lack preparation. Succession planning is consistently postponed with familiar rationalizations: no one is leaving anytime soon; we will deal with it when it becomes necessary; we are too busy right now; we do not want to create anxiety; or it is HR's responsibility. These explanations feel reasonable until a transition arrives, at which point the lack of preparation becomes immediately apparent.

Leadership transitions rarely come neatly packaged. They arrive through retirements that happen faster than expected, health issues that force sudden exits, competitive poaching of key talent, rapid organizational growth, or disruptions no one anticipated. Organizations without succession plans experience higher leadership transition costs and longer ramp-up times when key leaders depart. These numbers represent millions in lost productivity, damaged relationships, and strategic drift. Leaders know that hope is not a strategy. Neither is denial.

THE DEMOGRAPHIC REALITY LEADERS CANNOT IGNORE

The pressure on succession planning is not abstract. It is demographic and immediate. More than 10,000 Baby Boomers reach retirement age every day, a trend that will continue throughout this decade. Generation X leaders are not far behind, and research suggests they are retiring younger than the generation that preceded them. The leaders who built your organization, know your customers, understand your culture, and carry decades of institutional knowledge are leaving, and the pace is accelerating.

National research shows that more than 34 million small businesses are operating in the United States, with more than half owned by people over 50. While 78 percent of those owners intend to transition their businesses upon retirement, only 30 percent have developed a viable succession plan. That gap between intention and preparation is where organizational value quietly disappears.

For larger organizations, the challenge is different but equally pressing. A CNBC survey found that in companies with over 500 employees, 62 percent of employees report they would be more engaged and motivated if their company had a clear succession plan. For employees aged 18 to 34, that number rises above 90 percent. Your employees want succession planning. They need to see a path forward. Without it, your best people leave for organizations that invest in their future. When discussing what people need from their leaders, employees stay where they see growth and leave where they see stagnation.

WAITING TOO LONG: WHAT IT ACTUALLY COSTS

The cost of delayed succession planning is not theoretical. We have watched it unfold in real organizations with real consequences.

One mid-sized professional services firm experienced this directly. Their managing partner retired with six months' notice. The firm had no formal succession plan. They promoted the next-most-senior partner based on tenure rather than readiness. Within 18 months, the firm lost 30 percent of its client base. The new managing partner was an excellent practitioner but a poor manager. He could not delegate. He micromanaged. He alienated key clients who had built personal relationships with his predecessor. The firm survived, but barely. Recovery took three years. A well-designed succession plan would have either prepared a ready successor or clearly identified the need to look outside the organization.

An organization with a charismatic founder delayed succession planning for years. The founder believed no one could replicate his relationships, instincts, or vision. When health issues forced a sudden exit, the organization scrambled. Internal candidates were unprepared. External hires struggled to gain traction. Trust eroded. Performance declined. Recovery took years. Proper succession planning would have significantly softened the impact.

SUCCESSION PLANNING IS ABOUT READINESS, NOT REPLACEMENT

One of the most common mistakes leaders make is treating succession planning as a list of names. Name-based planning answers the wrong question. The right question is not "Who replaces whom?" It is "What capabilities must exist for this organization to remain stable, competitive, and true to its mission?"

Succession planning is about roles and readiness, not people and titles. Every organization has critical roles that, if left vacant, would create disruption. These roles may or may not sit at the top of the organizational chart. Some are operational. Some are relational. Some are strategic. All of them matter, and all of them need a backup.

Readiness includes judgment under pressure, decision-making ability, emotional regulation, organizational credibility, contextual understanding, and the capacity to lead others through difficulty. As we explored in Chapter 3 on strategic decision-making, leaders who have practiced making difficult calls with incomplete information develop a kind of judgment that cannot be manufactured quickly. A high performer without that judgment is not ready for senior leadership, regardless of how strong their technical skills are. A loyal employee without leadership capability is not ready, regardless of their tenure. Potential is not the same as preparedness, and confusing the two is among the most costly mistakes in succession planning.

We worked with a technology company where the founder identified his VP of Engineering as his successor. On paper, the choice made sense. The VP was technically brilliant, well-liked, and deeply committed to the company. When the founder stepped down, the VP struggled immediately. He could solve technical problems beautifully. He could not make strategic decisions under pressure. He avoided conflict. He delayed difficult personnel decisions. Within six months, three senior leaders left. The founder had confused technical excellence with leadership readiness. As we discussed in previous chapters, when examining what work leaders should personally execute, technical expertise and leadership judgment are distinct capabilities. Organizations that treat them as interchangeable pay for that confusion at the moment of transition.

THE COST OF NOT HAVING A BENCH

Organizations that neglect succession planning pay for it repeatedly. They experience leadership gaps during crises, overreliance on external hires who lack context, loss of institutional knowledge that was never documented, political infighting among leaders who expected advancement, cultural instability as direction becomes unclear, and burnout among remaining leaders who absorb responsibilities beyond their bandwidth.

Organizations without bench strength become reactive rather than resilient. When no backup exists, remaining leaders absorb the load. They work longer hours. They make rushed decisions. They take on responsibilities outside their expertise. Capacity erodes. And the organization that was performing well begins to falter, not because the work changed, but because the human infrastructure supporting it was never built deep enough. The irony is consistent. Succession planning feels optional until it becomes urgent, and by then, it is usually too late to do it well.

WHY LEADERS RESIST SUCCESSION PLANNING

Resistance to succession planning is rarely rational. It is emotional. Common sources include fear of being replaced, identity tied too tightly to a specific role, concern about losing control, discomfort with the political dynamics that development conversations can create, and genuine discomfort with discussing what happens after they are gone.

Some leaders resist because they worry that developing others diminishes their own relevance. In reality, the opposite is true. If the organization cannot function

> **IF THE ORGANIZATION CANNOT FUNCTION WITHOUT YOU, YOU ARE NOT INDISPENSABLE. YOU ARE A LIABILITY.**

without you, you are not indispensable. You are a liability. Leadership is stewardship, not ownership. When exploring how values shape leadership priorities, leaders who think beyond their own tenure build legacies that outlast their presence. Leaders who protect their position at the expense of organizational continuity leave their organizations weaker than they found them.

We coached a CEO who resisted succession planning for years. When we asked why, he said, "If I train someone to do my job, the board might decide they don't need me anymore." We responded, "If you don't train someone to do your job, the board might decide the organization is too risky to sustain." He paused. That reframing changed his perspective. Six months later, he had identified three internal candidates, created development plans, and begun systematically sharing institutional knowledge. His relevance did not decrease. His credibility increased. The board saw him as a leader building for the long term rather than protecting his position. That is the shift that succession planning requires.

A COMPANY THAT TREATED SUCCESSION AS STEWARDSHIP

Gore and Associates, best known for its innovative products, offers a powerful example of long-term bench-building embedded into organizational design. Gore operates with a flat, lattice-based structure that emphasizes leadership readiness rather than positional titles. Leaders emerge through credibility and demonstrated capability rather than through appointment or hierarchy. Because leadership development is continuous and distributed rather than centralized, succession is not a crisis event at Gore. It is a natural transition.

At W.L. Gore and Associates, leadership readiness is not built through formal succession charts or job titles; it is built through daily practice. Because the lattice structure requires every associate to self-commit to projects, influence others without authority, and earn followers through demonstrated expertise rather than rank, people develop leadership instincts continuously and organically throughout their careers.

By the time Gore selects a leader, including at the CEO level, they are choosing from a pool of people who have already been leading in real conditions for years, which is precisely why, when CEO Chuck Carroll retired in 2005, the board asked a broad cross-section of employees who they would be willing to follow rather than simply appointing a successor from above.

The lesson is not that every organization should imitate Gore's structure. The lesson is about intent. Succession planning works best when it is embedded in how the organization operates every day rather than addressed episodically when a transition becomes imminent.

BUILDING BENCH STRENGTH AT EVERY LEVEL

Succession planning is not reserved for the C-suite. Organizations that future-proof effectively identify critical roles at every level, including mission-critical operational positions, single-point-of-failure roles where one person holds irreplaceable knowledge, positions requiring high trust or complex judgment, and roles whose vacancy would create immediate disruption to customers, clients, or internal operations.

Bench strength means more than having a name on a backup list. It means more than one person understands how a critical role functions; that knowledge is documented and accessible rather than held exclusively in one person's memory; that decision authority is distributed appropriately rather than concentrated; and that development is intentional rather than accidental. Depth matters more than hierarchy. Leaders who hoard knowledge create organizations that depend entirely on their continued presence. Leaders who share knowledge build organizations that can sustain performance through any transition.

One hospital system we worked with had an exceptional director of nursing who had been with the hospital for 23 years. She knew every system, every protocol, every physician preference, and every relationship that kept the floor running smoothly. When she announced her retirement, quiet panic set in. No one else had her knowledge. No one else had her relationships. No one else could step into her role without significant disruption to patient care and staff performance. The hospital scrambled to document her knowledge, shadow her intensively for six months, and accelerate development for her eventual replacement. It worked, but barely, and only because she was generous with her time and willing to stay longer than originally planned. Had the hospital built bench strength five years earlier, the transition would have been seamless rather than stressful.

THE FIVE CRITICAL ROLES EVERY ORGANIZATION MUST PROTECT

Not every role requires formal succession planning. Some require it urgently. The following categories represent the positions in which a vacancy poses the greatest risk to the organization.

1. Roles with irreplaceable relationships are client or stakeholder-facing positions in which trust is personal rather than organizational. If the person leaves, does the client-partner relationship leave with them?

2. Roles with specialized technical knowledge are positions where critical expertise is not documented, not shared, and not transferable quickly. If the person leaves, does essential work stop or deteriorate significantly?

3. Roles with high decision-making authority are positions in which judgment under pressure determines organizational outcomes. If the person leaves, do decisions stall, slow, or decline in quality?

4. Roles with cultural influence are held by leaders who shape how people think, behave, and engage with the organization's mission. If the person leaves, does morale collapse or direction become unclear?

5. Roles with strategic vision connect daily operational work to long-term organizational direction. If the person leaves, does the organization drift or lose its sense of direction?

Identify the roles in your organization that fit these descriptions. Then build a backup before you need one.

DEVELOPING PEOPLE WITHOUT PROMISING JOBS

One of the most delicate aspects of succession planning is how development conversations are conducted. Leaders must develop talent without guaranteeing outcomes, which requires a kind of honesty that many leaders find uncomfortable.

Effective development conversations include an honest assessment of the individual's current strengths and genuine gaps, exposure to broader responsibilities that build context beyond their current role, stretch assignments supported by coaching and feedback, and clear expectations about what growth is required and over what timeline. Development is about building readiness, not creating entitlement. When leaders prematurely promise roles, they create complacency and political risk. When they avoid development conversations entirely, they create fragility. The balance is honesty delivered with integrity.

We worked with a leader who told a high-potential employee, "You're next in line for my job when I retire." The employee stopped growing. He assumed the role was secured. He became complacent, stopped seeking feedback, and stopped pursuing the development experiences that would have actually prepared him for senior leadership. When the leader retired three years later, the board conducted an external search. The "next in line" employee was passed over. He left the organization bitter and angry, and the organization lost someone who could have been a strong contributor for years. The leader's intention was kind. The impact was damaging.

A better approach sounds like this: "I see real potential in you for senior leadership. Here is what that role requires. Here is where you are genuinely strong. Here is where you need to grow. I am committed to helping you develop those capabilities. The final decision will be made when the time comes, based on readiness and organizational needs at that moment." That is honest. That is fair. It builds capability without creating entitlement, and it protects both the individual and the organization.

SUCCESSION PLANNING IN TIMES OF UNCERTAINTY

Uncertainty accelerates leadership risk. Economic shifts, technology disruption, regulatory change, demographic pressure, and unexpected departures all increase the likelihood and frequency of leadership transitions. Static succession charts built around today's organizational structure do not survive significant volatility. As we explored in Chapter 3 on strategic decision-making, planning under uncertainty requires scenario thinking rather than single-path assumptions.

Future-proofing succession requires asking: What if this leader leaves unexpectedly rather than on the planned timeline? What if the next generation of leaders needs fundamentally different skills than the current generation? What if growth or disruption requires a leadership profile that the organization has never developed internally? Succession planning must evolve with the organization rather than reflecting a snapshot of what leadership looked like at the moment the plan was created.

One manufacturing company had a succession plan built entirely around continuity. Leadership assumed the next generation would manage the same business model their predecessors had built. Then their industry shifted. Automation changed the technical requirements of every senior role. The skills that had made current leaders successful were not the skills needed for the future they were entering. Rather than waiting for the gap to become a crisis, the company proactively adjusted its succession plan. They added external candidates with expertise in technology and digital transformation. They cross-trained internal candidates in areas beyond their operational comfort zones. They shifted development focus from operational excellence to strategic innovation. Flexibility, not the original plan, saved them. This mirrors what we discussed in Chapter 10 about building organizational resilience. The organizations that weather disruption best are not the ones with the most detailed plans. They are the ones who build adaptive capacity before they need it.

INTERNAL VERSUS EXTERNAL SUCCESSORS

There is no universal answer to whether internal or external candidates make better successors. Both have genuine advantages, and both carry genuine risks.

Internal successors offer cultural continuity, a faster ramp-up, existing relationships, and institutional knowledge that external candidates can take years to build. External successors offer fresh perspectives, new capabilities, accelerated change, and the ability to challenge assumptions that insiders have stopped questioning. The strongest organizations prepare for both, rather than defaulting to a single approach based on habit or convenience.

We coached a retail company facing CEO succession at a moment when their industry was changing faster than their internal bench had adapted. They had strong internal candidates but recognized that they were optimized for a business model that was already beginning to shift. They hired externally for the CEO role while simultaneously promoting two strong internal candidates into new C-suite positions created to support the transition. The external CEO brought strategic vision and a fresh market perspective. The internal leaders provided cultural continuity, operational knowledge, and the organizational relationships that allowed the new CEO to move quickly without losing the trust of the existing team. The combination worked in ways neither approach alone would have.

Internal development also increases the long-term success rate of external hires by providing the organizational stability and contextual knowledge that new leaders need to make good decisions quickly. Organizations with strong internal benches get more from external hires because external hires are not carrying the full weight of organizational knowledge alone.

BOARD AND EXECUTIVE RESPONSIBILITY

Succession planning is a governance issue, not just a leadership development program. Boards are responsible for overseeing CEO succession, assessing leadership continuity risk, and ensuring long-term organizational health. Executives are responsible for developing talent pipelines, identifying vulnerabilities honestly, and communicating readiness with transparency rather than defensiveness. CEO succession should never come as a surprise at a board meeting. Transparency prevents panic. Silence creates speculation, and speculation breeds the kind of uncertainty that destabilizes organizations from the inside.

One board we worked with had not formally discussed CEO succession in the past 5 years. The CEO was in his late seventies. Everyone in the room assumed he would retire eventually. No one raised the topic directly. When the CEO experienced a serious health scare, the board scrambled. They had no plan, no identified candidates, no development timeline, and no criteria for evaluating readiness. The CEO recovered, but the experience was a clear signal. The board now reviews succession planning quarterly. They have identified internal candidates, clarified development plans, established readiness criteria, and created a communication protocol for various transition scenarios. That is governance done properly, not because a crisis forced it, but because the health scare made visible what had always been true: the absence of a plan is itself a significant organizational risk.

SUCCESSION AS CULTURE, NOT AN EVENT

The organizations that manage leadership transitions most effectively are not the ones with the most detailed succession binders. They are the ones where leadership development is so embedded in daily operations that transitions feel like natural evolutions rather than organizational crises.

Room to Read is a global nonprofit founded in 2000 that focuses on childhood literacy and gender equality in education. When co-founder and CEO Erin Ganju decided to step down in 2018, the transition was handled with the same intentionality the organization brings to its educational programs. Rather than scrambling for a replacement, the board ran a genuine six-month search that included external candidates while also assessing internal talent. Dr. Geetha Murali, who had joined Room to Read in 2009 and risen to Chief Development and Communications Officer, emerged as the right choice not because she was handed the role, but because she had earned it.

What made this succession work was the years of development that came before the announcement. Murali had spent nearly a decade being stretched across global fundraising, communications, and stakeholder relationships, working directly with the organization's largest investors. The transition was also timed strategically, planned ahead of Room to Read's next five-year planning cycle, allowing Murali to own that process from the start rather than being thrust into immediate decisions. Ganju remained an Emeritus Board member, providing continuity without interference.

The results confirm what good succession planning makes possible. Since Murali took the helm, Room to Read has served as many children in four years as it did in its first twenty, and has expanded its digital library to over 3,000 titles in 41 languages. The organization never skipped a beat, because the people inside it were never left unprepared. That is the real lesson: the best succession plans are invisible by the time they are needed, because the work was done long before anyone had to ask for it.

The strongest organizations talk openly about growth and development, reward leaders who develop others rather than only rewarding leaders who deliver results, treat succession as an ongoing process rather than a periodic event, and value preparation over heroics. When a leader departs from these organizations, the question is not "Who do we call?" It is "Which of the prepared candidates is the right fit for this moment?"

THE MILITARY MODEL: SUCCESSION BY DESIGN

In the military, succession planning is not optional. It is mission-critical and built into the structure of every assignment from the beginning.

Every military leader knows they will only hold a given role for two to three years. Everyone knows they will be replaced. Part of your current job, from the first day you arrive, is to ensure that your replacement, when they arrive, is positioned to succeed. You are responsible for a systematic turnover process in which your successor shadows you, learns from you, and absorbs not just the technical requirements of the role but also the relationships, judgment calls, and institutional context that make the role function effectively.

Imagine designing an organization around 33 to 50 percent leadership turnover as a standard expectation rather than a crisis. Military leaders took pride in ensuring that the person who would succeed them would be well-prepared. In the Navy, Commanding Officers have Executive Officers as their second-in-command. After serving as Executive Officer for two years, the Executive Officer becomes the Commanding Officer. That structured pipeline ensures that knowledge is transferred systematically, relationships are introduced deliberately, and when the transition happens, it is seamless rather than disruptive. The missions continue without interruption because continuity was designed in, not hoped for.

Corporate organizations could learn significantly from this model. Instead of treating succession as a crisis event triggered by a departure, treat it as a planned evolution. Instead of waiting until departure is imminent to begin knowledge transfer, make it continuous. Instead of protecting institutional knowledge as a source of personal relevance, share it systematically as a leadership responsibility. Leaders who hoard knowledge are not protecting themselves. They are creating organizational fragility that will eventually become everyone's problem.

We worked with a financial services company that embedded succession directly into its performance review process. Every leader was evaluated on two equally weighted criteria: their own individual performance results and their demonstrated ability to develop successors. Leaders who hoarded knowledge, created dependency, or failed to invest in their team's development were penalized in their evaluations regardless of their individual results. Leaders who built bench strength, generously shared knowledge, and created ready successors were recognized and promoted. The result was a pipeline of ready leaders at every level of the organization, not because individuals were unusually talented, but because the system made development an expectation rather than an optional contribution.

COMMON PITFALLS IN SUCCESSION PLANNING

Even organizations that commit to succession planning encounter predictable mistakes. Recognizing these pitfalls before they occur is far less costly than recovering from them afterward.

Confusing Loyalty with Capability

Long tenure does not equal leadership readiness. Loyalty matters and should be recognized. Capability matters more when organizational continuity is at stake.

Doug Ivester's rise to CEO of Coca-Cola in 1997 is one of the most studied cases of loyalty-based succession in corporate history. When the beloved CEO Roberto Goizueta died suddenly of lung cancer, the board did not deliberate long. Ivester had been Goizueta's right-hand man for a decade, a brilliant CFO who had engineered many of the financial structures behind Coke's remarkable growth. The board believed they were honoring their late CEO's wishes. What they were actually doing was confusing devotion to a leader with readiness to become one.

The problems surfaced almost immediately. Ivester was high in analytical intelligence and relentless in his work ethic, but he lacked the emotional and political instincts the role demanded. When dozens of Belgian schoolchildren fell ill after drinking Coke products, he maintained silence for more than a week before traveling to apologize, a delay that cost the company 65 million cans in recalled product and serious brand damage. He alienated European regulators, major customers, and his own board by working in isolation and shutting out the advisors who might have helped him. Return on shareholder equity dropped from 56% to 35%, and earnings declined for two consecutive years. Ivester resigned after less than two years in the role. The lesson boards still struggle to absorb is: loyalty and long service are qualities worth honoring, but they are not, on their own, a leadership development strategy.

Assuming Development Happens Naturally

Development requires intention, structure, and accountability. Hoping people grow through exposure alone is not a plan. Leaders cannot expect outcomes without creating the conditions that make them possible.

Jack Welch is still celebrated as one of the great talent developers in corporate history, and with good reason. He built Crotonville, GE's renowned leadership training facility, invested heavily in 360-degree reviews, and spent years identifying and grooming his top executives. By the time he retired in 2001, he had narrowed his succession race to three exceptional internal finalists: Jeff Immelt, James McNerney, and Robert Nardelli. The process was heralded at the time as a model for every company to follow. What Welch did not anticipate was what the race itself would cost him. The moment Immelt was named CEO, the other two finalists left for top roles at other companies, taking years of institutional knowledge and leadership depth with them. Immelt inherited the top job without the senior team that had been built alongside him.

The deeper gap was not in development; it was in design. Welch's horse-race model assumed that competition would sharpen his successors, and it did. What it failed to account for was that a succession process that pits talented leaders against one another publicly creates winners and losers, and that organizations rarely get to keep the losers.

Deliberate development would have looked different. It would have included not just competition for the top role, but structured pathways that retained the runners-up, gave each finalist genuine enterprise-wide experience rather than division-level success, and built a senior team capable of supporting whoever ultimately led.

Treating Succession as a Secret

Transparency builds trust. Secrecy breeds speculation and anxiety. As we explored in Chapter 5 on trust, people fill information vacuums with assumptions, and those assumptions are almost always more alarming than the truth. Organizations that treat succession planning as a confidential exercise conducted behind closed doors create exactly the uncertainty they were trying to prevent.

Focusing Only on the CEO

Leadership depth matters at every level. Succession planning that stops at the top of the organization leaves the middle and operational layers vulnerable, and those layers are often where organizational knowledge and customer relationships actually live.

Creating Entitlement

Identifying potential is not a promise. Development does not guarantee promotion. When organizations communicate succession planning poorly, they create expectations that become political liabilities when transitions do not unfold as anticipated.

HOW TO START SUCCESSION PLANNING THIS QUARTER

If your organization does not have a succession plan, the best time to start was five years ago. The second-best time is now. Here is how to begin with the resources and information you currently have.

Step 1: Identify your critical roles. List the five positions in your organization that, if vacant tomorrow, would create the most immediate disruption to operations, customer relationships, or strategic direction. These are your highest-priority succession planning targets.

Step 2: Assess current readiness honestly. For each critical role, ask three questions: If this person left today, who is genuinely ready to step in? Who could be ready within 6 to 12 months of focused development? Who is not yet identified as a potential successor, suggesting a pipeline gap that needs immediate attention?

Step 3: Create development plans with specificity. For each identified successor, move beyond general statements of intent. What specific experiences do they need that they do not currently have? What knowledge gaps must be closed and how? What relationships need to be built deliberately? Development plans without specific actions and timelines are intentions, not plans.

Step 4: Document institutional knowledge now. Do not wait until a departure is announced to begin capturing what critical leaders know. Start now. Create documentation systems, conduct knowledge-transfer conversations, and identify the tacit knowledge that resides only in experienced leaders' heads and needs to be made explicit before it walks out the door.

Step 5: Communicate appropriately and transparently. Let people know the organization is actively building bench strength and investing in leadership development. Transparency about the process, even without revealing specific succession decisions, reduces anxiety and signals organizational commitment to people's futures. People trust leaders who communicate intention clearly, even when all the details are not yet determined.

WHY THIS CHAPTER MATTERS

Leadership is tough because its most important responsibilities are often the ones most avoided. Succession planning sits at the top of that list.

Every discipline explored in this book, making sound decisions under pressure, building trust through consistent communication, holding people accountable with clarity and empathy, developing resilience as a leadership capacity, managing time and energy as strategic resources, ultimately serves an organization only as long as capable leaders are available to practice those disciplines. When leadership continuity is not planned, the investment made in developing individual leaders is lost at the moment of transition rather than compounded through the pipeline.

Succession planning is tough because it requires leaders to act in an organization's future rather than their own present. It requires admitting vulnerability, sharing knowledge that feels like power, developing people who may eventually exceed you, and thinking about legacy rather than tenure. These are not comfortable disciplines. They run directly against the instincts that drive many high-achieving leaders: the instinct to be needed, to be the one who knows, to be irreplaceable.

But leadership at its best is stewardship. It is the willingness to build something that outlasts your own time in the role. When exploring how values shape leadership priorities, leaders who think only about their own performance leave organizations that are strong today but fragile tomorrow. Leaders who build bench strength, share knowledge generously, and develop successors deliberately leave organizations that are stronger for their having been there.

That is the standard succession planning holds leaders to. Not the standard of being good at the job, but the standard of making the organization better prepared for every job that comes after yours.

KEY TAKEAWAYS:

- **Succession planning is risk management, not HR paperwork.** Organizations without plans pay significantly more when transitions occur than organizations that prepared in advance.

- **Bench strength stabilizes organizations during transitions.** Organizations without depth become reactive rather than resilient when leadership changes occur.

- **Readiness matters more than titles or tenure.** Judgment under pressure is built over time and cannot be manufactured quickly when a transition arrives.

- **Development is a leadership responsibility, not a perk.** Leaders who invest in others' growth build organizational capacity. Leaders who hoard knowledge build organizational fragility.

- **Waiting creates vulnerability and increases costs.** The time to build a bench is before you need one, not after a transition reveals the gap.

- **Great leaders are great stewards.** The leaders who build lasting legacies think beyond their own tenure and prepare the organization for what comes next.

- **Succession planning works best when embedded in culture.** Organizations that normalize development and reward leaders for building successors create continuity as a byproduct of daily practice.

- **Transparency builds trust faster than secrecy.** People fill information vacuums with assumptions. Communicate your succession planning intentions clearly.

- **Internal and external candidates both have value.** The strongest organizations prepare for both, rather than defaulting to a single approach based on habit.

- **The strongest plans evolve with the organization.** Planning under uncertainty requires scenario thinking rather than single-path assumptions.

REFLECTION QUESTIONS:

1. Where is my organization most vulnerable to leadership loss, and how long has that vulnerability existed without being addressed?

2. Which roles have no backup, no documented knowledge, and no identified development path for a successor?

3. Who on my leadership team is actively developing talent, and who is protecting knowledge in ways that create organizational risk?

4. How honest are we about the difference between potential and genuine readiness for the roles we need filled?

5. What happens to this organization if I leave sooner than expected, and is that answer acceptable?

6. What legacy am I building beyond my own role and tenure, and what evidence supports that answer?

7. Do our board discussions regularly include succession planning as a standing agenda item, or does it only surface when a transition becomes imminent?

8. Are we treating succession as a periodic event or as an embedded cultural practice?

9. What would it take to begin meaningful succession planning this month, and what is the real reason it has not started yet?

10. Who needs development now to be genuinely ready when the next leadership transition occurs?

CHAPTER **13**

MENTORSHIP IS A DECISION
ADVICE FOR PURPOSEFUL DEVELOPMENT

Chapter 12 answered one fundamental leadership question: who comes next? This chapter answers the more difficult and far more consequential question. How do we develop people so they are ready to lead when the time comes?

Too many organizations treat succession planning as an inventory exercise. Names are placed in boxes. Readiness labels are assigned. Assumptions are made. Leaders reassure themselves that the future will be handled without doing the disciplined work required to make it viable. Succession planning without mentorship creates false confidence. Mentorship without succession planning creates wasted effort. When aligned, they form a continuous leadership pipeline that transforms organizational vulnerability into organizational strength.

Succession planning defines where the organization is exposed. Mentorship develops the judgment required to close that exposure. Rotational, intentional mentoring exposes leaders to diverse perspectives and decision styles. Integrated learning programs reinforce readiness across the organization. In short, Chapter 12 identifies future leaders. This chapter prepares them to lead. That

247

alignment transforms leadership development from a hopeful aspiration into a disciplined system, and it is why mentorship is not a favor, a side project, or a personality match. Mentorship is a leadership decision. And like all leadership decisions, it requires discipline.

FROM ADVICE TO ACCELERATION: WHY MENTORSHIP MUST EVOLVE

For decades, mentorship was treated as a nice-to-have. Informal. Optional. Often invisible. Someone senior took someone junior under their wing, offered advice when time allowed, and hoped something useful rubbed off. That model is no longer sufficient.

> **MENTORSHIP IS NOT A FAVOR, A SIDE PROJECT, OR A PERSONALITY MATCH.**
> - **MENTORSHIP IS A LEADERSHIP DECISION.**

Organizations today operate in environments defined by accelerated change, thinner leadership benches, rising accountability, and constant complexity. The demographic pressure on leadership pipelines is real and accelerating. Developing leaders cannot be left to chance. It must be intentional, structured, and aligned with strategic priorities. From our combined decades of consulting and military leadership, we know that organizations with structured mentorship programs report higher leadership readiness scores and lower turnover among high-potential employees. That is not a coincidence. That is proof that intentional development works.

THE PROBLEM WITH OLD-SCHOOL MENTORSHIP

Traditional mentorship was built on a one-way assumption. The mentor had the knowledge, and the mentee needed to receive it. That approach worked when careers were linear, change was slow, and expertise aged well. That world no longer exists.

Today's leaders face incomplete information, competing priorities, technological disruption, and constant pressure to adapt. In that environment, one-way mentorship fails. It creates dependency instead of capability. It reinforces hierarchy instead of learning. It privileges tenure over insight. Most importantly, it fails to accelerate judgment, which is the real goal of leadership development.

We worked with a financial services company that had a formal mentorship program. On paper, it looked impressive. Senior executives were paired with high-potential managers. Meetings happened quarterly. Progress was tracked. But when we dug deeper, the problem became clear. Mentees were not developing faster. They were becoming dependent on their mentors for answers instead of learning to think through problems themselves. One mentee told us, "I just wait to ask my mentor what to do. It is easier than figuring it out myself." That is not mentorship. That is an abdication of responsibility and sheer laziness. The mentor, a well-meaning executive, did not realize he was creating dependency. He thought he was helping. He was actually stunting growth.

When a mentee becomes dependent on their mentor for decisions, the relationship has quietly shifted from development to delegation. The mentee stops forming judgments and starts outsourcing them. They bring problems to the mentor not to think them through, but to receive answers. This dynamic can feel productive on the surface because decisions still get made and the mentee appears to be learning, but what is actually happening is sophisticated mimicry rather than genuine growth. The moment the mentor steps back or becomes unavailable, the mentee is exposed. They have been in the room for years, but they have never truly led.

The dependency usually develops for understandable reasons. The mentor is experienced, decisive, and trusted. The mentee is eager to get things right and naturally gravitates toward the person who seems to have the answers. Some mentors, without meaning to, reinforce the pattern by enjoying being needed or by stepping in too quickly when the mentee struggles. Comfort in a development relationship is often a signal that real development has stopped.

Restructuring the relationship requires an honest conversation and a deliberate shift in how the two people interact. When the mentee brings a problem, the mentor's first response should not be a solution but a question: What do you think, and what would you do if I were not available? This repositions the mentor as a thinking partner rather than a decision-maker. Both parties should also agree on clear boundaries: decisions that fall within the mentee's role belong to the mentee, full stop. The mentor can be consulted, but the mentee must own the outcome and live with it, because that ownership is where real development lives. The truest measure of great mentorship is a mentee who, over time, needs the mentor less, not because the relationship has ended, but because the mentee has genuinely grown into their own authority.

WHY HIGH PERFORMERS OFTEN STALL AS LEADERS

Understanding why mentorship must change requires understanding the most common development failure organizations make. High performers succeed by doing more themselves. They close deals that others cannot. They solve problems faster. They outwork everyone around them. Organizations reward that behavior and then promote those same people into leadership roles where those exact behaviors become liabilities.

As we explored in Chapter 11 on managing time and energy, the transition from individual contributor to leader requires a fundamental shift in how people define their value. It is no longer about personal output. It is about organizational capacity. Without intentional mentorship to guide that transition, organizations promote execution and hope that leadership will follow. It rarely does.

We coached a high-performing sales manager who was promoted to director. As a manager, she had succeeded by being the best salesperson on her team. She

HIGH PERFORMERS BECOME GREAT LEADERS WHEN THEY LEARN THAT LEADERSHIP IS NOT ABOUT BEING THE BEST.

closed deals others could not. She worked longer hours. She outperformed everyone. As a director, those behaviors hurt her. She could not do everyone's job. She tried anyway. Her team became frustrated. "She does not trust us," they told us privately. We worked with her to shift her mindset. "Your job is no longer to be the best salesperson. Your job is to build the best sales team." That required letting go, delegating, trusting, and coaching instead of doing. It was uncomfortable. But over six months, she made the transition. Her team's performance improved. She stopped working 70-hour weeks. And she developed her team members into stronger performers because she had a mentor who asked her the right questions rather than telling her what to do.

High performers become great leaders when they learn that leadership is not about being the best. It is about making others better. That lesson rarely arrives on its own. It requires mentorship that challenges assumptions rather than reinforcing comfortable habits.

WHAT MODERN MENTORSHIP MUST BECOME

Modern mentorship must move from advice to purpose of development. This accelerates decision-making, perspective, judgment, confidence, and readiness. That does not happen through occasional conversations or unstructured relationships. It happens when leaders make deliberate choices about how people learn, grow, and lead. Listening to understand rather than listening to respond is the foundation of effective communication. The same principle applies to mentorship. Good mentorship develops people. Great mentorship accelerates judgment.

During my time in the Navy, I saw this distinction clearly. The best commanding officers did not tell junior officers what to do. They asked questions that **GOOD MENTORSHIP DEVELOPS PEOPLE. GREAT MENTORSHIP ACCELERATES JUDGMENT.** forced those officers to think through problems on their own. "What are your options?" "What happens if you choose that path?" "What would you do if I were not here?" Those questions-built judgment. They forced people to practice decision-making in real time with a safety net. As we explored in Chapter 3 on strategic decision-making, judgment under pressure is built through repeated practice, not through instruction. Over time, that practice created confident, capable leaders who could operate independently. Corporate mentorship should work the same way.

MENTORSHIP IS NOT ABOUT TIME SERVED

One of the most damaging assumptions in leadership development is that experience alone makes someone an effective mentor. Experience matters, but it is not sufficient on its own. Some leaders have twenty years of experience. Others have one year repeated twenty times. Effective mentors are reflective. They ask better questions than they answer. They challenge assumptions instead of reinforcing habits. They understand that leadership is contextual, constrained, and rarely clear-cut.

Just as importantly, effective mentees bring value. They offer fresh perspectives, technological fluency, frontline insight, and cultural awareness that experienced leaders frequently lack. As we explored in Chapter 4 on working well with others, the most productive professional relationships are reciprocal ones where learning flows in both directions. Mentorship must embody that same principle.

We coached a technology company where a 28-year-old engineer was paired with a 62-year-old executive. The executive initially resisted. "What can I possibly learn from someone with five years of experience?" We challenged him to try. Three months later, he admitted, "I learned more about our customers' digital expectations in those sessions than I learned in the previous five years. She sees things I miss completely." That is reciprocal mentorship. Both people grow. Both people lead better because of it.

WHY MENTORSHIP MUST BE INTENTIONAL

When mentorship is informal, it becomes inequitable. The same people gain access to the same leaders. High performers are overloaded with mentorship requests. Quiet talent is overlooked entirely. Bias, often unconscious, shapes who gets developed and who does not. Intentional mentorship corrects that inequity before it becomes a cultural liability.

Leaders must decide deliberately who should mentor, who is not yet ready to mentor, the specific purpose of each mentoring relationship, its duration, what success looks like, and when it should end. Ending a mentorship is not a failure. It is maturity. Clarity of expectations is what separates development from wishful thinking. Vague mentorship produces vague results.

Rotational mentorship broadens perspective, prevents stagnation, reduces dependency, and protects organizations from informal power structures that concentrate development among the familiar few. One healthcare organization we worked with implemented mandatory mentorship rotation every six months. Leaders initially resisted. "Why fix what is not broken? My mentee and I have a great relationship." We explained the limitation. "That relationship may be great for you. But it limits your mentee's exposure to different leadership styles, decision-making approaches, and organizational perspectives. Rotation strengthens them, not weakens them." Within two years, leadership bench strength improved measurably because people were learning from multiple perspectives rather than from a single one.

MENTORSHIP AS A SYSTEM, NOT AN EVENT

One of the most common leadership mistakes is treating mentorship as a standalone initiative. It should not stand alone. Mentorship works best when embedded in a broader leadership development system, one that stretches how people think, decide, and lead in real work. This is where mentorship and leadership development converge, and where the question this chapter answers becomes most consequential.

Leadership development fails when it relies on encouragement instead of design. Leaders cannot expect outcomes without building the conditions that make those outcomes possible. People attend programs, read books, and complete assessments, then return to environments that reward speed over judgment and activity over thinking. Most capable professionals want to grow. What they lack is structure, not ambition. Leadership development must be embedded in work itself. That requires programs, not platitudes.

The following eight programs implement mentorship and turn it into measurable leadership growth. Each is strengthened by mentorship and weakened without it. Together, they form the development system required for succession planning.

DEVELOPING LEADERSHIP SKILLS AT WORK: PROGRAMS THAT ACTUALLY WORK

1. Rotational Leadership Assignments

Temporary leadership roles allow people to practice leadership without permanent risk, which is exactly what mentorship is designed to support. When a mentee takes on a rotational assignment, the mentor's role shifts from advisor to thinking partner, helping the mentee process decisions rather than avoid them. These assignments are time-bound for three to six months, carry clear authority and scope, include defined learning objectives, and end with structured feedback facilitated by the mentor.

We worked with a manufacturing company that implemented rotational leadership assignments for high-potential employees. One strong individual contributor was given responsibility for leading a cross-functional project to improve production efficiency. She struggled initially. She was accustomed to doing the work herself, and leading others required a fundamentally different skill set. Her mentor met with her weekly, not to tell her what to do, but to ask the questions we describe in Chapter 6, which form the foundation of genuine understanding. "What is blocking progress?" "What have you tried?" "Where are you avoiding a difficult conversation?" Those questions forced her to think like a leader instead of an expert. By the end of the six-month assignment, she had successfully led the project and developed the judgment that two years of advice-giving would never have produced. She was promoted to a senior leadership role two years later. She was ready because she had practiced leading in a structured, supported environment with a mentor who accelerated her thinking rather than substituting for it.

2. Decision-Making Labs

Leadership is ultimately about decisions, yet most people are never taught how leaders actually think through complexity. Decision-making labs create structured forums where leaders present real decisions, discuss constraints and trade-offs, and examine outcomes afterward. Judgment under pressure is built through repeated practice and reflection, not through classroom instruction. Mentorship reinforces these sessions by guiding thoughtfulness rather than providing answers, which builds judgment faster than any training program.

One financial services firm created monthly decision-making labs where leaders brought real, current decisions they were facing. The rule was simple: no one could tell the decision-maker what to do. They could only ask questions and share relevant experiences from their own leadership. After the decision was made and executed, the leader returned to the group to debrief. What worked? What did not? What would they do differently? Over time, participants developed the pattern recognition that is identified as the foundation of strategic decision-making. They learned to identify decision traps, anticipate consequences, and move faster with greater confidence by repeatedly practicing the thinking process in a safe environment.

3. Leadership Book Clubs With Application

Books provide shared language. Mentorship provides application. Without the application component, book clubs become discussion groups rather than development tools. The connection to mentorship is direct: mentors help participants translate ideas into behavior, reinforcing learning through action and holding mentees accountable for experimentation rather than just comprehension.

Effective leadership book clubs focus on leadership judgment and ethics, use structured discussion questions, require real-world application within 30 days, and rotate facilitation responsibilities so that every participant practices the communication and influence skills.

We coached an executive team that started a leadership book club following this model. Every member had to identify one concept from each book and apply it within their team in the following 30 days. At the next meeting, they shared what they tried, what happened, and what they learned. One leader read a section on delegation and realized he was holding onto too much work. He identified three tasks he could delegate and trained team members to handle them. Thirty days later, he reported back. "I freed up six hours per week. My team members are more engaged because they have more responsibility. And I realized my hesitation to delegate was about my own need for control, not their capability." That level of self-awareness does not happen from reading alone. It happens when mentorship combines learning, application, and reflection.

4. Stretch Projects With Executive Sponsorship

Stretch assignments develop leaders only when adequate support exists. Without mentorship, stretch becomes sink-or-swim. With it, stretch becomes acceleration. Effective stretch projects include a real business challenge, an executive sponsor who asks strategic questions rather than solving problems, scheduled check-ins focused on thinking rather than reporting, and formal debriefs that turn outcomes into learning. As shown in our succession planning chapter, readiness is built through supported challenge, not just exposure.

We worked with a retail company that assigned a high-potential manager the responsibility for opening a new store. It was a significant stretch. She had never managed a project of that scale. Her executive sponsor met with her biweekly to ask the questions that accelerate judgment. "What keeps you up at night about this project?" "Where are you most uncertain?" "What decision are you avoiding?" Those conversations helped her think more strategically and build the self-awareness that Chapter 6 identified as foundational to empathetic leadership. She made mistakes, but she learned from them in real time with guidance. The store opened successfully. More importantly, she developed the experience she needed for larger leadership roles because her sponsor accelerated her thinking rather than protecting her from difficulty.

5. Peer Leadership Forums

Leadership is isolating, and isolation erodes judgment over time. Peer forums address that isolation directly by normalizing challenges and creating mutual accountability among leaders who face similar pressures. Mentorship complements peer learning by personalizing the insight those forums generate, helping each leader apply shared learning to their specific context and development needs.

One technology company created peer leadership forums for its mid-level managers. They met monthly without executives present, fostering the psychological safety we identified in Chapter 9 as essential for honest dialogue. Topics included handling difficult employees, managing upward, navigating organizational politics, and balancing workload. The power was not in having answers. The power was in realizing that others faced similar challenges. One manager shared her struggle with a difficult team member. Three others had faced similar situations. They shared what worked, what did not, and how they handled the stress. She left with practical strategies and the confidence to address the issue. Two weeks later, she had the difficult conversation successfully. She reported back to the group, reinforcing the peer accountability that makes these forums more powerful than individual coaching alone.

6. Meetings as Leadership Development

Meetings are leadership laboratories hiding in plain sight. Rotating responsibility for facilitation, agenda design, time management, and follow-through develops communication, influence, and accountability, all core leadership skills that Chapter 4 identified as foundational to working well with others. Mentorship strengthens this program by helping participants debrief each facilitation experience and extract learning that might otherwise go unexamined. We worked with an executive team that rotated the facilitation of monthly meetings. Initially, some resisted. "I do not have time to prepare an agenda."

We pushed back. "If you cannot manage a one-hour meeting, how will you lead a division?" Within three months, meeting quality improved measurably because facilitators became more intentional about time, preparation, and outcomes. And watching others facilitate taught everyone what effective leadership presence looks like in practice.

7. Feedback and Cycles

Leaders who skip reflection may miss the lesson it contains. Mentorship supports reflection by asking the questions that turn experience into insight rather than simply turning experience into history. Without a mentor asking "What decision stretched you most?" or "Where did you hesitate?" or "What would you repeat or avoid next time?" most leaders move from one challenge to the next without extracting the learning each challenge contains.

A healthcare COO implemented a simple practice that his mentor helped him establish and sustain. At the end of every week, he thought hard on three questions: What tough decision did I make this week? What did I learn from it? What will I do differently next time? That 10-minute reflection compounded over time. He developed the pattern recognition as the foundation of sound strategic judgment. He noticed he was avoiding certain decisions, rushing without thinking, or letting emotions drive choices in specific situations. Thinking about how he could be better made him a better leader, not only because he made fewer mistakes, but because he learned from them faster. His mentor provided the accountability that kept the practice from becoming optional.

8. Leadership Readiness Reviews

Succession planning identifies who might be next. Leadership development determines who will actually be ready. Readiness reviews close the gap between those two realities by focusing on judgment, decision quality, accountability, and capacity for broader responsibility. Mentorship assignments and leadership programs should flow directly from these reviews, ensuring that development is targeted at specific gaps rather than distributed generically.

One organization conducted quarterly leadership readiness reviews, asking four questions for each high-potential employee: Can they make decisions without constant oversight? Do they demonstrate sound judgment under pressure? Are they accountable for results in the way Chapter 8 defines accountability? Can they lead others effectively? If the answer to any question was no, they designed specific mentorship and development experiences to close the gap. This created clarity for both mentors and mentees. Development was purposeful and measurable rather than general and aspirational. Mentors knew exactly what they were developing toward. Mentees understood specifically what readiness looked like and what was required to achieve it.

MENTORSHIP AS CULTURE IN ACTION

Culture is not what leaders say, it is what they design and reinforce. When mentorship and leadership development are structured, visible, and disciplined, the message to every person in the organization is unmistakable: leadership is built here, not inherited, not assumed, and not reserved for the fortunate few who happen to know the right people.

MENTORSHIP BECOMES VISIBLE IN A CULTURE WHEN LEADERS STOP TREATING IT AS SOMETHING THAT HAPPENS NATURALLY AND START TREATING IT AS SOMETHING THAT REQUIRES DESIGN, ACCOUNTABILITY, AND MEASUREMENT.

Henry Schein, the global healthcare products and services company, offers one of the more honest and instructive examples of what it takes to make mentorship a genuine cultural practice rather than a program that lives in an HR brochure. The company's leaders were candid about a problem many organizations share. Informal mentoring leaves too much to chance. Only those confident enough to ask for a mentor, or lucky enough to be noticed by one, received the benefit. Everyone else was quietly left out, and the inequity tended to compound over time.

Rather than accepting this as inevitable, Henry Schein built what they called "Mentoring Reimagined," a structured program designed to give every team member, whom they call Team Schein Members, agency over their own development. Critically, mentees were empowered to identify their own gaps and choose their own mentors, rather than having the process managed entirely from above.

What separates Henry Schein's approach from a typical mentoring initiative is that leadership treated it as a cultural commitment rather than a checkbox. Senior leaders modeled the behavior publicly, and the organization tracked outcomes with the same rigor it applied to business performance. Their internal research found that tenure increased by one year for employees who engaged in formal mentoring relationships, and that the promotion rate for participants was 33% higher than for those who did not participate. In their 2022 survey, 49 out of 50 questions were rated more favorably by mentoring participants than by non-participants. These are not soft measures. They reflect an organization that understood mentorship not as a feel-good initiative but as a driver of business results.

The deeper lesson from Henry Schein is that mentorship becomes visible in a culture when leaders stop treating it as something that happens naturally and start treating it as something that requires design, accountability, and measurement.

THE TOUGH DECISION LEADERS MUST MAKE

The hardest part of mentorship is not starting it. It is committing to structure, rotation, accountability, and integration with real work over time. Casual mentorship wastes time. Deliberate mentorship builds the leaders that succession planning requires.

One manufacturing CEO strongly resisted structured mentorship. "It feels too rigid. I want relationships to develop naturally." We challenged him directly. "How is that working?" He paused. "Not well. We keep promoting people who are not ready. We keep losing high-potential employees because they do not see a path forward." We reframed his resistance. "What if structure is not the enemy of good relationships? What if structure creates better relationships because expectations are clear, development is intentional, and people grow faster?" He tried it.

BUILDING A MENTORSHIP PROGRAM THAT WORKS

A well-structured mentorship program begins long before the first mentor-mentee meeting. The organization starts by identifying what it is trying to develop, whether that is leadership readiness, cross-functional thinking, or the ability to navigate senior stakeholder relationships, and then selects participants based on those criteria rather than availability or seniority alone. Mentors are matched to mentees not by title but by the gap the mentee needs to close.

If your organization does not have a structured mentorship program, the connection between succession planning and leadership readiness described in this chapter remains theoretical. Here is how to make it real.

Step 1: Define the purpose with specificity. Why are you implementing mentorship? What outcomes do you need? Common purposes include accelerating leadership readiness for roles identified in your succession plan, improving retention of high-potential employees, building the judgment that readiness reviews reveal is missing, and deepening the pipeline that Chapter 12 identified as essential. Vague goals produce vague results.

Step 2: Identify mentors deliberately. Not every senior leader is ready to mentor. Effective mentors are reflective, ask better questions than they answer, challenge thinking without providing all the answers, and commit genuinely to the mentee's growth rather than their own visibility. Interview potential mentors. Assess their readiness honestly. Provide training on the question-based approach established in this chapter as the foundation of effective mentorship.

Step 3: Select mentees strategically. Who needs development most? Who has the highest potential? Who is at risk of leaving because they cannot see a path forward? Use the succession-planning readiness framework from Chapter 12 and your leadership readiness reviews to identify mentees based on organizational needs rather than personal familiarity.

Step 4: Create a structure with clear expectations. Define the duration, which we recommend be six to twelve months with rotations after each cycle; the frequency of meetings, monthly or biweekly; and the specific learning objectives tied to the gaps identified in readiness reviews. The same principle applies to mentorship structure.

Step 5: Integrate with the eight mentor development programs described above. Mentorship works best when combined with stretch assignments, decision-making labs, peer forums, and feedback cycles. Do not treat mentorship as a standalone relationship. Embed it in the broader development system that this chapter has described.

Step 6: Monitor and adjust with the same discipline you apply to any other leadership process. Are mentees developing faster? Are retention rates improving? Are leadership readiness scores increasing? Are the gaps identified in succession planning being closed? If not, adjust. Mentorship requires continuous improvement, just as every other leadership discipline does.

COMMON PITFALLS IN MENTORSHIP PROGRAMS

Even organizations that commit to structured mentorship encounter predictable mistakes. Recognizing these before they occur is far less costly than recovering from them afterward.

Treating mentorship as a one-time event is the most common failure. Mentorship is ongoing. One conversation does not create a leader, and one program cycle does not build a pipeline.

Most mentorship programs fail. The story tends to unfold the same way. A company announces its new mentorship program with visible excitement. Senior leaders send a message to all staff. Pairs are matched over a few weeks, an orientation session is held, and for the first month or two, the energy is genuine. Mentors show up prepared. Mentees arrive with real questions. HR receives positive early feedback. Then, quietly, the meetings start to thin. A mentor reschedules once, then again. A mentee stops setting the agenda because no one told her she was supposed to. Without a coordinator checking in, without goals tied to anything measurable, and without senior leaders visibly continuing to invest their own time, the program drifts. Within six months, participation has dropped significantly. Within a year, the program will exist on paper but not in practice. This pattern is so common that mentorship researchers have given it a name: the "set it and forget it" approach, and it is consistently cited in the literature as the single most frequent reason well-intentioned programs fail.

What makes this particularly costly is that the people most harmed by the fade are rarely the most senior or most confident employees, those who have the networks and visibility to find support elsewhere. They are the high-potential employees from underrepresented groups, the newer professionals who joined because the program was part of the culture they were promised, and the mid-level leaders who were quietly counting on the relationship to help them navigate a pivotal career moment. Research from Cornell University's School of Industrial and Labor Relations found that formal mentorship programs, when sustained, boosted minority representation at the management level by 9% to 24%, compared to little or negative movement from other diversity initiatives. When programs fade, those gains evaporate with them, leaving the organization with the reputational cost of a promise it did not keep.

Allowing mentors to solve problems rather than develop thinking is the failure that the financial services example at the opening of this chapter illustrated. Mentors who provide all the answers create dependency. Great mentors ask questions that force mentees to think, consistent with the listening principles in Chapter 6 on empathy.

Failing to rotate mentorships creates stagnation. Long-term mentorships can become comfortable at the expense of being challenging. Rotation broadens perspective, prevents dependency, and builds the leadership bench that Chapter 12 identified as the goal of the entire development process.

WHY THIS CHAPTER MATTERS

Leadership is tough because developing others requires leaders to invest in something they may never personally see through to completion. The leaders who build the strongest organizations are the ones who develop people who eventually surpass them, who ask questions rather than provide answers, who create systems that produce leaders long after they have moved on. That is not comfortable. That is not instinctive. And for many leaders, it does not feel like leadership at all.

> **LACK OF ACCOUNTABILITY MAKES MENTORSHIP OPTIONAL, AND OPTIONAL DEVELOPMENT PRODUCES OPTIONAL RESULTS.**

It is the most important leadership work there is.

Every discipline explored in this book requires leaders who have been developed deliberately. The trust we explored in Chapter 5 must be taught and modeled. The accountability in Chapter 8 must be practiced under guidance before it becomes instinctive. The resilience developed in Chapter 10 must be built through supported adversity. The time and energy discipline of Chapter 11 must be coached through the transition from individual contributor to leader. The Chapter 12 succession plan identifies who needs to be ready. This chapter provides the mechanism that actually makes them ready.

Mentorship is tough because it requires patience when urgency feels more productive. It requires asking questions when answering feels more efficient. It requires letting people struggle when rescuing them feels kinder. It requires committing to development that takes months and years to produce results in organizations that reward quarterly performance. But the leaders who make that commitment, who treat mentorship as a strategic discipline rather than a generous impulse, are the ones who build organizations that outlast their own tenure. That is what transformative leadership looks like in practice. That is why mentorship is a leadership decision, and not the easiest one.

KEY TAKEAWAYS:

- **Mentorship and succession planning are interdependent disciplines.** Succession planning identifies who comes next. Mentorship prepares them to lead.

- **Old-school mentorship creates dependency.** Modern mentorship accelerates judgment by asking questions rather than providing answers.

- **Reciprocal mentorship produces better leaders at every level.** Learning must flow in both directions for mentorship to reach its full potential.

- **Intentional mentorship corrects the inequity of informal development.** When mentorship is left to chance, the same people gain access to the same leaders. Design corrects that.

- **Rotation prevents stagnation and builds perspective.** Long-term mentorships can become comfortable at the expense of being developmental.

- **High performers stall as leaders without intentional development.** The transition from doing to leading requires a fundamental shift that mentorship must guide.

- **Leadership development must be embedded in real work.** The eight programs in this chapter operationalize mentorship through stretch assignments, decision labs, peer forums, and reflection cycles.

- **Structure creates accountability in development.** Clarity of expectations is what separates development from wishful thinking.

- **Mentorship shapes culture by signaling who gets developed and how.** Organizations that invest visibly in development send an unmistakable message about what leadership means here.

- **The hardest mentorship decision is committing to doing it well.** Structure, accountability, and discipline separate leadership development that builds leaders from leadership development that merely feels supportive.

REFLECTION QUESTIONS:

1. How intentional is our current approach to mentorship, and where are we relying on informal relationships or assumptions instead of deliberate structure?

2. Which leadership roles identified in our succession plan are most vulnerable right now, and how specifically does our mentorship approach address that vulnerability?

3. Do our mentoring relationships accelerate judgment, or do they primarily provide advice and reassurance that creates dependency rather than capability?

4. Where might we be allowing mentorship relationships to last too long, creating comfort instead of challenge and stagnation instead of growth?

5. Are we developing leaders broadly across the organization, or concentrating development among a familiar few in ways that create inequity?

6. How effectively do we integrate mentorship with on-the-job development programs such as stretch assignments, decision-making forums, and peer learning?

7. What leadership skills are people expected to develop in our organization, and how deliberately do our programs build those specific capabilities?

8. How often do leaders in our organization reflect on decisions rather than simply moving on to the next issue, and what structures support that reflection?

9. What signals does our mentorship approach send about who

gets access, opportunity, and organizational investment?

10. What is one leadership decision we need to make differently in the next twelve months to strengthen our bench and prepare the next generation of leaders before succession planning makes the gap undeniable?

CHAPTER 14

LEADING YOUR BOARD
WITHOUT LOSING CONTROL

Working with a board is one of the most misunderstood and mishandled responsibilities in leadership. Boards carry authority without proximity. They have accountability without daily immersion. They are legally responsible for outcomes, yet are ofter far removed from the operational realities that create them. That tension alone makes board relationships uniquely complex.

Consider that most board members are accomplished professionals. They are or were CEOs, attorneys, financial experts, elected officials, and community leaders, and you have a group accustomed to being listened to, deferred to, and respected.

This is not a problem. But it is a reality executives must navigate skillfully.

With the exception of the CEO, boards are not your boss in the way many leaders assume they are. Nor are they your peers in the way some leaders wish they were. They govern. You lead. When that distinction is understood and respected on both sides, organizations thrive. When it is blurred, organizations stall, fracture, or quietly bleed momentum over time.

This chapter is not about governance mechanics or bylaws. It is about relational leadership at the highest level, where credibility is fragile, trust is cumulative, and missteps linger longer than leaders expect.

THE BOARD REALITY LEADERS DON'T LIKE TO ADMIT

Boards are made up of people who care deeply about the organization. Many are volunteers. Many are mission-driven. Nearly all believe they are acting in the organization's best interest. They also bring:

- Limited time and partial information
- Uneven understanding of operations
- Strong opinions shaped by past success
- Personal reputations they want to protect
- Varying levels of governance maturity

Boards are not monolithic. They are collections of individuals with diverse motivations, risk tolerances, and definitions of success. Effective leaders acknowledge this reality without resenting it.

Ineffective leaders either over-defer and slowly surrender leadership authority or over-control and alienate the very body meant to support them. Both paths lead to dysfunction.

Over time, overly deferential CEOs become order-takers. Their confidence erodes. Boards begin to fill the vacuum, not because they want to, but because they feel they must. On the other hand, over-controlling CEOs treat boards as obstacles rather than partners. They filter excessively, defend reflexively, and eventually lose credibility. The goal is not control. The goal is to be a partner without abdication.

THE LEADER–BOARD RELATIONSHIP IS BUILT BEFORE THE MEETING

If you want a productive board meeting, start long before the agenda is finalized. Strong leaders understand that board meetings are not for first exposure. They are for confirmation, discussion, and decision.

Surprises feel like betrayal in a boardroom. A decision that feels thoughtfully developed to a leader can feel reckless to a board that encounters it cold. Resistance in meetings is rarely about the substance alone. It is about trust.

BOARDS ASK HARD QUESTIONS PUBLICLY WHEN THEY FEEL UNINFORMED PRIVATELY.

When Howard Schultz returned as CEO of Starbucks in January 2008, he inherited a company whose stock had fallen more than 40 percent and whose stores, according to his own internal memo, had lost the warmth and identity that made the brand great. The board had already seen enough to bring him back. What Schultz did next is instructive. Rather than arriving with a finished plan and seeking approval, he communicated transparently from the first day, accepting responsibility for the company's failures and laying out the work ahead with honesty and specificity. He did not wait for board members to read about the crisis in the press. He brought them into the thinking before the decisions were made. The board's confidence in his leadership held through two years of painful restructuring, including store closures, executive departures, and a full retraining of the company's workforce. The trust he built before the hard decisions made those decisions possible.

One CEO learned this painfully. She brought a strategic pivot to the board for approval, confident it was the right move. The data was solid. The market timing was right. Her team was aligned. The board's reaction was swift and sharp. Board members questioned risk, leadership judgment, and preparedness, not because the strategy was flawed, but because they had not been brought along earlier.

Contrast that with another leader facing a similar pivot. Weeks before the formal meeting, he met with board members individually. He shared early thinking. He asked where they saw risk. He listened carefully, not to be swayed by every opinion, but to understand concerns. By the time the issue reached the boardroom, the discussion was rigorous but constructive. Approval followed. Same governance process. Different leadership disciplines.

RESPECT, NOT DEFERENCE

Working well with a board does not mean agreeing with everyone on the board. Boards respect leaders who think clearly, take positions, and explain their reasoning. They lose confidence in leaders who hedge, waffle, or ask for permission on matters that clearly fall within management's role.

BAD NEWS DELIVERED EARLY EARNS TRUST. BAD NEWS DELIVERED LATE ERODES IT.

One of the fastest ways to invite micromanagement is to appear unsure of your own authority. Language matters more than most leaders realize. There is a meaningful difference between saying "I'd like your thoughts on this" and "My recommendation is X, and here's why." There is a difference between asking "What do you want us to do?" and presenting "Here are the options, the risks, and my recommendation."

Strong leaders know when they are seeking approval and when they are seeking alignment, and they are explicit about the difference. Deference masquerading as collaboration weakens the credibility of leadership. Over time, boards begin to question whether the leader can lead decisively when conditions worsen.

KEEPING THE BOARD STRATEGIC AND OUT OF THE WEEDS

Boards think. Staff do. Boards drift into operations when leaders allow it. Micromanagement rarely starts as a power grab. It usually starts as a concern. When leaders fail to provide context, boards seek detail. When leaders avoid clarity, boards probe deeper. Altitude discipline is the leader's responsibility.

Effective leaders frame issues at the right level:

- Strategic tradeoffs
- Risk implications
- Long-term consequences

They answer operational questions without surrendering decision-making authority.

One executive director found herself fielding questions about staffing schedules, vendor contracts, and software choices. She felt scrutinized and undermined. The issue was not the board's intent but her framing of it. She changed how information was presented, providing less detail, more context, and clearer boundaries between governance and management. The board adjusted quickly.

Boards respond to what leaders train them to do.

BAD NEWS IS THE CURRENCY OF TRUST

Boards do not expect perfection. They expect honesty. Credibility is built in difficult moments, not successful ones. Bad news delivered early earns trust. Bad news delivered late erodes it, even if the outcome itself is understandable.

RadioShack's collapse, which ended in bankruptcy in 2015 after 94 years in business, is one of the most documented cases of leadership denial in modern retail history. The warning signs were visible for years: eleven consecutive quarters of losses, a failed strategy pivot, and a brand that had lost its identity. Yet, according to multiple post-mortem accounts, executives consistently dismissed the severity of the situation and failed to confront it honestly with their board until options had narrowed to almost none. By the time the full picture was clear, the board had little room to act, no runway to correct course, and no remaining confidence that they had been given an accurate view of the organization's health. The question that often haunts boards in these situations is not "why did this happen?" but "why didn't we know sooner?" That question, once it takes root, is nearly impossible to answer in a way that restores trust.

Boards forgive bad outcomes more readily than they forgive withheld information. Transparency is not weakness. It is leadership.

INDIVIDUAL BOARD MEMBERS: POWER, POLITICS, AND BOUNDARIES

Not all board challenges occur in formal meetings. Some emerge through side conversations, well-meaning emails, or "just checking in" phone calls that quietly bypass the chain of authority.

This pattern is one of the most common governance challenges leaders face, and one of the most avoided. A board member begins giving directions to staff, asking for reports directly, or offering unsolicited guidance to a program manager. The board member genuinely believes they are helping. They are not. What they are doing is creating confusion about who is actually in charge, and staff almost always feel caught in the middle.

Governance experts consistently identify the same principle: board members have no individual authority over staff. Authority belongs to the board as a whole, not to individual directors acting outside of formal meetings. When a single board member acts as though they have management authority, even with good intent, they undermine the very leadership they are supposed to support.

Strong leaders address this early and privately. The conversation does not need to be combative. It can begin with acknowledgment: "I know you care deeply about this organization, and I genuinely value your experience. I also need your help in making sure our staff has clear lines of authority, because when they receive direction from more than one place, it creates confusion that affects our work." Most board members, when approached with that kind of directness and care, will course-correct. Those who do not need to be brought to the board chair. Silence is never a solution. Silence in the face of role confusion is not diplomacy. It is abdication, and it costs the leader credibility with both the board and the staff over time.

Carly Fiorina's departure from Hewlett-Packard in February 2005 is among the most instructive examples in modern corporate history of what happens when the relationship between a CEO and a board breaks down beyond repair. Fiorina arrived at HP in 1999 as a celebrated outsider, the first woman to lead a Fortune 500 company, and she moved quickly and boldly. She pushed through a controversial $19 billion merger with Compaq, fought a bruising proxy battle to make it happen, and significantly reorganized the company.

The problems were not simply strategic. They were relational. The board and Fiorina sparred repeatedly over executive appointments, reorganization plans, and suggestions that she hire a chief operating officer. Board members felt excluded from key decisions and, as performance deteriorated, increasingly uninformed and sidelined rather than consulted and included. In early January 2005, the board discussed with Fiorina a list of issues they had been holding back, and within weeks, she was gone. HP's stock rose 10 percent the day her departure was announced, a painful but clear signal of how much confidence had eroded, not just in her strategy but in the leadership relationship itself.

Fiorina's story illustrates that a leader can be bold, visionary, and even right about a company's direction and still lose the board. Credibility with a board is not earned solely through confidence. It is built through consistent communication, transparency about problems as they emerge, and a genuine willingness to treat board members as thinking partners rather than obstacles to manage. When those habits are absent, even strong leaders find that the board's patience runs out quietly and often faster than they expect.

THE BOARD CHAIR RELATIONSHIP

No board relationship matters more than the one with the chair. And yet it is the relationship that many leaders deliberately invest in least, assuming that goodwill and regular meetings are enough.

The chair is not a shield. They are a partner, and the nature of that partnership shapes everything else. A leader who communicates openly with the chair, shares concerns before they become crises, and aligns on expectations before key meetings will find that even difficult board dynamics are manageable. A leader who keeps the chair at arm's length, shares only what is required, or uses the chair primarily to manage political tension will eventually find that the relationship offers no real support when they need it most.

Strong leaders use the chair relationship as a genuine thinking partnership. They bring half-formed ideas, not just finished recommendations. They ask the chair where the board's concerns are running before they surface in a meeting. They are honest about their own doubts, because a chair who trusts the leader's candor will advocate for the leader when others do not. When this relationship is strong, board dynamics stabilize. When it breaks down, every issue becomes harder, and the leader often does not realize how much support they have lost until it is missing. CEOs ignore this relationship at their peril.

WHEN THE BOARD ITSELF BECOMES THE PROBLEM

In 2011, activist investor Bill Ackman joined the J.C. Penney board and urged his colleagues to hire Ron Johnson, the executive behind Apple's celebrated retail stores, as the company's new CEO. The board agreed, and Johnson moved quickly, eliminating the coupons and clearance sales that had defined the retailer's relationship with its customers for decades. By summer 2012, sales had collapsed, and board members were privately expressing concern. Yet they did not act. Month after month, as losses mounted to $985 million and the stock fell more than 50 percent, the board watched and waited, unable to reach a collective decision on what to do next. When Johnson was finally fired in April 2013, it was too late to undo the damage. Sources close to the board later acknowledged they had known much earlier that something was deeply wrong.

Firing Johnson did not restore the board's ability to function. It destroyed it. Ackman publicly turned on his colleagues, accusing directors of prioritizing personal relationships over the company's interests and demanding the removal of the chairman in letters he released directly to the media. The chairman fired back, calling Ackman's conduct disruptive and counterproductive. The board, already managing a company in crisis, was now managing open warfare within itself. The episode exposed not simply a disagreement over strategy but a board with no shared sense of purpose, no functioning leadership at its center, and no way to hold competing agendas in check. Ackman resigned in August 2013, locking in a $500 million loss. J.C. Penney filed for bankruptcy in 2020.

The lesson for every CEO is both clear and sobering. When board members arrive at the table representing their own interests rather than the organization's future, the chair cannot hold them accountable, and you cannot lead effectively beneath them. The J.C. Penney board had capable individuals around the table. What it lacked was the collective will to act as one body, set aside personal agendas, and make hard decisions before the crisis made them irreversible. A board divided against itself does not just paralyze the boardroom. It paralyzes the entire organization — and by the time that becomes visible, the window for recovery has usually already closed.

Building a functional board relationship is not something you do when trouble arrives. It is the work you do every quarter, in every conversation, long before anyone is under pressure. That investment is what makes collective action possible when it counts.

THE LONG VIEW: LEAVING THE ORGANIZATION STRONGER

Great leaders think beyond their tenure. They build governance relationships that outlast them. They leave boards confident, not confused. They create clarity that endures beyond personalities.

Boards remember leaders who:

- Respected governance boundaries
- Communicated honestly
- Made their role easier, not harder
- Led with clarity and courage

Your leadership legacy includes board confidence. Not control or popularity, but faith and trust that you will make the right decisions at the right time and keep them informed.

WHY THIS CHAPTER MATTERS

Leadership is tough because authority without relationship is fragile. Boards carry legal accountability for organizations they do not run day-to-day, which means the gap between what leaders know and what boards understand is always present and always consequential. Closing that gap requires the same disciplines this book has built throughout every preceding chapter: trust through consistent communication, courage to deliver difficult news early, clarity about roles and expectations, and the accountability to hold the line when pressure mounts to defer, deflect, or disappear into the details.

Leaders who manage board relationships poorly do not usually fail dramatically. They fail quietly, through eroding credibility, lost confidence, and the slow accumulation of missed moments when transparency would have built trust and silence would have built suspicion instead. By the time the relationship breaks down visibly, the damage is rarely new. It is simply finally visible.

Board relationships are tough because they require leaders to be simultaneously confident and humble, decisive and consultative, transparent and appropriately discreet. That balance does not happen by accident. It is practiced, refined, and earned through the same intentional disciplines that effective leadership requires everywhere else. Leaders who treat their board as a governance partner rather than an obstacle to manage discover that the relationship becomes one of their most valuable strategic assets. Leaders who do not usually discover the cost too late to recover it.

KEY TAKEAWAYS:

- **Boards govern; leaders lead.** Confusing the two creates dysfunction.

- **Strong boards have strong relationships.** Strong board relationships are built before meetings, not during them.

- **Surprises erode trust.** Preparation builds it.

- **Respect does not mean deference**. Clarity builds credibility.

- **Leaders need to have a strategy.** Leaders who lack strategy and discipline train their boards to micromanage.

- **Bad news delivered early strengthens trust.** Delayed honesty destroys it.

- **Lean in to issues.** Individual board dynamics must be addressed intentionally, not avoided.

- **Boards can be a great asset.** Your leadership legacy includes how well the board functions after you are gone.

REFLECTION QUESTIONS:

1. Do I treat my board as partners or as obstacles?

2. How often do board meetings surface surprises that should have been handled earlier?

3. Am I clear about when I am seeking approval versus alignment?

4. Where might I be inviting micromanagement through how I present information?

5. How comfortable am I delivering bad news early and directly?

6. Are there individual board dynamics I am avoiding instead of addressing?

7. How strong is my relationship with the board chair, and what would improve it?

8. If I left tomorrow, would the board have confidence in the organization's direction?

CHAPTER 15

BECOMING A TRANSFORMATIVE LEADER

Transformation is not an action or an event but a lifelong learning experience. It is not a title, a role, or a moment of recognition. It is not charisma, visibility, or even success. Transformation is what happens when leadership changes, not just what gets done, but how people think, decide, and lead after you are gone.

> **TRANSFORMATION IS WHAT HAPPENS WHEN LEADERSHIP CHANGES, NOT JUST WHAT GETS DONE, BUT HOW PEOPLE THINK, DECIDE, AND LEAD AFTER YOU ARE GONE.**

Many leaders are effective. Fewer are transformative. Transformative leadership is not louder, faster, or more impressive than effective leadership. It is deeper. It endures. It shows up over time in people who are stronger, organizations that are steadier, and cultures that do not depend on one individual to survive.

This final chapter is about that kind of leadership. Not the kind that looks good in the moment, but the kind that lasts. Everything explored in the chapters before this one, the decisions, the trust, the accountability, the resilience, the time discipline, the succession planning, the mentorship, has been building toward a single question: Are you becoming the kind of leader whose impact outlasts your tenure? This chapter is about answering that question with intention rather than hope.

TRANSFORMATION IS A CHOICE, NOT A CAREER STAGE

One of the most persistent myths in leadership is that transformation happens automatically with time and experience. It does not. Experience alone makes leaders more practiced. It does not necessarily make them wiser, more courageous, or better at handling power. Leadership is tough precisely because its demands grow as responsibility increases. Experience without learning means making the same mistakes with more authority.

Transformation begins when leaders stop asking "What do I need to do?" and start asking "Who must I become?" That question requires honesty. It requires humility. And it requires leaders to confront the uncomfortable reality that many of their habits, while once useful, may no longer serve the organization or the people who depend on it.

We have worked with thousands of leaders. The leaders who transform organizations are not necessarily the most talented. They are the most intentional. They choose transformation. They do not wait for it. Transformative leaders are not finished products. They are leaders who remain willing to evolve.

THE DIFFERENCE BETWEEN EFFECTIVE AND TRANSFORMATIVE

Effective leaders get results. They meet goals. They solve problems. They keep operations running smoothly. These are important contributions.

Transformative leaders operate differently. Their impact is greater even when they are not present. They change how the organization operates long after they are gone.

- An effective leader fixes a problem; a transformative leader builds a system that prevents the problem from recurring.

- An effective leader delivers results this quarter; a transformative leader develops people who deliver results every quarter.

- An effective leader makes good decisions; a transformative leader teaches others how to make good decisions.

> **AN EFFECTIVE LEADER FIXES A PROBLEM; A TRANSFORMATIVE LEADER BUILDS A SYSTEM THAT PREVENTS THE PROBLEM FROM RECURRING.**

The distinction matters because organizations built around effective leaders are fragile. Organizations built by transformative leaders are resilient.

We coached two CEOs in similar industries. Both were successful by conventional measures. Revenue grew. Market share increased. Employees were generally satisfied. The first CEO was brilliant strategically. He made every major decision. He reviewed every significant proposal. He approved every budget. But when he retired, the organization struggled immediately. Decisions stalled. Strategy drifted. His successor inherited a capable team that did not know how to move forward without him. He had built effectiveness, not transformation.

The second CEO was equally strategic. But she spent half her time developing her leadership team. She pushed decisions down. She taught people how to think through complex problems. To ensure the people she had built up were ready to carry the work forward without her. She shifted her focus from doing and deciding to developing and delegating. In practical terms, she identified two or three people with genuine leadership potential and began giving them visible, high-stakes opportunities approximately two years before she was planning to retire. She made her thinking transparent, inviting her team into strategic conversations they might have previously watched from the outside, so they understand not just what decisions get made but also how and why.

Creating these situations allowed her team to develop confidence in their own judgment, not just in their competence in their tasks. She stepped back from meetings she would normally lead, letting her emerging leaders run them, and offered coaching afterward rather than correction in the moment. Creating a clear succession plan, communicating it openly, and celebrating early wins from her emerging leaders signals to the whole organization that the transition is intentional and that the future is in strong hands.

When she retired, the transition was seamless. The organization continued growing because she had built leaders, not dependents. Both CEOs were effective. Only one was transformative.

WHAT TRANSFORMATIVE LEADERS UNDERSTAND

Transformative leaders recognize truths that others resist. Understanding these truths is not the result of reading about them. It is the result of practicing the disciplines explored in this book across fourteen chapters.

- Leadership is stewardship. You hold responsibility for a period of time. You do not possess it forever. Leaders who build organizations that cannot function without them have confused dependency with effectiveness.

- Authority is temporary, while influence is cumulative. Titles fade. Behaviors endure. As we explored in Chapter 5, trust is built through patterns over time, and those patterns outlast any organizational role.

- Culture outlasts strategy. Plans change. People remember how they were treated. How leaders treat people defines them more durably than any strategic achievement.

- How you lead matters as much as what you accomplish. Results achieved at the expense of trust, values, or people are inherently fragile, as we explored throughout Chapters 5, 7, and 8.

- Leadership is not about being indispensable. It is about

building something that can function and thrive without you. The goal of mentorship is not to create followers. It is to create leaders.

During my naval career, I watched as commanding officers came and went. The ships, submarines, and squadrons continued operating. Missions continued to be executed. Why? Because Navy systems are designed to transcend individuals. The best commanding officers understood this. They did not try to make themselves irreplaceable. They built teams that were prepared for their departure from day one. Corporate organizations struggle with this concept. Too many leaders build organizations that depend on them personally, confusing dependency with effectiveness. Transformation requires a different mindset entirely.

COURAGE LOOKS DIFFERENT AT THE TOP

Before leaders can transform organizations, they must be willing to lead with a kind of courage that looks different from what earned them their position in the first place.

Early in leadership, courage looks like speaking up. Later, it looks like a restraint. It looks like saying no to short-term wins that undermine long-term health. It looks like holding the line on values under intense pressure, making unpopular but necessary decisions, creating clarity when ambiguity would be easier, and developing successors who could eventually replace you. As we explored in Chapter 9, this is where leadership becomes both lonely and meaningful at the same time. Transformative leaders accept that not everyone will understand their choices in the moment. They lead anyway, grounded in purpose rather than approval.

We coached a CEO facing pressure from her board to cut training budgets during a downturn. The board argued, "We need to preserve cash. Training is a luxury we cannot afford right now." She disagreed. "Training is not a luxury. It is how we build future capability. If we cut training, we signal to our people that growth and development do not matter. We will lose our best talent. Short-term savings will cost us our long-term competitiveness." She held the line. She protected training budgets. She made cuts elsewhere. The board was initially unhappy. Two years later, the organization emerged from the downturn stronger than its competitors. Talent retention was higher, and capabilities were deeper. The CEO's courage to protect long-term health over short-term optics proved transformative.

BEFORE LEADERS CAN CHANGE ORGANIZATIONS, THEY MUST BE WILLING TO EXAMINE THEMSELVES. NOT PERFORMATIVELY. NOT DEFENSIVELY.

This is the courage that Chapter 7 identified as the willingness to let values guide decisions even when pressure pushes in a different direction. Transformative leaders do not abandon their principles when the cost of holding them becomes visible. That is precisely when principles matter most.

THE INNER WORK OF TRANSFORMATION

Transformational leadership begins internally. Before leaders can change organizations, they must be willing to examine themselves. Not performatively. Not defensively. Honestly. This includes confronting blind spots, patterns of avoidance, control behaviors, emotional triggers, and comfort zones disguised as principles. Empathy begins with self-awareness. Transformative leaders do not outsource that awareness. They pursue it deliberately.

They ask: Where do I default under pressure? What behaviors do I rationalize because they get results? What feedback have I dismissed that I need to examine? Where am I protecting myself instead of the organization?

This work is uncomfortable. That is why many leaders avoid it. Without it, transformation remains a concept rather than a practice. You cannot transform organizations if you are unwilling to examine yourself.

INNER WORK IS NOT OPTIONAL FOR TRANSFORMATIVE LEADERSHIP. IT IS FOUNDATIONAL.

We worked with a senior executive who completed a 360-degree leadership assessment. The feedback was clear. He was strategic, driven, and results-oriented. He was also controlling, dismissive of input, and intimidating. His initial reaction was defensive. "They don't understand the pressure I'm under. They don't see what I see." We asked one question. "If your behaviors don't change, what happens to the organization when you leave?" He paused. "It collapses," he admitted.

To create lasting change, we recommended three actions to this leader. The first is learning to pause before responding, especially in moments of disagreement or pressure. Most controlling behavior is not intentional; it is a habit driven by urgency. A deliberate pause interrupts that habit before it causes damage. The second is redesigning the decision-making process. A controlling leader tends to centralize choices that others are fully capable of making. By deliberately stepping back from those decisions, he sends a clear signal that he trusts his team's judgment. The third, and perhaps most sustaining, is finding a coach or trusted advisor who will give him honest feedback over time, because this kind of growth does not happen in a single workshop or with a single good intention. It happens through consistent reflection, real accountability, and the willingness to keep asking whether the people around him feel genuinely heard and valued.

CREATING YOUR PERSONAL LEADERSHIP VISION

Transformative leaders operate from a clear sense of who they want to become, not just what they want to achieve. This requires developing a personal leadership vision that integrates the values we explored in Chapter 7, the self-awareness we built in Chapter 6 on empathy, the trust disciplines of Chapter 5, and the legacy thinking in Chapter 12 on succession planning. A personal leadership vision is not about your company's mission. It is about how you want to be seen and remembered as a leader.

Ask yourself: ideally, what picture do I want to create for myself as a leader? How do I want to be seen in three to five years by my employees, peers, board, and customers? What are the guiding principles and non-negotiable values that should drive my leadership? What barriers will I have to overcome to take my leadership from its current state to my desired future?

Write a first draft. Do not limit yourself. This is aspirational. This is who you want to become, not necessarily who you are today. Here is an example of a strong personal leadership vision: "I am a leader who develops other leaders. I create environments where people think clearly, communicate honestly, and perform at their best. I make tough decisions with integrity. I build organizations that thrive long after I am gone. I am remembered not for what I accomplished, but for who I developed."

Your vision will be different. It should be. But it should be clear enough to guide your daily choices. Transformative leaders revisit their vision regularly and ask, "Are my actions aligned with who I said I want to become?" When the answer is no, they adjust. That question, repeated honestly over time, is what separates transformation from intention.

LETTING GO: THE PRICE OF TRANSFORMATION

Every transformative leader eventually faces the same reckoning. What skills, disciplines, mindsets, and habits are you willing to change? What are you willing to let go? Transformation requires releasing what once worked: trying to be the smartest person in the room, being the final decision-maker on everything, needing validation, being central to every success, and being the bottleneck.

Letting go does not mean disengaging. It means redistributing strength. Leaders who refuse to let go often believe they are safeguarding standards. In reality, they are limiting growth. Control feels productive but is expensive. It exhausts leaders, disempowers teams, and constrains the organization's future.

One director we worked with held every approval authority. Every budget decision. Every personnel change. Every vendor contract. He believed this ensured quality. What it actually ensured was dependence. When he took a two-week vacation, the organization nearly came to a halt. As we explored in both Chapter 11 and Chapter 12, this is not a sign of indispensability. It is a single point of organizational failure. We challenged him. "What would happen if you were hit by a bus tomorrow, or better yet, you won the Mega Lottery?" He looked uncomfortable. "The organization would struggle," he admitted.

He began to align new behaviors with his personal leadership vision. He delegated systematically. He clarified decision rights. He trained his team. He built accountability without requiring his personal involvement in every decision. He created succession plans so he would not remain the single point of failure. Six months later, he took another two-week vacation. The organization functioned smoothly. When he returned, he realized something profound. His value was not in making every decision. It was in building a team that could make good decisions without him. That is transformation.

THE DAILY DISCIPLINES OF TRANSFORMATIVE LEADERS

Transformation is not achieved through grand gestures. It is built through small, consistent actions repeated over time, the same way trust is built through daily patterns rather than single moments. The following disciplines are not new to readers of this book. They are the integration of everything built in the preceding chapters.

Ask Better Questions

The question-based approach in Chapter 13, as the foundation of effective mentorship, becomes, at the transformative level, a daily leadership discipline rather than a deliberate mentorship technique. Transformative leaders do not just answer questions. They teach others how to think by asking better questions.

Instead of "Here is what to do," they ask, "What do you think we should do?" Instead of "Let me fix that," they ask, "How would you approach this?" Instead of "I have decided," they ask, "What are we missing?" Better questions build better thinkers, and better thinkers build stronger organizations.

Teach, Don't Just Tell

When someone asks for direction, transformative leaders resist the urge to simply provide the answer. The distinction between advice and acceleration is between giving someone a solution and developing their capacity to find solutions independently. Teaching takes longer than telling. But teaching builds capacity. Telling builds dependency.

"Here is how I would think through this problem. What factors would you consider? What risks do you see? What alternatives exist?" That sequence, practiced consistently, develops the judgment that Chapter 3 identified as the foundation of sound decision-making under pressure.

Make Your Thinking Visible

Transformative leaders do not just share decisions; they also make them. They share the reasoning behind them, building the decision-making culture. "Here is what I decided and why. Here are the factors I weighed. Here are the trade-offs I considered. Here is what I am still uncertain about." Making thinking visible helps others learn how to make similar decisions in the future. It also builds the trust we explored in Chapter 5, because transparency about reasoning demonstrates respect for the people who must live with the outcomes.

Celebrate Development, Not Just Results

Culture is shaped by what leaders celebrate. Transformative leaders recognize those who develop others, not just those who deliver outcomes. "Thank you for mentoring Sarah. She handled that client situation beautifully because you invested time in her." "I noticed you delegated that project to Mark. That took courage. Thank you for developing him." What gets celebrated gets repeated. And when development is consistently celebrated, it becomes cultural rather than individual.

Normalize Failure as Learning

Adversity only builds capacity when leaders extract learning from it. Transformative leaders create environments where failure is analyzed rather than punished, building the psychological safety that Chapter 9 identified as essential for honest dialogue and genuine connection. "That did not work. What did we learn? What would we do differently? How can we apply that learning going forward?" Organizations that punish failure stop innovating. Those who learn from failure keep improving.

Ed Catmull, co-founder and longtime president of Pixar Animation Studios, built one of the most deliberate cultures of psychological safety in modern business history. He did it not with a policy memo or a values poster on the wall, but by changing what failure meant within the organization. Catmull was open about Pixar's meltdowns because he believed that being open about problems is the first step toward learning from them and that the cost of failure should be treated as an investment in the future. That was not an abstract philosophy. It was a standard he modeled personally and expected his leaders to live out every day.

The lesson for leaders is that psychological safety around failure doesn't happen by accident or because a leader announces it. It happens when a leader builds systems that normalize honest feedback, models vulnerability from the top, and makes it structurally safe for people to say, "This isn't working yet." Catmull did all three, and the result was a studio that produced some of the most celebrated films of its generation.

A Quiet Example of Transformative Leadership

Consider Menlo Innovations, a mid-sized software company in Michigan that deliberately structured its leadership and culture to outlast any single individual.

Menlo focused obsessively on decision-making, people development, the sharing of leadership responsibilities, and the normalization of learning. Leaders were expected not only to deliver resu ts but also to develop future leaders. Promotions were tied to development, not heroics. Knowledge was shared deliberately. Succession was not a confidential exercise. It was cultural. Menlo did not become known for a single leader. It became sustainable because leadership was treated as a system rather than a personality. The transformation happened quietly and endured.

WHAT TRANSFORMATION LOOKS LIKE IN PRACTICE

Transformative leadership is visible, not abstract. You can see it in meetings where people speak honestly without fear, in decisions that are clear even when difficult, in leaders who are calm under pressure, in teams that solve problems without escalation, and in successors who are ready rather than rushed.

In transformative organizations, accountability is firm and fair. Trust is assumed but verified. Time is treated as precious. Development is intentional. Succession is normal rather than threatening. These outcomes do not happen by accident. They result from consistent leadership choices made over time across every discipline addressed in this book.

One manufacturing company embedded transformation into performance reviews by evaluating every leader on both their own performance and their ability to develop successors. Leaders who hoarded knowledge were not promoted. Leaders who built bench strength were rewarded. The result was a pipeline of ready leaders at every level where succession was expected rather than feared. That organization's approach illustrates what transformation looks like when succession planning and mentorship work together.

> **YOUR VALUE IS NOT IN BEING PRESENT FOR EVERY DECISION. IT IS IN BUILDING A TEAM THAT MAKES GOOD DECISIONS WHEN YOU ARE NOT.**

THE TRANSFORMATION TEST: THREE QUESTIONS

How do you know if you are becoming a transformative leader? The following three questions integrate the disciplines this book has built across every chapter. Ask them regularly and answer them honestly.

Question 1: Can the organization function without me? If the answer is no, you are a bottleneck rather than a leader. Transformative leaders build organizations that operate smoothly in their absence by creating systems, developing people, and distributing authority. Your value is not in being present for every decision. It is in building a team that makes good decisions when you are not.

Question 2: Am I developing leaders or dependents? If your team constantly needs your input, you have created the dependency that Chapter 13 identified as the failure of old-school mentorship. Transformative leaders develop people who can make decisions, solve problems, and lead others without constant oversight. The question-based approach, the stretch assignments, the peer forums, and the reflection cycles of Chapter 13 exist precisely to build that independence.

Question 3: What will last after I leave? If the answer is unclear, you are managing rather than transforming. Transformative leaders build the capabilities, cultures, and systems that Chapter 12 identified as the goal of succession planning: organizations that remain strong not because of who is present but because of what has been built. These questions are uncomfortable. Answer them honestly.

WHAT TRANSFORMATION REQUIRES YOU TO RESIST

Not every leader who commits to transformation succeeds. The obstacles are rarely external. They are internal, the habits, instincts, and patterns that made leaders successful at earlier stages but now limit their ability to lead at the transformative level.

Resist Confusing Activity With Transformation

Launching initiatives, attending training, and creating programs are not a transformation. They are activities. Leadership development fails when it relies on encouragement instead of design. Transformation occurs when behavior changes, systems improve, and people grow. The test is not what you started. It is what changed.

Resist Delegating Without Authority

As articulated in Chapter 11 on managing time and energy, delegation without authority is not delegation. It is micromanagement with additional steps. "I want you to own this project, but you need my approval for every decision" creates frustration and dependence, which are identified as the primary failures of ineffective mentorship. True delegation transfers both the task and the authority to complete it.

Resist Developing People Without Accountability

Development without accountability creates entitlement rather than capability. Transformative leaders develop people and hold them to results with the same consistency and clarity that Chapter 8 defined as the foundation of effective accountability. Both matter equally. One without the other produces either resentment or complacency.

Resist Focusing Only on High Performers

Transformative leaders develop everyone, not just the stars identified in succession planning reviews. Middle performers who grow into strong contributors often become the organizational backbone that sustains performance through transitions. Investing only in obvious high-potential candidates creates the inequity identified as the primary failure of informal mentorship.

Resist Giving Up Too Soon

Transformation takes time. Endurance is built through discipline and reflection, not toughness alone. Leaders who expect immediate results quit before change takes hold. The same patience required to build trust is required to build transformation. Both compound slowly and visibly, only in retrospect.

YOUR LEADERSHIP LEGACY

Legacy is not what people say at your retirement. Legacy is what remains operational after you leave. Ask yourself: What systems will continue? What leaders will step forward? What behaviors will persist? What standards will be met? What values will still guide decisions?

Transformative leaders measure success not only by the outcomes achieved but also by the capabilities transferred. They leave organizations better prepared for the future, not dependent on the past. The values that guide daily leadership decisions are the same values that determine what endures when the leader is gone.

One financial services CEO we deeply admired announced her retirement. At her farewell, the board chair said, "Your greatest accomplishment is not the growth you led. It is the people you developed and the people who learned from you. This organization is stronger because you built a team that no longer needs you. That is transformation."

LEADERSHIP IS TOUGH, AND THAT'S THE POINT

Leadership is tough because people are complex, trade-offs are real, decisions have consequences, time is finite, and responsibility is heavy. But leadership is also meaningful because you shape environments where others grow, you create stability during uncertainty, and you influence decisions you will never personally make. You leave something stronger than you found it.

TRANSFORMATIVE LEADERSHIP DOES NOT MAKE LEADERSHIP EASIER. IT MAKES IT WORTHWHILE.

Transformative leadership does not make leadership easier. It makes it worthwhile.

Throughout this book, we have explored the realities that make leadership tough. In Chapter 1, why leadership demands more than most people anticipate, and why that weight is worth carrying. In Chapter 2, we explored what it takes to lead others through change without losing their trust in the process. In Chapter 3, we built a framework for making sound decisions under pressure with incomplete information. In Chapter 4, we examined what it actually means to work well with others at the level required by leadership. In Chapter 5, we view trust as the foundation that enables every other leadership discipline. In Chapter 6, we explored empathy not as a soft skill but as a strategic discipline that determines how leaders see and develop others. In Chapter 7, we examined how values and priorities shape every leadership decision, whether leaders acknowledge it or not. In Chapter 8, we built the accountability framework that separates leaders who develop people from leaders who simply manage them. In Chapter 9, we named the loneliness that comes with leadership responsibility and gave it a discipline rather than a stigma. In Chapter 10, resilience is a capacity that must be built deliberately rather than assumed. In Chapter 11, we explored how time and energy, when managed with discipline, become the foundation for sustained leadership performance. In Chapter 12, we built the succession planning framework that future-proofs organizations against the inevitable. In Chapter 13, mentorship is the mechanism that turns succession planning from a document into a pipeline. In Chapter 14, the governance dimension of leadership is critical because it connects individual leaders to their broader organizational responsibilities.

None of these disciplines are easy. All of them matter. Leadership is tough because it asks more of you than you often want to give. It asks for courage without applause, discipline without certainty, and humility without recognition. But leadership is also an extraordinary opportunity to shape people, organizations, and futures you may never fully see.

BECOMING THE LEADER THE MOMENT REQUIRES

Transformation does not require perfection. It requires intention. It calls for leaders to choose growth over comfort, stewardship over ego, long-term health over short-term ease, and people over personal validation.

> **LEADERSHIP IS TOUGH BECAUSE IT ASKS MORE OF YOU THAN YOU OFTEN WANT TO GIVE.**

You will not always get it right. But you can always choose to lead with integrity, discipline, and purpose. That choice, made repeatedly under pressure, is what transforms leaders. And transformed leaders transform organizations.

FINAL REFLECTIONS:

As you close this book, we want to leave you with this truth. You have everything you need to be a transformative leader. You have the experience. You have the capability. You have the opportunity. What you choose to do with those gifts will determine not just your success but your legacy.

- Will you lead in a way that makes people dependent on you? Or will you lead in a way that makes people stronger without you?

- Will you build an organization that collapses when you leave? Or will you build one that thrives because you invested in its future?

- Will you protect your position? Or will you develop your successors?

- Will you manage for today? Or will you transform for tomorrow?

- Will you be remembered for what you accomplished? Or for who you developed?

These choices are yours. Make them wisely. Make them consistently. Make them with the long view in mind. Leadership is tough. And the world needs leaders willing to do the tough work of transformation.

Choose to be one of them. That is your legacy.

ABOUT THE AUTHORS

MARY C. KELLY, PhD
Commander, U.S. Navy (Retired)
CEO, Productive Leaders

Mary C. Kelly specializes in leadership development that boosts organizational profitability and productivity, particularly in finance, insurance, real estate, and manufacturing. One of the first female graduates of the U.S. Naval Academy, Mary served 25 years on active duty, primarily in Asia, where she led multicultural teams across nine countries. Her distinguished military career included roles as an intelligence officer, chief of police, HR director, and chief of staff.

Mary was a professor of leadership and economics at the Naval Academy, the Air Force Academy, and Hawaii Pacific University. She holds a PhD in economics and brings a unique blend of military discipline, economic insight, and real-world leadership experience to every engagement.

She is the author of over 20 business books, including her bestseller *Master Your World: 10 Dog-Inspired Leadership Lessons to Improve Productivity, Profits, and Communication*, named a "must-read" by MENSA and MOAA, *Why Leaders Fail and the 7 Prescriptions for Success* (profiled in Forbes and Success magazines), *Who Comes Next? Leadership Succession Planning Made Easy* (Benjamin Franklin Gold Medal winner), *The Five-Minute Leadership Guide, 15 Ways To Grow Your Business in Every Economy, You Next: A Step-by-Step Guide to Taking Charge of Your Career, In Case of Emergency, Break Glass!* and

Stop Procrastinating Tomorrow.

Mary is a Hall of Fame Speaker with the National Speakers Association and a Hall of Fame Author in Colorado. She is listed among the Top 50 World Sales Speakers and the 56th Most Influential Economist in the World, and she is consistently named one of the Top Global Gurus in Organizational Culture.

As a leadership economist, executive coach, and keynote speaker, Mary partners with businesses, associations, and corporations worldwide. Her clients seek her expertise in leadership development, business growth strategies, and organizational culture transformation. She offers content-rich, highly entertaining, and strategically designed programs to help clients achieve maximum results.

Mary's team wants you to know that in real life, she is both fun and funny, and that she loves spending time with her husband, Greg, and her dog.

Connect with Mary:

- Website: www.ProductiveLeaders.com
- Email: mary@productiveleaders.com
- Office: (719) 357-7360
- LinkedIn: LinkedIn.com/in/DrMaryKelly

PETER B. STARK
President, Peter Barron Stark Companies

Peter B. Stark is President of Peter Barron Stark Companies, a leadership consulting firm based in San Diego, California. For more than 35 years, Peter and his team have partnered with organizations worldwide to build workplaces where employees love to come to work and customers love to do business.

Peter is a sought-after consultant, executive coach, and keynote speaker specializing in leadership development, employee engagement, organizational culture transformation, and negotiation. He holds the prestigious dual designations of Certified Speaking Professional (CSP) from the National Speakers Association and Accredited Speaker from Toastmasters International, placing him among an elite group of professional speakers worldwide.

Throughout his career, Peter has coached and advised more than 500 executives, directors, and senior managers in the art of leading people. His client list includes the NFL, Qualcomm, WD-40, Kaiser Permanente, CVS/Aetna, The Phoenix Suns, Western Alliance Bank, Farmers Insurance, Sempra Energy, Lowe's Home Improvement, MetLife, and more than 200 other leading organizations.

Peter has been published worldwide in over 300 articles and has authored or co-authored ten books, including *The Only Leadership Book You'll Ever Need*, *The Competent Leader*, *The Only Negotiating Guide You'll Ever Need*, *Engaged: How Leaders Build Organizations Where Employees Love to Come to Work*, and *Why Leaders Fail and the 7 Prescriptions for Success*.

His expertise has been featured by *The New York Times*, *Newsweek*, *USA Today*, *Inc.com*, *CNBC*, *Bloomberg*, and *U.S. News & World Report*.

Peter's firm specializes in employee engagement surveys, leadership assessments, 360-degree feedback, and organizational diagnostics, having gathered insights from more than a quarter million leaders and employees.

When he's not working with clients or traveling for speaking engagements, Peter enjoys spending time with his wife, Kathleen; their three children, Barron and his wife, Elena; Brooke and her husband, Jake; and Brianne and their two grandchildren, Brady and Callan.

Connect with Peter:

- Website: www.peterstark.com
- Email: peter@peterstark.com
- LinkedIn: LinkedIn.com/in/PeterBStark

www.ingramcontent.com/pod-product-compliance
Lightning Source LLC
Chambersburg PA
CBHW051755050726
47598CB00006B/2293